Peachtree® For Dummies, 2nd Edition

Cheat Sheet

D1308017

Debit and Credit Rules

To *increase* an *asset* account, **DEBIT** it.

To *decrease* an *asset* account, **CREDIT** it.

To *increase* a *liability* or *equity* account, **CREDIT** it.

To *decrease* a *liability* or *equity* account, **DEBIT** it.

To *increase* a *revenue* account, **CREDIT** it.

To *increase* an *expense* account, **DEBIT** it.

Important Web Addresses

Peachtree Software: www.peachtree.com

Wiley Publishing, Inc.: www.wiley.com

Microsoft Corporation: www.microsoft.com

Internal Revenue Service: www.irs.gov

Small Business Administration: www.sba.gov

United States Post Office: www.usps.gov

Table C-1	Keyboard Shortcuts
Press This	*To Get This*
Alt+S	Save
F1	Help
Shift+F1	Field Help
Ctrl+C	Copy selected text to the Windows clipboard
Ctrl+X	Cut selected text to the Windows clipboard
Ctrl+V	Paste selected text to the Windows clipboard
Ctrl+E	Erase the current record
Ctrl+O	Open an existing Peachtree company
Ctrl+P	Display the Print Forms dialog box
Ctrl+N	Create a new Peachtree company
Ctrl+F	Display the Find Transactions window
Ctrl+B	Backup Peachtree data files
Ctrl+R	Restore Peachtree data files

For Dummies: Bestselling Book Series for Beginners

Peachtree® For Dummies, 2nd Edition

Button	Name	Function
	ChangeID	Change customer, vendor, employee, account, or inventory item ID
	Close	Close the current window
	Delete	Delete the current transaction/report/form
	Design	Customize invoices, checks, and other forms
	E-mail	Send a report or form via e-mail
	Estimate	Determine UPS shipping charges
	Event	Create a customer, vendor, or employee event
	Help	Access Peachtree Help system
	Journal	Display the "Accounting-Behind-The-Scenes" journal transaction
	Letters	Create a mail merge letter with Microsoft Word
	Log	View a list of events for a selected customer, vendor, or employee
	New	Create a new record
	Note	Add a note to the current transaction
	Open	Modify a previously created transaction
	Print	Print and post or save the current transaction
	Recur	Create a repeating transaction for future months or accounting periods
	Save	Store the current transaction
	SerialNo	Select or enter serial numbers for serialized inventory items
	Template	Create and save different task window formats

Table C-2 **Frequently Used Peachtree Toolbar Buttons**

For Dummies: Bestselling Book Series for Beginners

Peachtree® FOR DUMMIES®
2ND EDITION

By Elaine Marmel and Diane Koers

WILEY

Wiley Publishing, Inc.

Peachtree® For Dummies®, 2nd Edition

Published by
Wiley Publishing, Inc.
111 River Street
Hoboken, NJ 07030-5774

Copyright © 2004 by Wiley Publishing, Inc., Indianapolis, Indiana

Published by Wiley Publishing, Inc., Indianapolis, Indiana

Published simultaneously in Canada

WILEY

About the Authors

Elaine Marmel: Elaine is President of Marmel Enterprises, LLC, an organization that specializes in technical writing and software training. Elaine has an MBA from Cornell University and worked on projects to build financial management systems for New York City and Washington, D.C. This prior experience provided the foundation for Marmel Enterprises, Inc., which helps small businesses implement computerized accounting systems.

Elaine spends most of her time writing; she is a contributing editor to *Peachtree Extra* and *QuickBooks Extra*, monthly magazines. She also has authored and coauthored over 25 books about software products, including *Quicken for Windows, Quicken for DOS, Excel, Microsoft Project, Word for Windows, Word for the Mac, 1-2-3 for Windows*, and *Lotus Notes*.

Elaine left her native Chicago for the warmer climes of Florida (by way of Cincinnati, Ohio; Jerusalem, Israel; Ithaca, New York; and Washington, D.C.) where she basks in the sun with her PC and her dog Josh and her cats, Cato, Watson, and Buddy, and sings barbershop harmony.

Diane Koers: Owns and operates All Business Service, a software training and consulting business formed in 1988 that services the central Indiana area. Her area of expertise has long been in the word-processing, spreadsheet, and graphics area of computing as well as providing training and support for Peachtree Accounting Software. Diane's authoring experience includes over 30 books on topics such as PC Security, Microsoft Windows, Microsoft Office, Microsoft Works, WordPerfect, Paint Shop Pro, Lotus SmartSuite, Quicken, Microsoft Money, and Peachtree Accounting, many of which have been translated into other languages such as Dutch, Bulgarian, Spanish, and Greek. She has also developed and written numerous training manuals for her clients.

Diane and her husband enjoy spending their free time traveling and playing with her grandsons and her Yorkshire Terriers.

Dedications

Elaine's dedication: To my brother . . . he knows why.

Diane's dedication: To Jan and Chris: Thanks for letting me think of myself as the "third" sister.

Authors' Acknowledgments

We are deeply indebted to the many people who worked on this book. Thank you for all the time, effort, and support you gave and for your assistance.

Oh, where to start? First, thank you Tiffany Franklin for your confidence in us, your support in pushing to get this book published, and for listening to us whine throughout the process.

Thank you to all of our many editors and production staff, especially Beth Taylor for your patience and guidance, Virginia Sanders, Jean Rogers, and Susan Pink for your assistance in making this book grammatically correct, and Delicia Reynolds for your assistance in making sure that we weren't fibbing about the product.

We'd also like to express our gratitude to Kellie Jones and Cathy Strange at Peachtree Software for keeping us informed of the latest and greatest happenings at Peachtree Software. We know how frustrating we can be when we nag. Thanks for listening. . . .

Lastly, thanks to our families, for always being supportive of our stress tantrums and our late-night hours and keeping us supplied with chocolate.

Publisher's Acknowledgments

We're proud of this book; please send us your comments through our online registration form located at www.dummies.com/register/.

Some of the people who helped bring this book to market include the following:

Acquisitions, Editorial, and Media Development

Project Editor: Beth Taylor

Acquisitions Editor: Tiffany Franklin

Copy Editors: Susan Pink, Virginia Sanders, Jean Rogers

Technical Editor: Delicia Reynolds

Editorial Manager: Leah Cameron

Media Development Specialist: Kit Malone

Media Development Supervisor: Richard Graves

Editorial Assistant: Amanda Foxworth

Cartoons: Rich Tennant (www.the5thwave.com)

Composition

Project Coordinator: Courtney MacIntyre

Layout and Graphics: Jonelle Burns, Andrea Dahl, Lauren Goddard, Denny Hager, Stephanie Jumper, Heather Ryan, Julie Trippetti

Proofreaders: Laura Albert, Carl William Pierce, TECHBOOKS Production Services

Indexer: TECHBOOKS Production Services

Publishing and Editorial for Technology Dummies

Richard Swadley, Vice President and Executive Group Publisher

Andy Cummings, Vice President and Publisher

Mary Bednarek, Executive Acquisitions Director

Mary C. Corder, Editorial Director

Publishing for Consumer Dummies

Diane Graves Steele, Vice President and Publisher

Joyce Pepple, Acquisitions Director

Composition Services

Gerry Fahey, Vice President of Production Services

Debbie Stailey, Director of Composition Services

Contents at a Glance

Table of Contents

Introduction

*Y*ou're not a dummy, even if you think you are. But accounting by itself can be a challenge — and then, when you add the computer part to it . . . well, the whole thing can seem so overwhelming that you avoid it. (What? Never crossed your mind?)

Okay, if you're looking at this book, you've probably decided that you've "avoided" it long enough, and now you're going to do it — bite the bullet and computerize your accounting. We want to help you get the job done as quickly as possible with the least amount of pain. You've got other things to do, after all.

About This Book

Accounting isn't exactly a fun subject — unless, of course, you're an accountant . . . and even then it might not really be all that much fun. You might think that going to the dentist is more fun than playing with accounting software. We help you get past the ugly part so that you can start enjoying the benefits quickly.

What benefits? Well, computerizing your accounting can save you time and effort — and can actually be easier than doing it by hand and cheaper than paying somebody else to do it. Oh, we don't mean that you don't need your accountant, because you do. But you can save money by doing daily stuff for yourself — and paying your accountant for advice on making your business more profitable.

Peachtree For Dummies, 2nd Edition, shows you how to set up your company in Peachtree and then use Peachtree to pay bills, invoice customers, pay employees, produce reports about your financial picture, and more. But it's also a real-life-situation kind of book. We show you how to work in Peachtree by using everyday, real-life situations as examples. You know, the stuff you run into in the so-called real world that you need to figure out how to handle.

What You Can Safely Ignore

Throughout the book, we include Accounting Stuff tips — you can probably ignore those unless you're interested in that kind of stuff.

Oh, and the gray boxes that you see throughout the book? Those are called sidebars, and they contain extra information that you really don't *have* to know but that we thought you might find useful and interesting. So feel free to skip the sidebars as well.

Foolish Assumptions

We'll be honest — we had to assume some things about you to write this book. So, here's what we assume about you:

- You already know a little something about the day-to-day stuff that you need to do financially to run your business — you know, write checks, bill customers, pay employees, and so on. We *don't* assume that you know how to do all that on a computer.

- You have a personal computer (that you know how to turn on) with Microsoft Windows 98, Windows XP, or Windows 2000. We wrote this book by using Windows XP.

- You bought Peachtree and installed it on your computer.

The Flavors of Peachtree

Peachtree comes in four versions: Peachtree First Accounting, Peachtree Accounting, Peachtree Complete Accounting, and Peachtree Premium Accounting. (Peachtree Premium is available in industry-specific versions such as manufacturing, distribution, and accounting.) In this book, we cover Peachtree Premium Accounting.

Peachtree Premium Accounting contains everything that you find in the other three products plus a few additional features, such as the capability to store three years' worth of budget information instead of the two years available in the other Peachtree products. Peachtree Premium and Peachtree Complete include a time and billing feature that you don't find in Peachtree First Accounting or Peachtree Accounting, and Peachtree Premium and Peachtree Complete are networkable as long as you make sure that you get the multiuser version. Peachtree Premium and Peachtree Complete contain a job *costing* feature, but you find only a job *tracking* feature in Peachtree First Accounting and Peachtree Accounting. (If you don't know the difference between job costing and job tracking, you probably don't need either one.) And you can customize reports and forms in Peachtree Premium Accounting, Peachtree Complete Accounting, and Peachtree Accounting, but not Peachtree First Accounting.

Throughout the book, when we cover a feature that you find in Premium but not in the other flavors, we include notes to let you know. And, throughout the book, when we refer to the product as *Peachtree,* we mean Peachtree Premium — if we want to talk about one of the other flavors, we give you the full product name.

How This Book Is Organized

Every great book needs a plan. We divided this book into four parts, each made up of two to eight chapters so that you can easily find the information that you need.

Part 1: Getting Started

If you're new to Peachtree, you probably want to read this part. We explain how to get around in Peachtree, how to create a company in Peachtree, how to make an effective chart of accounts, and how to set up default information that saves you lots of time later.

Part 11: The Daily Drudge

In this section, we cover the stuff that you do on a regular basis:

- ✔ Buy and pay for goods to sell to your customers (yep, we cover inventory, too)
- ✔ Bill the customers and collect your money (or you won't be *able* to pay the employees)
- ✔ Pay the employees (or they won't work!)

Stuff like that. We also cover paying for services that keep your business running, and we cover a couple of more esoteric topics, such as billing customers for time that you spend working and tracking project costs.

Part 111: The Fancy Stuff

In this section, we cover a variety of topics — most that you *don't* do every day. First, we show you how to customize forms and produce and modify reports — after all, you put information *into* Peachtree, so you should be able to get it out and see the effects of your business habits. Then we cover reconciling the bank statement and the stuff that you do monthly, quarterly, or annually. We also show you how to easily keep your accounting information safe — a *very* important chapter. Why? Because you spend so much time putting stuff into Peachtree that it would be criminal to lose it just because your hard drive crashes or your office is robbed.

Part IV: The Part of Tens

If you've ever read a *For Dummies* book before, you've seen the Part of Tens. This part contains a collection of ten-something lists. Our Part of Tens includes the following:

- Ten common error messages that you might see — and what they mean
- Ten things that you can get from the Web — not just Peachtree stuff like support and additional information, but fun stuff, too, just in case you've had a bad day and need a laugh

The Peachtree For Dummies Web Site

This book's Web site, www.dummies.com/go/peachtreefd, features useful information that's not necessarily mainstream knowledge. You can find the following Bonus Chapters:

- Bonus Chapter 1, in which you find out how to tailor Peachtree to support the way that you work.
- Bonus Chapter 2, in which we discuss how to use the Peachtree money management tools to analyze your business and help you manage cash, receivables, and payables.
- Bonus Chapter 3, in which we describe how to use Peachtree in a network environment.
- Bonus Chapter 4, in which we list as many companion products for Peachtree as we can find. These products can enhance the way that you work in Peachtree.
- Bonus Chapter 5, in which we discuss who to blame for the whole debit/credit thing and explain how debits and credits work.

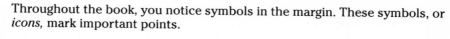

Icons Used in This Book

Throughout the book, you notice symbols in the margin. These symbols, or *icons,* mark important points.

This bull's eye appears next to shortcuts and tips that make your work easier.

When you see this icon, something could go wrong, so make sure that you read the paragraph anyway. This icon warns you of common mistakes and ways to avoid them.

This icon marks any point that you want to be sure to remember. You might want to reread paragraphs that are marked with this icon.

This icon identifies information related to accounting in general — not just Peachtree. You can skip this stuff if you don't care about accounting.

Where to Go from Here

Just getting started with Peachtree? Turn the page. Do you have a specific topic of interest? Use the index or the Table of Contents to find the topic and turn to that page.

Part I
Getting Started

The 5th Wave   By Rich Tennant

"WELL, SHOOT! THIS EGGPLANT CHART IS JUST AS CONFUSING AS THE BUTTERNUT SQUASH CHART AND THE GOURD CHART. CAN'T YOU JUST MAKE A PIE CHART LIKE EVERYONE ELSE?"

In this part . . .

Every project has a beginning point. If you are just getting acquainted with Peachtree, this part is the place to start. In this part, you find out how to navigate through the Peachtree screens and how to set up your existing company records in Peachtree.

Chapter 1

Mastering Peachtree Basics

· ·

· ·

*I*f you have been keeping your financial records using manual methods, you know how time consuming it can be. Plus, keeping books manually provides too many opportunities for human error. Using Peachtree saves you both time and money; in addition, you can know at any moment in time your complete financial status. We know you're eager to get started. Operating a business is a nonstop process, but to computerize your accounting, you have to put first things first.

To work effectively, take some time to get comfortable with some of the features unique to Peachtree. In this chapter, you find out how to navigate in the software as well as open and close companies as needed. We also show you where you can turn for additional assistance. If you're ready, dig in.

Starting the Program

You have a choice: You can start Peachtree the easy way or the hard way. We prefer the easy way. When you installed Peachtree, with your permission, it placed a Peachtree icon on your Windows desktop. Assuming (we know, we're not supposed to assume) that you haven't thrown that icon into the Recycle Bin, you can simply double-click the Peachtree icon (the one with the peachy little peach on it), and the program starts.

To make sure that Peachtree always starts in a full-sized (maximized) window, right-click the Peachtree icon and click Properties. In the resulting dialog box, click the drop-down arrow in the Run box, select Maximized, and then click OK to accept the changes.

If you did throw the icon away or you have so many icons on your desktop that you can't see it, okay, you can start Peachtree the hard way. Choose Start➪ All Programs➪Peachtree Premium Accounting 2005➪Peachtree Premium Accounting 2005— for a total of four mouse clicks.

Choosing opening options

After you start Peachtree, what do you do with it? The Peachtree Start Screen appears as shown in Figure 1-1, beckoning you to do one of several things. You can select any of the following options or click the Close button to close the window:

- ✔ **Open an existing company:** Use this option to open a company already existing in Peachtree.

- ✔ **Create a new company:** Select this option to set up your business with the Peachtree Setup Wizard. (Chapter 2 covers this wizard.)

- ✔ **Explore a sample company:** Use this option to explore one of several fictitious companies. One company, Bellwether Garden Supply, is a retail and service company that uses most of the features of Peachtree, including inventory and job costing. Depending on the Peachtree edition you are using, you may have additional sample companies to investigate. You explore one of these in the steps in the following section.

- ✔ **Take a Guided Tour of Peachtree:** Wander down this path when you've got some extra time and try to spot some of the things that you see in this book.

- ✔ **Convert from a QuickBooks or One-Write Plus Company:** If you have finally come to your senses and want to transfer to Peachtree from *that other software,* click this choice. Peachtree helps to make the conversion pretty painless.

Exploring a sample company

You can best explore Peachtree's features by opening the Bellwether Garden Supply sample company and finding out how to move around in Peachtree. To open a sample company, follow these steps:

1. **Click Explore a Sample Company.**

   If you're using Peachtree First Accounting or Peachtree Accounting, Bellwether Garden Supply immediately opens.

   If you're using Peachtree Complete Accounting or Peachtree Premium Accounting, the Explore a Sample Company dialog box opens.

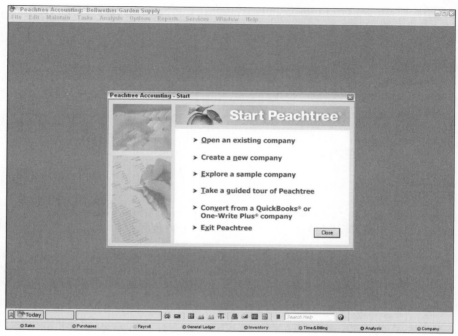

Figure 1-1:
Make a
selection
from the
Start
Screen.

2. **Click the radio button next to the sample company that you want to explore.**

   For this example, click Bellwether Garden Supply.

3. **Click OK.**

   As with other Windows programs, the name of the currently open company appears at the top of the window in the Peachtree title bar.

Getting around town

When you first open a sample company, the Peachtree Today window appears. (See Bonus Chapter 2 on this book's Web site for more information about the Peachtree Today window.) For now, click the Close box to close the Peachtree Today window.

Although the main menu window of Peachtree looks pretty plain, don't skip too lightly through it. The window actually displays several pieces of information. At the bottom of the screen, the Windows-style status bar (see Figure 1-2) displays information about the field, window, or menu choice that you happen to be using, as well as the current date, a toolbar, and the current accounting period. We think that the toolbar Calculator tool is especially helpful!

Hover your mouse over each tool on the main application toolbar to see a Tool Tip description of its function.

Figure 1-2:
The current accounting period appears on the status bar.

Current accounting period

Peachtree Today

System date

Choosing menu commands

The pull-down menus should be a familiar sight from your other Windows programs. Even though the other menu choices are important, you're likely to spend the majority of your time in Peachtree using the following three main menu choices:

- **Maintain:** This menu offers choices for working with data records. For example, you can store vendor, customer, inventory, and employee information, including names, addresses, and phone numbers.

  A *record* is all the information about one person, product, event, and so on. Every record in a database contains the same fields. A *field* is one item of information in a record, such as an ID, name, or transaction number. To explore the parts of the information that you store in Peachtree, see the "Exploring fields and records" section, later in this chapter.

- **Tasks:** This menu is where you do your normal day-to-day work. You can bill your customers, buy materials, and pay your workers by using the Tasks menu.

- **Reports:** This menu is where it all comes together and where you can see the results of all your hard work.

Opening a Company

Maybe you need to keep numbers for more than one business. Peachtree enables you to account for the financial information of more than one company. Although you can open only one company at a time, you can switch back and forth between companies very easily.

Opening a Peachtree company from within Peachtree

The steps to open a company differ, depending on whether you're opening a company while already in a Peachtree company or whether you're opening a company from the Peachtree Start Screen. (See Bonus Chapter 1 on this book's Web site to find out how to hide the Start Screen and have Peachtree open directly to your company.) If you're already in a Peachtree company and want to open a different one, follow these steps:

1. **Choose File⇨Open Company (or press Ctrl+O).**

   You get an annoying little message telling you that you're closing the current company. Peachtree allows only one open company at a time.

   Click the Do not display this message again check box to permanently disable the message box.

2. **Click OK to acknowledge the message.**

   The Open dialog box appears.

3. **From the Open dialog box, click the company name and then click OK.**

   The newly opened company name appears at the top of the screen. No matter which company you open, the menu choices remain the same.

Opening a recently used Peachtree company

If you find yourself frequently switching back and forth between several companies, Peachtree provides an easier method; the Open Previous Company option. This option lists up to ten previously opened Peachtree company names from which you can select. Follow these steps to open a previously open company:

1. **Choose File⇨Open Previous Company.**

   A list of previously open Peachtree company names appears.

2. **Click the company name that you want to open.**

   The annoying little message that we mention in the previous section appears unless you turned it off.

3. **Click OK to acknowledge the message.**

   The selected company opens on the screen.

Opening a company from the Peachtree Start Screen

If you're opening a company from the Peachtree Start Screen, a different dialog box appears. To open a company from the Peachtree Start Screen, follow these steps:

1. **Click Open an existing company to display the Open an Existing Company dialog box.**

   This dialog box lists the companies that you recently opened in Peachtree. If the company name that you want to open doesn't appear, click the Browse button and make your selection from the Open dialog box.

2. **Click the company name that you want to open and then click OK.**

   The selected company opens.

Exploring Peachtree's Windows

Most windows in Peachtree are similar. They have places for you to fill in information and buttons that you use to take actions in that particular window. The Maintain Customers/Prospects window is typical of many other windows that you use in Peachtree. For an example, open Bellwether Garden Supply and choose Maintain➪Customers/Prospects. Take a stroll around this window.

Managing window sizes and placement

Depending on your screen size and resolution, you might not see enough of a window to suit your needs. Some windows, such as the Sales/Invoice window, display more lines when made larger. If you resize the window manually, Peachtree remembers that setting and uses it each time. You can also maximize the window, and Peachtree remembers that you like it maximized.

Place your mouse pointer around the border of any window until the pointer displays as a double-headed arrow. Click and drag the border until the window is the appropriate size.

Exploring fields and records

The main part of a Peachtree window consists of fields. Stop for a moment and ponder these components. When we refer to fields, we're not talking about the place corn grows. *Fields* are pieces of information that fit into a *record,* which is a type of electronic 3 x 5 index card. A record is all the information about one customer, vendor, employee, or inventory part, but a field is one piece of the record such as the ID, name, or phone number. In Figure 1-3, the record is all of the information about Archer Scapes and Ponds, and Nancy Archer is in the Contact field.

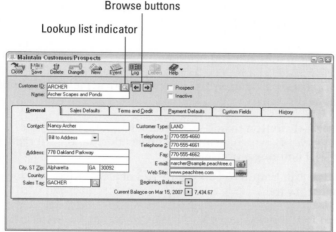

Browse buttons

Lookup list indicator

Figure 1-3:
Each record
has many
different
fields.

Looking up information

Some fields, such as Customer ID, have a magnifying glass next to them. These fields contain *lookup lists* that display a list of your customers (or vendors, accounts, employees, inventory items, and so on). You can choose a record from a lookup list. Depending on the global options that you set, a lookup list may automatically appear as you type any character in the field, or you can click the lookup list indicator (the magnifying glass) to display the list that's relevant to the current field. (See Figure 1-2.)

Optionally, to display the lookup list, either click the right mouse button in a lookup box or press the Shift key along with the question mark (?).

You can do any of the following while in a lookup list:

✔ Select a customer (vendor, item, and so on) and then click OK. Peachtree selects the highlighted record and closes the lookup list.

✔ Click Cancel to close the lookup list without selecting a record.

✔ Use the Find feature to search for a string of characters. The search covers any text that you can see in the displayed list. The Find feature is not case sensitive. Press Enter after you type the lookup text in the entry box. Peachtree highlights the first item that matches your request.

✔ Click Find Next to find the next instance of the previously entered Find text. If no next instance exists, the Find feature skips to the first instance in the lookup list. If no instance exists at all, the Find Next feature does nothing.

✔ Click Sort to sort the displayed list either alphabetically by the ID or name. (Numbers come before letters.)

✔ Use the Help option if you need it.

Some lookup lists, particularly the ones in the Task menu selections, have two additional buttons.

✔ Use the New button to add customers, vendors, employees, or inventory items *on-the-fly,* which means Peachtree adds the record right in the middle of entering a transaction.

✔ Click the Edit button to edit the record of a customer, vendor, employee, or inventory item.

Just browsing

Similar to buttons you use with a Web browser, Peachtree includes browse buttons to quickly scan the next record or the previous record. If you're in a maintenance window, such as Maintain Customers/Prospects or Maintain Inventory Items, the browse buttons move between the records in the order of customer ID or inventory item ID.

If you're in a Task window, the browse buttons move between the previous transaction and the next transaction.

Making a date

Many Peachtree windows have date fields where you need to enter data based on the calendar. If you're a keyboard-type person, you can simply type the date. Dates need to be typed as numbers. If you want, you can type the date by using the / (slash) key, but the slash isn't necessary. For example, to enter September 16, 2004, type **091604** or **09/16/04.** Be aware that Peachtree doesn't allow you to use a dash (-) in a date.

TIP

In most Peachtree date fields, you can get away with entering just the first four digits of a date. Peachtree then enters the year. The year is based on the system date displayed on the Peachtree status bar.

Now if you're like us, we need a calendar in front of us to select dates. Fortunately, Peachtree fields that require you to select a date also include a calendar, shown in Figure 1-4, so you can click that to select a date. To select a date from the calendar, follow these steps:

1. **Click the calendar icon next to a date field to display the current month.**

2. **Click the left-pointing arrow next to the month name to display a previous month or click the right-pointing arrow to display a future month.**

3. **Click the date that you want for the date field.**

   The small calendar closes, and the date appears in the field.

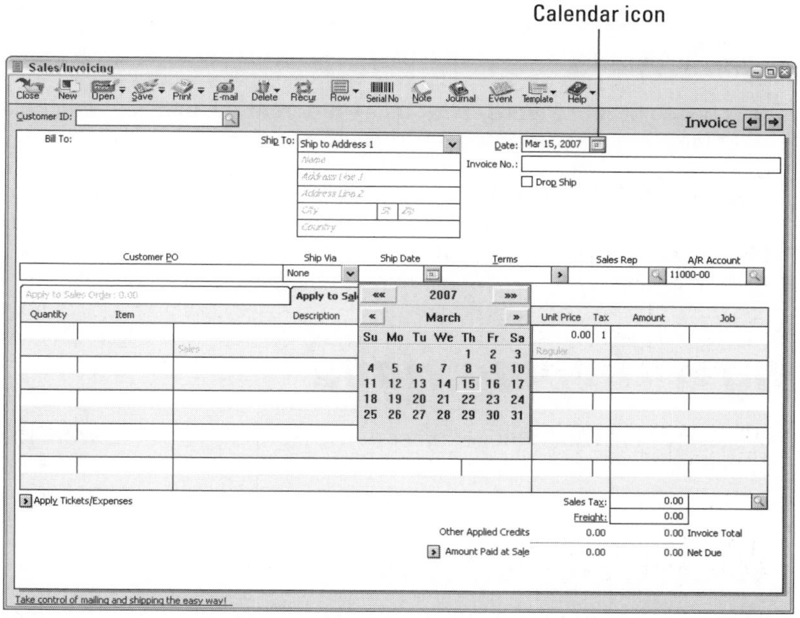

Calendar icon

Figure 1-4:
Click a date
to insert
it into a
Peachtree
date field.

Using the window toolbar

Earlier in this chapter, we mention the Peachtree toolbar, which appears on the status bar at the bottom of your screen. Most Peachtree windows include their own toolbars located across the top of the window. You use the Peachtree toolbar across the top of the window to complete the various tasks involved with the selected window.

The exact buttons vary slightly from window to window, but most of them have a Close button. To get out of a Peachtree window, you can use the Close button or the Windows Close button (X).

If you position the mouse pointer over any button on the toolbar, a small yellow box called a *Tool Tip* appears to explain the use of the button. Tool Tips are great for those CRS moments when you look at a button and cannot remember its function. CRS (Can't Remember Stuff) is a widespread disease that affects people of all ages, races, religions, and hair colors.

You also use the Save button frequently. The Save button appears on the toolbar if you're modifying data records, such as customers, from the Maintenance menu or if you're using a transaction entry window under the Tasks menu, such as Payroll Entry or Inventory Adjustments. You click the Save button to save the displayed transaction, and if you're using the *real-time* posting method, Peachtree also posts the transaction to the General Ledger (G/L). (See Chapter 2 for an explanation of posting methods.)

Post is one of those words with many different meanings. It can be a noun like the place you tie your horse, or it can be a verb and mean *to send*. Of course, the latter is how the word *post* is used in accounting, and it means *to save and send*. In Peachtree, you're sending transactions to the general ledger (G/L); then, when you want to find out whether you've made any money this month, Peachtree is able to show you.

Getting a Helping Hand

We really hope that you get most of the answers you need from this book. However . . . sometimes you need additional assistance.

What's this all about?

If you're in a Peachtree window and don't quite know what a particular field represents or what you're supposed to enter in that field, you can use the What's This feature, which is similar to features that you've probably used in other Windows applications. In Peachtree, right-click the field where you need a hint. Then choose What's This from the menu that appears. A summary definition of the field appears. To close a What's This text box, click inside it.

For our next demonstration . . .

Peachtree includes a series of demonstrative movies to help you with some key practices. The demos include topics such as how to make backups, change accounting periods, drill down in reports, and a variety of other subjects.

1. **Choose Help⇨Show Me How To to display a list of demo topics.**

2. **Select the demo that you want to see.**

   A demonstration window appears. Sit back, relax, and enjoy the show. Be nice and share the popcorn!

Using the Help Contents

The Peachtree Help system works in an HTML format, which simply means that it looks and works similar to a Web page. For easy navigation, the help windows have Back and Forward buttons as well as a Home button. To open the Help Contents, follow these steps:

1. **Choose Help⇨Contents and Index to open the Peachtree Help window.**

   The Contents tab appears on top. The Help Contents feature presents help information in a book-like format, making browsing available topics easy. If you've used the Help Contents tab in other Windows programs, you already know how to use the Help Contents in Peachtree.

2. **If they aren't already displayed, click the Contents tab to display a list of topics available in Peachtree Help.**

3. **Double-click a book to open that topic.**

4. **Continue opening books until you find the topic that you want to read.**

5. **Click the page icon to display the topic.**

   The help information is displayed on the right side of the screen. From this point, you can click the underlined hyperlinks to jump to related topics or print a topic.

Using the Help Index

Use the Help Index to look up a keyword or phrase in the extensive online index. The Peachtree Help Index feature works the same as the Help Index in other Windows applications. To use the Help Index, follow these steps:

1. **Choose Help⇨Contents and Index to open the Peachtree Help window.**

2. **Click the Index tab.**

3. **Scroll through the index to locate the term that you're looking for.**

   Peachtree lists the index in alphabetical order.

4. **Double-click a keyword.**

   Peachtree displays a list of topics relevant to the keyword you selected.

5. **Double-click the topic you want.**

   Peachtree displays the topical information on the Help window's right panel.

If all else fails, you can also access the Peachtree manuals from the Help menu.

Chapter 2

Setting Up Your Company

· ·

In This Chapter

▶ Supplying your company information

▶ Specifying an accounting method

▶ Identifying accounting periods

· ·

*P*eachtree tracks all kinds of information, including the names and addresses of your customers, vendors, or employees, and any business transactions that you've made with them. But before Peachtree can do any of that, you have to tell the software about your company. You need to tell it the usual stuff such as name and address. (That's so you don't forget who you are. . . .) You also need to tell it when you want to pay Uncle Sam taxes on the money that you earn and spend. (Sorry, but *never* is not an option.)

Keep this important fact in mind: Two of the options that you determine when setting up a Peachtree company are written in stone — no going backward. One is whether you run your business on a cash or an accrual basis, and the other is the time frame of your accounting year. We talk about these issues in the accounting method and accounting period sections of this chapter.

Starting the New Company Setup Wizard

When you want to create a new company, the New Company Setup Wizard simplifies the task for you. It asks you the basic questions in the order that Peachtree needs to set up your business. (If you're not setting up a new company but are simply changing settings, see Chapter 4.)

You access the New Company Setup Wizard when you click Create a new company from the Peachtree start screen. Like most wizards, the New Company Setup Wizard guides you through the process. You've probably used wizards dozens of times (not to mention when you install most applications, such as Peachtree), so we keep things short and sweet.

If you're already in Peachtree and want to create a new company, choose File➪New Company to start the New Company Setup Wizard.

When you're done checking out the opening screen, click Next to move to the next screen.

The following sections walk you through each step of the New Company Setup Wizard.

Introducing Your Business to Peachtree

The left half of the New Company Setup Wizard screen is pretty self-explanatory. Fill in your business name, address, city, two-letter state name, and, optionally, country. Notice we say *country* — not *county!* Many people misread this line. You see country fields other places in Peachtree. Use the Tab or Enter keys to fill in or skip through the fields.

The first item on the right side of the screen asks for your business type. To fill in the rest of the screen, follow these steps:

1. **Click the drop-down list to display and select a Business Type.**

   Options are Corporation, S Corporation, Partnership, Sole Proprietorship, or Limited Liability Company. Selecting a type of business tells Peachtree how to determine equity accounts.

   Equity is what's left after you subtract the company's liabilities from the assets. The equity is the value of a company to its owners. In a corporation, the equity is divided among the stockholders, but if the business is a sole proprietorship or partnership, the equity belongs to the individual owner or owners, respectively. If you're not sure what type of business you have, talk with your accountant.

2. **Enter your information in the Federal Employer, State Employer, and State Unemployment IDs fields.**

   If your state doesn't use employer IDs or unemployment IDs, leave these fields blank.

3. **Click Next to move to the Chart of Accounts screen.**

4. **Select a Chart of Accounts option (see Figure 2-1) and then click Next.**

   If you're not sure which option to select, read the section "Selecting a Chart of Accounts," later in this chapter.

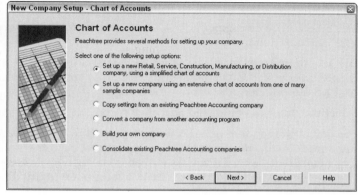

What you see next depends on the option that you selected. For example, if you chose to set up a new company based on one of the several sample companies, a list of business descriptions appears. Don't worry if the descriptions of the accounts that you select don't match yours completely; you can edit them after you're done with the New Company Setup wizard. (Chapter 3 shows you how to customize the Chart of Accounts.)

If you choose to copy settings from an existing Peachtree company, a list of existing Peachtree companies appears. Peachtree asks whether you want to copy default information from these other companies. Usually, you do want to copy default information.

5. **Select the sample Chart of Accounts that most closely matches your business or click the company from which you want to copy; then click Next.**

   The Accounting Method screen appears.

6. **Select an accounting method and then click Next.**

   For important information on choosing an accounting method, see "Selecting an Accounting Method" later in this chapter.

   The accounting method is one of the two items that you can't change after you finish creating your Peachtree company. Be sure of your method before proceeding.

7. **Select a posting method and then click Next.**

   To understand posting methods, see "Selecting a Posting Method," later in this chapter.

   The Accounting Periods screen appears.

8. **Select an accounting period structure option and then click Next.**

   See "Selecting Accounting Periods," later in this chapter, if you're not sure which option to select.

   The accounting period is the second of the two items that you can't change after you finish creating your Peachtree company. Be sure of your accounting periods before proceeding.

9. **Select the dates as requested and click Next.**

   The default screen that appears next displays how Peachtree sets up the standard (default) information for your vendors, customers, and inventory items. Don't worry if you don't plan on using one of these modules, or if the information is incorrect. (See Chapter 4 for information on changing the default information.)

10. **Click Next.** The final setup screen appears.

    Congratulations! You're almost finished with the New Company Setup Wizard. Optionally, you can have Peachtree display a checklist of steps to continue setting up your company information.

    We recommend using the Back button to double-check that the accounting method and accounting periods are correct before you click Finish. After you click Finish, you can't change them.

11. **Click Finish.**

    Peachtree creates a set of data files for your company and displays the Peachtree Today screen.

    The Peachtree Today screen includes a Setup Guide that's designed to walk you through the remainder of the setup process.

Selecting a Chart of Accounts

The New Company Setup Wizard also asks you to choose how you want to start your Chart of Accounts. If you're a new business, you might want to choose one of the samples provided by Peachtree, or you might already have a Chart of Accounts supplied by your accountant.

The Chart of Accounts lists the names that you use to classify transaction information and categorizes the accounts so that they appear in appropriate places on financial statements. If you're not sure which Chart of Accounts to select, you can choose one of the sample Charts of Accounts that are supplied by Peachtree. Peachtree has listed dozens of business types (6.25 dozen, or 75, to be exact), and each one includes accounts typical to the selected business type. For example, the accounts that a shoe store uses are different from those that a drugstore or a dentist uses.

Accounts are the systematic arrangement of numbers and descriptions to keep records of the business that your company transacts. Each time you buy or sell something, you record the transaction and assign it to one or more accounts. Accounts help you organize information by grouping similar transactions together.

Peachtree has several Chart of Accounts options (refer to Figure 2-1):

- ✔ **Set Up a New Retail, Service, Construction, Manufacturing, or Distribution Company, Using a Simplified Chart of Accounts:** This option allows you to select from one of the predefined Charts of Accounts that comes with Peachtree. The simplified Chart of Accounts includes the basic accounts that a retail, service, construction, manufacturing, or distribution company might use.

- ✔ **Set Up a New Company Using an Extensive Chart of Accounts from One of Many Sample Companies:** This option allows you to select from one of the seventy-five detailed predefined charts of accounts that are industry specific such as florist, auto repair, beauty repair or video rental businesses.

- ✔ **Copy Settings from an Existing Peachtree Accounting Company:** This option copies the Chart of Accounts from a Peachtree company that's already set up. Use this option if you're starting your Peachtree company books over or starting another company with a similar Chart of Accounts.

- ✔ **Convert a Company from Another Accounting Program:** Select this option if you're switching from Peachtree Complete Accounting for DOS, Quicken, or Quickbooks.

- ✔ **Build Your Own Company:** Use this choice if your accountant has supplied you with an account list or you're starting with a manual system that uses account numbers.

- ✔ **Consolidate Existing Peachtree Accounting Companies:** If you're using one of the Peachtree Premium versions, you can select this option to combine the Charts of Accounts of other existing Peachtree companies to create a new consolidated Chart of Accounts.

Selecting an Accounting Method

At the beginning of this chapter, we mention that you enter two pieces of permanent information in the New Company Setup Wizard. Selecting your accounting method is one of those two pieces of info. Your business can be accrual-based or cash-based.

Because you must report your accounting method to the IRS, don't just arbitrarily pick one. If you're not sure, ask your accountant. Doing so might just keep you out of jail.

Accrual or cash: What's the difference?

An *accrual*-based business is one that recognizes income in the month an invoice was issued to a customer, regardless of when that customer decides to pay. Also, accrual-based businesses recognize a purchase as an expense in the month that you make the purchase, not whenever you write the check to your supplier.

A *cash*-based business is one that declares income in the month that you receive the payment from your customer and expenses in the month that you actually write the check to your supplier. Dates of customer invoices and vendor bills play no role in a cash-based business.

Say, for example, that you sell a $20,000 service to Smith and Sons on December 13th. You invoice them right away, but they don't pay you until April 2nd of the next year. Do you declare that $20,000 as part of your sales for December? If the answer is yes, you're running an accrual-based business. If that $20,000 doesn't show up on your income statement until April 2005, you're running a cash-based business.

Selecting a Posting Method

The *posting* method determines how Peachtree processes or transfers the transactions that you enter from the individual journals to the general ledger. You have two options: real-time or batch posting. You can switch posting methods at any time.

Journals are electronic or paper records of accounting transactions. Peachtree has many different types of journals. For example, the Cash Receipts journal stores transactions of money that you receive, and the Cash Disbursements journal stores transactions of the money that you spend. Through posting, the journals ultimately go into the General Ledger (G/L), where Peachtree sorts the information and reports it to you on financial statements.

If you choose real-time posting, Peachtree posts the transactions to both the individual journals (like Cash Receipts) and to the G/L as you enter and save transactions. This posting method immediately updates the company's financial information. For example, if an accrual-based business using real-time posting enters an invoice to a customer and then prints an income statement, that invoice is included in the income totals.

Real-time posting can save you a lot of time. We recommend that you use the real-time posting method.

If you choose batch posting, Peachtree saves the transactions and then posts them in a group when you initiate the posting process. When you use batch posting, you can print registers and check the batch of transactions before posting them to the journals.

While using batch posting, Peachtree prompts you to post journals when necessary. For example, before you enter a customer receipt, you need to have all the invoices posted.

Selecting Accounting Periods

According to a calendar in our office (the one with the Yorkshire Terriers all over it), a new year starts on January 1. Some businesses, however, start their business years, or *fiscal* years, at different times. You can't watch Dick Clark as the new fiscal year rolls in, but I guess if you want, you could have champagne and throw confetti. (For details on closing a fiscal year, see Chapter 17.)

Entering the fiscal periods correctly in Peachtree is very important. Selecting the accounting periods is the second of the two permanent items you set in the New Company Setup Wizard. After you create fiscal periods, you can't change them.

You can choose from two options on this screen:

- ✔ **Twelve Monthly Accounting Periods:** Each accounting period's starting and ending dates match those of the 12 calendar months. On the next screen, you can choose the month to start your fiscal year.

- ✔ **Accounting Periods That Do Not Match the Calendar Month:** Select this option if you want to set up a custom fiscal year structure. For example, you might want four accounting periods per year or possibly 13 four-week accounting periods per year.

On the next screen, Peachtree prompts you to choose the year and month that you want to begin entering data. If you choose to set your own fiscal calendar month, Peachtree also asks you to enter the number of accounting periods that you want to use. Most businesses use 12 accounting periods, based on the calendar months.

Visit this book's Web site for more information on Peachtree.

Chapter 3

Designing the Chart of Accounts

*W*e know you're eager to start using the software. But before you dive in, we need to tell you a little about the Chart of Accounts, which serves as the foundation for all your reports. To make sure that you get the reports you want, you might find that a little planning at this stage is wise. Some of the material in this chapter might seem a little dry because it deals with accounting principles and information that you need for your big picture financial tracking, but understanding this information helps you set up the Chart of Accounts that produces the business reports that you want.

Understanding the Chart of Accounts

You use accounts to keep records of the business that your company transacts. Each time you buy or sell something, you record the transaction in the appropriate accounts. Accounts help you organize information by keeping similar transactions together. In today's world, for example, you probably get several different telephone bills for your regular phone, your fax phone, your cellular phone, your pager, and so on. But when you think of the big picture, all the bills are related to *telephone* expenses. So when you pay these bills, you record all the transactions in the Telephone Expense account.

The *Chart of Accounts* is nothing more than the list of all your accounts. The Chart of Accounts doesn't show any amounts — just titles and numbers that you assign to each account. But like any list, you can and *should* organize the Chart of Accounts to make the best use of it. So where do you get a list of your accounts and their balances? Use the General Ledger Trial Balance report. See Chapter 14 for details.

Understanding account types

Good accountants and bookkeepers are typically very organized people — they would hate what they do (and probably wouldn't do it for long) if they weren't. So, it should come as no big surprise that they've invented a method to help them organize things further.

To organize the Chart of Accounts, accounting uses *account types*. Usually, accounts are broken down into five general categories of account types:

- **Assets:** Things that you own but don't sell to customers. Money in checking and savings accounts, computers, trucks, and money that others owe you are all assets.

- **Liabilities:** Debts that you owe to others. Bills from your vendors and bank loans are liabilities.

- **Equity:** Also known as *net worth*, equity represents the amount that owners have invested in the company. Some people prefer to think of equity as the owner's claim against the assets of the company (as opposed to liabilities, which are outsiders' claims against the business). Basically, if you used your assets to pay off your liabilities, what you'd have left is equity.

- **Income:** The sales that you make to your customers. *Income* and *revenue* are interchangeable terms.

- **Expenses:** The cost of staying in business to do business. The wages that you pay your employees and the money that you spend advertising are expenses.

You can break down these account types even further to organize them. In Table 3-1, you see the account types that are available in Peachtree, their general categories, and what they represent. The sidebar "Accounting terms for account types" gives the accounting details on these types.

Table 3-1	Account Types and What They Represent	
Account Type	*General Category*	*Represents*
Cash	Asset	Money in the bank that's available for transacting business, as well as undeposited funds (checks, money orders, and so on).
Accounts Receivable	Asset	Money that customers owe but haven't yet paid; required for accrual-based businesses.

Account Type	General Category	Represents
Inventory	Asset	The value of the goods that you have on hand and available for sale.
Fixed Assets	Asset	The value of things (property and equipment) that you own for long-term use (with an estimated life of longer than one year) in your business rather than for resale.
Accumulated Depreciation	Contra asset	The value by which fixed assets are reduced to indicate their decline in value, usually due to age. A truck doesn't last forever, no matter how hard you try to keep it in good running condition.
Other Current Assets	Asset	The value of nonworking capital that has a short life (usually less than a year). Employee advances and prepaid expenses, such as deposits made to utility companies, are examples of other current assets.
Other Assets	Asset	The value of nonworking capital that has a long life (usually longer than one year).
Accounts Payable	Liability	The value of the bills you owe to vendors that are usually due in 30 or 60 days (a short time frame); required for accrual-based businesses.
Other Current Liabilities	Liability	The value of debts that you must pay in less than one year. Short-term loans are other current liabilities.
Long-Term Liabilities	Liability	The value of debts that you must pay but you have longer than one year to pay them. A three-year bank loan to buy a truck is a long-term liability.
Equity–doesn't close	Equity	The value of things, such as common stock, that carries forward from year to year. Typically, you use this account type for a corporation that issues stock.

(continued)

Table 3-1 *(continued)*

Account Type	General Category	Represents
Equity–gets closed	Equity	The value of equity accounts that don't carry forward from year to year but instead become part of retained earnings. Use this account type for dividends that you pay to owners or shareholders.
Equity–Retained Earnings	Equity	The accumulated value of net profits or losses. Peachtree automatically updates this account for you when you close your year.
Income	Income	The value of sales that you make to your customers.
Cost of Sales	Expense	The known cost to your business of selling goods or services to customers. Generally, the price that you pay for purchased goods for resale or to use in manufacturing goods for resale is the cost of sales.
Expenses	Expense	The costs that your business incurs to operate, such as wages, rent, and electricity.

Accrual-based businesses must use an Accounts Receivable account and an Accounts Payable account, but many cash-based businesses also want to use these accounts to produce an aging report of customers' outstanding balances or of bills that are due to vendors. See Chapter 2 for more on accounting methods.

Keep a couple notes in mind about the account types and equity accounts in your Chart of Accounts: The account type that you choose for an account determines the financial report on which it appears and the placement on the financial report. Consider the three main financial reports: the Income Statement, the Balance Sheet, and the Trial Balance. Income and Expense accounts appear on the Income Statement, but not on the Balance Sheet. The Balance Sheet shows all Asset, Liability, and Equity accounts. The Trial Balance shows *all* account types, in the following order: Assets, Liabilities, Equity, Income, and Expense.

Accounting terms for account types

Nonworking capital is something that you own and don't sell to customers, but you could sell it to turn it into cash. Certificates of deposit (CDs) are an example of nonworking capital. The length of time before the CD matures determines whether it is an *other current asset* or an *other asset*. If your company owns CDs or bonds that don't mature for at least one year, you have *other assets*.

Income and *revenue* are interchangeable terms.

Some people call cost of sales, *cost of goods sold* — same thing.

The account type also determines how Peachtree handles the account when you close your year. For example, Peachtree zeros out Income and Expense accounts but doesn't zero out Asset or Liability accounts. Keep in mind the following points about equity:

- You can have only one Equity-Retained Earnings account.

- You should show the initial investment in the business as either Paid-In Capital, if your business type is a corporation, or Owner's Contributions, if your business type is a proprietorship (sole or partnership) or an LLC (Limited Liability Company). These are Equity-doesn't close account types.

- You should track withdrawals from the initial investment using a Dividends Paid (corporation) or Owner's Draw (proprietorship) account; these accounts are Equity-gets closed account types.

The sum of the Equity–Retained Earnings account and any Equity–doesn't close accounts (you can have more than one Equity–doesn't close account types) equals the net worth of the company prior to the current year.

Numbering accounts

Okay, in the previous section, we discuss account types, which help you organize the appearance of accounts on financial statements. The account numbers that you use can also affect the information that you can present on financial reports.

First, understand that Peachtree places very few restrictions on the numbering scheme that you use. Be aware of the following points when you develop your account numbering scheme:

- ✔ Peachtree sorts Account IDs alphabetically — that means numbers first, and you need to use leading zeros to get numbers to sort in numerical order (I know that sounds stupid, but it's true). For example, to get the numbers 1, 27, 100, and 1000 to sort in the order just listed, you'd need to enter them as 0001, 0027, 0100, and 1000.

- ✔ Account IDs can contain any printable character except the asterisk (*), the plus sign (+), and the question mark (?).

- ✔ Account IDs cannot contain leading or trailing blanks, but you can use blanks in the middle.

- ✔ Account IDs are case sensitive; cash and CASH are two different accounts.

Most people use numbers, not letters, for Account IDs, and they use letters for the account's description. The description appears on all reports; the Account ID appears on only some reports.

Because Peachtree places so few restrictions on the Account ID, you can use any scheme you want, but we strongly suggest that you keep it logical. For example, many companies number all asset accounts in the 10000 range, liability accounts in the 20000 range, equity accounts in the 30000 range, income accounts in the 40000 range, cost of sales accounts in the 50000 range, and expense accounts in the 60000 range or higher.

Handling departments or locations

Suppose that your business has multiple geographic locations, and each location generates income and expenses. Or suppose that you don't have geographic locations but you do have multiple departments, and each department generates income and expenses that you want to track. Of course, you want to produce a company-wide income statement, but how do you want it to look?

Perhaps you want a detailed Income Statement that's broken down by department, like the one in Figure 3-1. Or, maybe you want an Income Statement that summarizes the information for all departments, like the one in Figure 3-2. Or maybe you want to be able to produce Income Statements for individual departments, like the one shown in Figure 3-3.

Because we show you all three formats, it's safe to assume that you can produce any of these reports in Peachtree. But to do so, you must correctly set up the numbering of your Chart of Accounts.

Bellwether Garden Supply
Income Statement
For the Three Months Ending March 31, 2007

	Current Month			Year to Date
Revenues				
Sales	$	175.00	0.21	$	175.00
Sales - Aviary		5,628.01	6.67		50,153.16
Sales - Books		149.75	0.18		7,293.10
Sales - Ceramics		0.00	0.00		0.00
Sales - Equipment		15,139.29	17.94		57,492.78
Sales - Food/Fert		1,006.96	1.19		5,204.15
Sales - Furntiture		15,000.00	17.77		15,000.00
Sales - Hand Tools		729.67	0.86		7,058.12
Sales - Landscape Services		7,469.43	8.85		16,977.53
Sales - Miscellaneous		0.00	0.00		45.00
Sales - Nursery		31,200.48	36.97		65,042.56
Sales - Pots		5,905.08	7.00		9,469.51
Sales - Seeds		1,457.43	1.73		8,661.39
Sales - Soil		655.02	0.78		9,082.55
Sales - Statuary		0.00	0.00		0.00
Sales - Topiary		0.00	0.00		0.00
Interest Income		0.00	0.00		0.00
Other Income		0.00	0.00		25,500.00
Finance Charge Income		0.00	0.00		0.00
Sales Returns and Allowances		0.00	0.00		0.00
Sales Discounts		(126.03)	(0.15)		(135.93)
Total Revenues		84,390.09	100.00		277,018.92

Figure 3-1: An Income Statement that shows all departments.

Bellwether Garden Supply
General Income Statement
For the Three Months Ending March 31, 2007

	Current Month			Year to Date
Revenues				
Sales	$	84,516.12	100.15	$	251,654.85
Interest Income		0.00	0.00		0.00
Other Income		0.00	0.00		25,500.00
Finance Charge Income		0.00	0.00		0.00
Sales Returns and Allowances		0.00	0.00		0.00
Sales Discounts		(126.03)	(0.15)		(135.93)
Total Revenues		84,390.09	100.00		277,018.92
Cost of Sales				
Product Cost		11,582.04	13.72		60,523.68
Direct Labor		1,750.00	2.07		3,062.50
Materials Cost		6,261.35	7.42		10,491.45
Subcontractors		335.50	0.40		335.50
Total Cost of Sales		19,928.89	23.62		74,413.13
Gross Profit		64,461.20	76.38		202,605.79

Figure 3-2: An Income Statement that rolls up all departmental numbers.

Bellwether Garden Supply
Income Statement
For the Three Months Ending March 31, 2007

	Current Month			Year to Date
Revenues				
Sales - Aviary	$ 5,628.01	100.00	$	50,153.16
Total Revenues	5,628.01	100.00		50,153.16
Cost of Sales				
Product Cost - Aviary	1,479.30	26.28		20,222.95
Total Cost of Sales	1,479.30	26.28		20,222.95
Gross Profit	4,148.71	73.72		29,930.21
Expenses				
Total Expenses	0.00	0.00		0.00
Net Income	$ 4,148.71	73.72	$	29,930.21

Figure 3-3:
An Income
Statement
for a single
department.

Setting up departmental account numbers

To produce these reports, Peachtree uses a concept called *masking* that
enables you, through the use of account numbers, to easily limit the information that appears on reports. To use masking, you divide your account
number into segments; you assign the account number, say, 40000, to the first
segment and then assign a digit or two to the second segment of the number
to represent the department or location. That is, 40000-01 might be income
for Department 1, and 40000-02 could be income for Department 2. The impli-
cation here is that the first segment of the account (40000) would appear several different times in your Chart of Accounts, but the second segment would
contain a different department number. And, you can set up a 00 level for the
account (that is, 40000-00) that Peachtree can use to display the sum of all
the departments and represent the company as a whole. You record sales
and purchases or payments by using the account number that represents the
department responsible for the sale, purchase, or payment. You would never
record a transaction in the 00 level account. Your expense accounts would
work the same way if you want to track costs separately for each department.

If your situation is more complex, and you want to track expenses for multiple locations *and* for multiple departments at each location, your account
number should include both a location segment and a department segment.
To track sales for Location 1, Department 1, your Sales account number
might be 40000-01-01, where the first 01 tracks the Location and the second
01 tracks the Department. Table 3-2 shows the various possible combinations
for Sales accounts that you might find in your Chart of Accounts if you had
three locations and three departments:

Table 3-2	Sample Combinations for Accounts Using Locations and Departments
Account Description	**Account Number**
Sales for Location 1, Department 1	40000-01-01
Sales for Location 2, Department 1	40000-02-01
Sales for Location 3, Department 1	40000-03-01
Sales for Location 1, Department 2	40000-01-02
Sales for Location 1, Department 3	40000-01-03
Sales for Location 2, Department 2	40000-02-02
Sales for Location 2, Department 3	40000-02-03
Sales for Location 3, Department 2	40000-03-02
Sales for Location 3, Department 3	40000-03-03

Be sure to allow the maximum number of characters that you need for your departments and locations and keep future growth in mind. For example, if you have ten or more departments, you need two digits for your department number. Don't forget to use a leading zero for department numbers less than ten (for example, 01, 02, 03, and so on).

If you are using any version of Peachtree *other than* Peachtree Premium and you want to use masking, do so when creating your chart of accounts by simply setting up the appropriate account numbers. If you are using Peachtree Premium, you can add masking to your existing chart of accounts. Follow these steps to identify your account segment structure in Peachtree.

1. **Choose Maintain⇨Default Information⇨General Ledger.**

   Peachtree displays the General Ledger Defaults dialog box shown in Figure 3-4.

2. **Click the Account Segments tab.**

3. **Click in the Segment Description text box and type a description of the portion of the account number that you want to define.**

4. **Click in the Length text box and type the value that represents the number of digits you want to assign to this segment of the account number.**

5. **Click the Separator drop-down list arrow and select a character to separate portions of the account number.**

6. **Repeat Steps 3 through 5 for each segment that you want to define.**

7. **Click OK.**

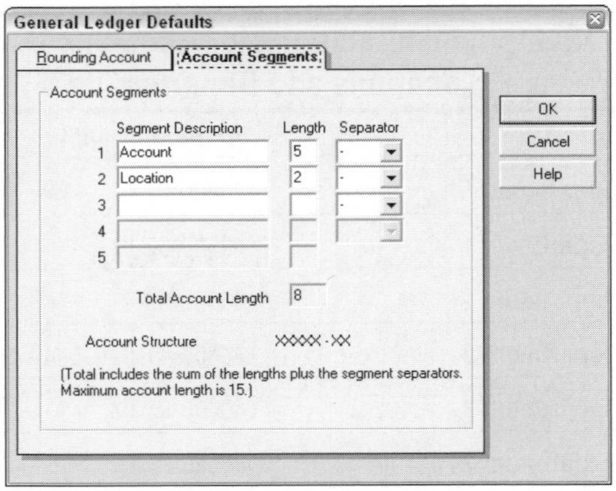

Figure 3-4:
Set up the
account
segments
that you
want to use
in your chart
of accounts.

If you're identifying segments for an existing Chart of Accounts, Peachtree displays a message that tells you how many accounts you currently have that don't match the segment structure that you defined when you clicked OK. Simply click OK when you see the message and edit your Chart of Accounts to provide the new segment numbers as appropriate by using the information in the next section. Remember, you don't *need* to assign numbers for any segment other than the first segment of your account number — the other segments are optional. Many people use them only for Income and Expense accounts.

Consolidating departmental figures

You can extend the department/location scenario from the previous section one step further. Suppose that you find yourself in the situation where you have two or three geographic locations that each need to use Peachtree — and you're not networked. You *can* set up separate companies in Peachtree, but at the end of an accounting period, you won't have a consolidated financial statement to show the true financial picture of your company. Or suppose that your check writing volume exceeds 200 transactions per month. In this case, Peachtree can begin to operate quite slowly; therefore, you might want to consider breaking your company into multiple companies and then consolidating to produce reports.

In Peachtree Premium, you can consolidate companies by creating a new company that contains — or consolidates — companies that you select.

If you are *not* using Peachtree Premium, you can purchase the Consolidation Wizard, an add-on product that allows you to use multiple companies in Peachtree and consolidate the information in those companies into one master company. For more information on the Consolidation Wizard and other add-on products for Peachtree, see Bonus Chapter 4 on this book's Web site.

If you segment the Chart of Accounts in each company in the same way (whether you use Peachtree Premium's consolidation feature or you use the Consolidation Wizard add-on product), consolidating is quick and painless and lets you produce departmental as well as company-wide financial statements.

Modifying the Chart of Accounts

Once you understand account types, numbering, and so on, you can dive in and make additions, changes, or deletions to the Chart of Accounts. To make *any* changes to the Chart of Accounts, use the Maintain Chart of Accounts window, shown in Figure 3-5.

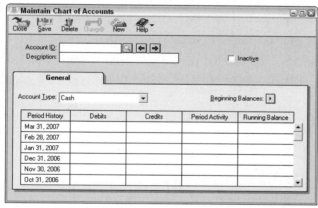

Figure 3-5: Use this window to make changes to the Chart of Accounts.

Adding new accounts

To add an account, follow these steps:

1. **Choose Maintain⇨Chart of Accounts and, in the Maintain Chart of Accounts window, type a number for the new account in the Account ID text box.**

   Peachtree opens the account list and shows you the number of the account that most closely matches the number you typed. Make sure that you type a new number — one that doesn't already exist.

2. **In the Description text box, type a name for the account as you want it to appear on reports.**

3. **Open the Account Type drop-down list box and select the correct account type for the account that you're adding.**

4. **Click Save.**

If you create an account number that doesn't match the segmenting scheme, you see a message. You can click OK and create the account despite the message.

Editing accounts

You can edit the Account ID, description, and account type of an account by following these steps:

1. **Choose Maintain⇨Chart of Accounts to display the Maintain Chart of Accounts window (refer to Figure 3-5).**

2. **Click the lookup list indicator to the right of the Account ID text box or type some characters of the Account ID to display the account list.**

3. **Highlight the account and click OK or press Enter.**

4. **Retype the description or change the account type.**

5. **To change the Account ID, click the ChangeID button on the toolbar.**

    Peachtree displays the Change Account ID dialog box shown in Figure 3-6.

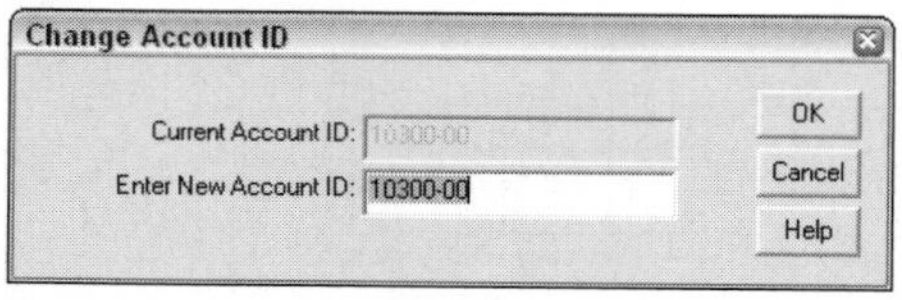

Figure 3-6:
Change an
account
number in
this box.

Change Account ID

Current Account ID: 10300-00

Enter New Account ID: 10300-00

OK

Cancel

Help

6. **Type a new Account ID and click OK.**

7. **Click Save.**

Deleting accounts

You can delete accounts that have no activity — that is, you haven't used them in any transactions. Choose Maintain⇨Chart of Accounts to display the Maintain Chart of Accounts window. Select the account; then click the Delete button.

If you try to delete an account that you've used in transactions, Peachtree tells you that it can't delete the account. You can, however, set the status of the account to Inactive. If you choose to hide inactive accounts, they don't appear in the list of any transaction window. In addition, hidden accounts don't appear on any report except the Chart of Accounts report. Only people who know the account's number are able to use it. To make an account inactive, display it in the Maintain Chart of Accounts window, select the Inactive check box, and click the Save button.

When you make an account inactive, you make it eligible for deletion when you purge. See Chapter 17 for information on purging.

Identifying the rounding account

Peachtree can round numbers on financial statements to either whole dollars or whole thousands of dollars. So, occasionally, when you prepare financial statements, Peachtree needs round numbers. Also, Peachtree needs a place to store the difference caused by rounding. Although the account can be any account, Peachtree recommends that you use the Retained Earnings account.

To make sure that Peachtree uses the Retained Earnings account for rounding, follow these steps:

1. **Choose Maintain⇨Default Information⇨General Ledger.**

   Peachtree displays the General Ledger Defaults dialog box (refer to Figure 3-4).

2. **Click the Rounding Account tab.**

3. **Confirm that Peachtree has selected the single account that you've designated as Equity–Retained Earnings.**

   If necessary, click the magnifying glass next to the account number to display the list. In the unlikely event that Peachtree chooses the wrong account, change it.

4. **Click OK.**

Opening balances

The odds are good . . . very good . . . excellent, in fact, that you've been in business for some time now and that you're starting to use Peachtree after you've done some business. In cases like these, you need to enter beginning balances into Peachtree to represent the business that you conducted before setting up your Peachtree company.

Timing the start of using Peachtree

And now is a good time to talk about timing. How do you know when you should go live with Peachtree? Well, ideally, try to start using a new accounting package on the first day of your accounting year — January 1, if your business operates on a calendar year; otherwise, the first day of your fiscal year. If you can't wait that long, then start using Peachtree on the first day of a quarter. And if you can't start using Peachtree on the first day of a quarter, then start on the first day of a month.

Why these target dates? Well, you have the least amount of setup work to do. For example, if your business operates on a calendar year and you start using Peachtree on January 1, you don't need to enter any beginning balances for payroll or any of your income or expense accounts because the balances of these accounts start at zero on January 1. If you start at the beginning of a quarter, and you're willing to forego monthly reports preceding that quarter, you can enter summarized information for preceding quarters. And, if you start on the first day of a month, you don't need to play catch-up for the month — which you'd need to do if you'd started mid-month.

Where do you get the numbers?

If you've used some other accounting package, you can print an Income Statement, Balance Sheet, and a Trial Balance as of the last month that you intend to use that accounting package. You can use a combination of the Balance Sheet and the Income Statement, or you can use the Trial Balance: The numbers on these reports in your old software represent the beginning balance numbers of your new Peachtree company.

If you've never used any other accounting package, contact your accountant. Provide the date that you want to start your company and ask for a Trial Balance, a Balance Sheet, and an Income Statement as of that date. Your accountant probably can't provide the information instantly, especially if you want to start on January 1, and you ask for the information in December of the prior year. Your accountant needs to prepare these reports *after* December 31 so that the reports include all your prior year transactions.

But don't worry; you can start working in Peachtree without beginning balance numbers; in fact, you might as well start working in Peachtree without beginning balance numbers. You just need to remember that year-to-date reports aren't accurate because they don't show the entire picture until you enter beginning balances.

Entering beginning balances

After you get the numbers, entering them into Peachtree isn't difficult. If you're going to start using Peachtree at any time other than the beginning of your business year, we suggest you use the alternative method described in the next section. If you're going to start using Peachtree at the beginning of your business year (calendar or fiscal), we suggest that you use Peachtree's Chart of Accounts Beginning Balances or Prior Year Adjustments window to enter beginning balances. Follow these steps:

1. **Choose Maintain⇨Chart of Accounts to display the Maintain Chart of Accounts window (refer back to Figure 3-5).**

2. **Click the Beginning Balances button to display the Select Period dialog box.**

3. **Select the period from the list.**

Until you have entered transactions, you can enter beginning balances in Peachtree by month for the year preceding your first open year, for your first open year, or for your second open year. If Period 1 for the company is January 2007, Peachtree makes available each month in 2006, 2007, and 2008; all balances prior to January 1, 2006, would be lumped together into Before 1/1/06.

4. **Click OK to display the Chart of Accounts Prior Year Adjustments window (see Figure 3-7).**

Figure 3-7:
Use this
window to
enter
account
balances
generated
before you
started
using
Peachtree.

		Chart of Accounts Prior Year Adjustments			
Cancel	OK	New	Find	Next	Help

Prior Year Adjustments as of Before January 1, 2006

Account ID	Account Description	Account Type	Assets, Expenses	Liabilities, Equity, Income
15400-00	Leasehold Improvements	Fixed Assets		
15500-00	Buildings	Fixed Assets	185,500.00	
15600-00	Building Improvements	Fixed Assets	26,500.00	
16900-00	Land	Fixed Assets		
17000-00	Accum. Depreciation-Furniture	Accumulated Deprecia		53,418.21
17100-00	Accum. Depreciation-Equipme	Accumulated Deprecia		31,872.92
17200-00	Accum. Depreciation-Vehicles	Accumulated Deprecia		47,271.59

The Trial Balance is made up of the balances of all accounts. In order for the Trial Balance to be in balance, the sum of Assets and Expenses should equal the sum of Liabilities, Equity, and Income.

Total:	508,706.78	508,706.78
Trial Balance: (Difference posts to Beg Bal Equity)		0.00

Net Income is the difference of Income and Expense account values. The Income and Expense values making up Net Income are already included in the total.

Income - Expenses:	0.00	0.00
Net Income:		0.00

5. **Using the numbers that you've gotten either from your old accounting system's Trial Balance or from your accountant, enter the balances for each account.**

If you have an unusual balance in an account (for example, your cash balance is a negative instead of a positive balance), enter a negative number for the account balance.

When you finish, the Net Income number at the bottom of the window should represent your Net Income for the period. Look for the Net Income at the bottom of your Income Statement.

6. **Click OK to store your beginning balances.**

You can find out more about posting transactions in Chapter 5 — and also in Chapters 6 through 9.

If you're out of balance . . .

You know that you're out of balance if the Trial Balance number in Figure 3-7 is *not* zero. In this case, Peachtree wants to post the difference to an Equity–doesn't close account called Beg. Bal. Equity. This account doesn't appear in the Beginning Balances window, but it *does* appear on financial statements, General Ledger reports, and in the Chart of Accounts list. The chances are good that you're out of balance due to a typing mistake; double-check the numbers that you've entered and make sure you've entered *all* the numbers.

If you still can't find the mistake, you can click through Peachtree's warning and let it create the Beg. Bal. Equity account. Your company is then in balance, and you can safely proceed to enter transactions. If you have to use this workaround, you need to live with the Beg. Bal. Equity account until you find the source of the problem. You can then correct it by clicking the Beginning Balances button in the Maintain Chart of Accounts window. Peachtree displays the Beginning Balances window if you *haven't* posted any transactions. If you *have* posted transactions, Peachtree displays the Prior Period Adjustment window, which looks and operates just like the Beginning Balances window. When the Beg. Bal. Equity account has a zero balance, you can delete the account.

An alternative method for entering beginning balances

If you start using Peachtree at any time other than the beginning of the business year, we suggest that you enter one (or more) journal entries to represent your beginning balances rather than using Peachtree's Chart of Accounts Beginning Balances or Chart of Accounts Prior Year Adjustments window. We find that using journal entries for midyear starts seems to be less confusing. You'd enter the journal entries to provide balances as of the first day of the first open month.

Because we're trying to avoid using the *d* word and the *c* word this early in the book (debits and credits), we save the discussion of journal entries for Chapter 17.

The B word — Budgeting

Nobody likes to live on a budget, but for most of us, budgets are a sad fact of life. In the business world, budgets can help you compare how your business is actually doing to how you *thought* it would do.

You can create budgets for each account in Peachtree; you can then print Budget vs. Actual reports to see how well you're doing. Although we'd love to walk you through the details on budgeting, space is limited. We know you're a pretty smart reader, so, here's a synopsis.

In Peachtree Premium, choose Maintain⇨Budgets. In the Maintain Budgets window that appears, select an Account ID for which you want to establish budget numbers. Then fill in budget amounts for each month in the available fiscal years. You can use the Adjust\Copy button to copy amounts from the first month to all other months — and save yourself some typing — or to copy amounts from one fiscal year to another. Click Save, select the next account, and repeat the process.

If you're using any other edition of Peachtree, you open the Maintain Budgets window by choosing Maintain⇨Chart of Accounts. In the Maintain Chart of Accounts window, click the Budgets tab. You can create budgets for three years instead of two.

Visit this book's Web site for more information on Peachtree.

Chapter 4

Setting Up the Background Information

. . . .

In This Chapter

▶ Setting purchasing preferences

▶ Determining sales preferences

▶ Setting up payroll preferences

▶ Choosing inventory preferences

. . . .

*B*efore you dive into the day-to-day stuff of managing your company's books, you need to set up preferences. Doing so will save you time when performing daily tasks because Peachtree uses the default information as a model whenever you create vendors, customers, employees, and inventory items, produce statements, and enter transactions (purchase orders, purchases, invoices, payroll checks, and so on). You can alter this global information when a particular person or item requires something other than the default.

Terminology alert: Peachtree switches back and forth between two terms when referring to bills that vendors send you: a *purchase* and an *invoice*. For the sake of clarity, we call vendor bills a purchase; invoices are the things you send to customers so that *you* can get paid.

Setting Purchasing Preferences

"What kind of information do you supply for vendors?" you ask. Well, you set up standard terms. *Terms* describe how long the vendor gives you to hold a bill before you need to pay it and how you want Peachtree to respond if vendors offer you a discount for paying early. You also identify the default account to assign to most vendor bills and vendor discounts. And you specify how you want Peachtree to *age* bills that you enter. Last, you can set up custom fields for vendors to track information you specify about the people from whom you buy goods or services.

Aging is the concept of holding onto a bill for a specified period of time before you apply payment terms to it.

Peachtree applies these preferences to all vendors you create and all purchases you enter. If a vendor or a transaction is unusual in some way, you make a change to the specific vendor or transaction. Using standardized information in this way saves you time because you need to change the standard information only for exceptions to the rule. And let's face it — we *all* like to save time. See Chapter 5 for information on setting up vendors.

Establishing default payment terms and accounts

Efficient bill paying is an art. You don't want to pay your bills too early or too late. For example, if your bank account earns interest, you don't want to pay a vendor's bill too soon, because you lose interest from the bank. On the other hand, if your vendor assesses late fees or finance charges for bills that you don't pay on time, you don't want to pay a bill too late.

Using Peachtree's Vendor Defaults dialog box, you can establish a typical set of terms to use for most vendors. In Chapter 5, you can find out how to create vendors and how Peachtree automatically assigns these default terms to each vendor. You need to change terms only for those vendors who *don't* use the typical terms.

To set default payment terms and accounts that most vendors use, follow these steps:

1. **Choose Maintain⇨Default Information⇨Vendors to display the dialog box shown in Figure 4-1.**

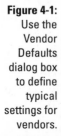

Figure 4-1:
Use the
Vendor
Defaults
dialog box
to define
typical
settings for
vendors.

2. **From among the Standard Terms option buttons, choose the option that best describes the terms most of your vendors offer you.**

   The terms shown in Figure 4-1 are 2% 10 Net 30, which means you can discount the bill by 2 percent if you pay it within 10 days; otherwise, the entire amount of the bill is due in 30 days.

3. **Fill in the appropriate boxes to the right of the terms you select in Step 2.**

   As you select an option button on the left, the boxes on the right change. For example, if you choose C.O.D. (cash on delivery) or Prepaid, only the Credit Limit box on the right remains available, because none of the other boxes apply.

4. **At the bottom of the Payment Terms tab, click the magnifying glass to select the account that you use most often when you post purchases from vendors.**

   If you don't select an account, Peachtree will prompt you for an account each time you create a new vendor.

5. **In the Discount GL Account text box, select the account to which you want Peachtree to post discounts that vendors give you for paying in the specified time.**

   To select the account, type its account number or click the Lookup list indicator (the magnifying glass) to the right of the account number to display a list. In the list, highlight the account number and click OK.

6. **Click OK to close the dialog box or leave it open to review additional defaults in the sections that follow.**

Keep two points in mind: First, you may never receive discounts from your vendors, but Peachtree expects you to set up the account anyhow. Second, you may want to increase the credit limit. If you exceed the credit limit when buying from a vendor, you can still buy from the vendor, but you see an annoying message telling you that you've exceeded the credit limit.

Aging vendor bills

When you age a bill, you hold onto it for a specified period of time before you pay it. You can age purchases (that is, you can tell Peachtree to count the number of days you hold the bill) from either the billing date or the due date.

To set account aging defaults, choose Maintain⇨Default Information⇨ Vendors. On the Account Aging tab, select a method to age bills: Invoice Date or Due Date. Optionally, you can change the number of days in each of the four columns on the Aged Payables report.

You may find the difference between the two aging methods easier to understand if you take a look at two Aged Payables reports, each prepared using one of the aging methods. In Figure 4-2, we set the Aging option to Due Date and then prepared a customized Accounts Payable Aging report for only one vendor, Akerson Wholesale Nursery, as of March 31, 2007. In Figure 4-3, we switched the Aging Option to Invoice Date and printed the same report for the same vendor and time frame. (Note that *invoice* here refers to bills your vendors send you.)

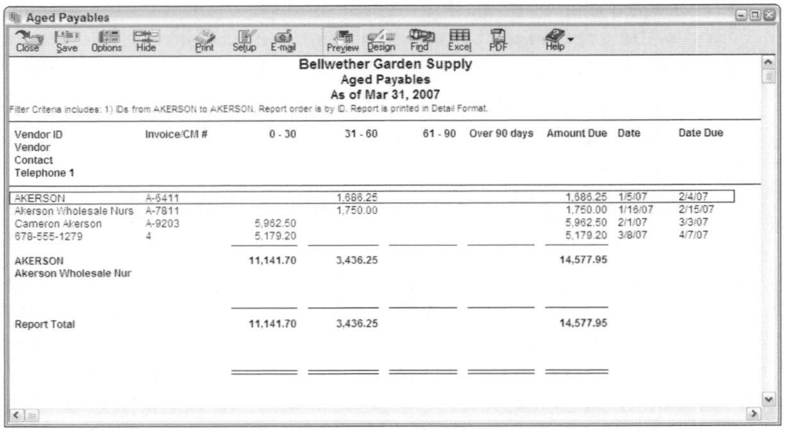

Bellwether Garden Supply
Aged Payables
As of Mar 31, 2007
Filter Criteria includes: 1) IDs from AKERSON to AKERSON. Report order is by ID. Report is printed in Detail Format.

Vendor ID / Vendor / Contact / Telephone 1	Invoice/CM #	0 - 30	31 - 60	61 - 90	Over 90 days	Amount Due	Date	Date Due
AKERSON	A-6411		1,686.25			1,686.25	1/5/07	2/4/07
Akerson Wholesale Nurs	A-7811		1,750.00			1,750.00	1/16/07	2/15/07
Cameron Akerson	A-9203	5,962.50				5,962.50	2/1/07	3/3/07
678-555-1279	4	5,179.20				5,179.20	3/8/07	4/7/07
AKERSON Akerson Wholesale Nur		11,141.70	3,436.25			14,577.95		
Report Total		11,141.70	3,436.25			14,577.95		

Figure 4-2: An Aging report showing bills aged by due date.

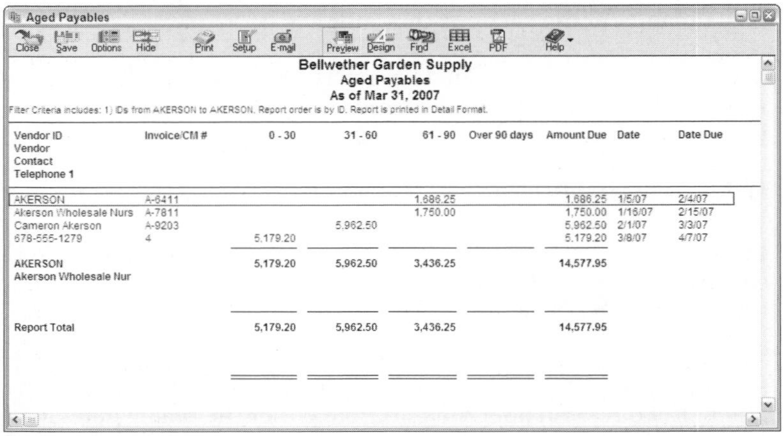

Bellwether Garden Supply
Aged Payables
As of Mar 31, 2007
Filter Criteria includes: 1) IDs from AKERSON to AKERSON. Report order is by ID. Report is printed in Detail Format.

Vendor ID / Vendor / Contact / Telephone 1	Invoice/CM #	0 - 30	31 - 60	61 - 90	Over 90 days	Amount Due	Date	Date Due
AKERSON	A-6411			1,686.25		1,686.25	1/5/07	2/4/07
Akerson Wholesale Nurs	A-7811			1,750.00		1,750.00	1/16/07	2/15/07
Cameron Akerson	A-9203		5,962.50			5,962.50	2/1/07	3/3/07
678-555-1279	4	5,179.20				5,179.20	3/8/07	4/7/07
AKERSON Akerson Wholesale Nur		5,179.20	5,962.50	3,436.25		14,577.95		
Report Total		5,179.20	5,962.50	3,436.25		14,577.95		

Figure 4-3: An Aging report showing bills aged by invoice date.

Both reports show four outstanding bills for Akerson Wholesale Nursery. Each bill, along with its date and due date, is listed on a separate line.

Notice the third bill — the one for $5,962.50. It was posted as of February 1, 2007, with terms of Net 30; the bill is due 30 days from the bill date of February 1 — on March 3. On the first report, the bill appears to be somewhere between 0 and 30 days old, while on the second report, it appears to be somewhere between 31 and 60 days old. In actuality, according to the first report, on March 31, 2007, the bill is somewhere between 0 and 30 days past the *due date* of the bill. According to the second report, on March 31, 2007, the bill is somewhere between 31 and 60 days past the *invoice date* of the bill.

This report is *not* showing you what is past due; it is showing you the bill's age based on the number of days *past* either the due date or the invoice date.

Many people choose to age vendor bills by Due Date because the bills look "less overdue" on the aging report.

Creating custom fields for vendors

Custom fields are a great way to store information about your vendors that doesn't fit elsewhere in Peachtree, such as details specific to your business or industry. For example, many businesses track a workers compensation certificate number for subcontractors to justify not covering the subcontractor on the company's workers compensation insurance. On the Custom Fields tab of the Vendor Defaults dialog box, you can create up to five fields for each vendor. Check a box and, in the Field Labels boxes, type identifying labels for the information you want to store.

When you set up vendors, you can fill in this information for each vendor. (See Chapter 5 for more information on creating or editing vendor information.) On some reports in Peachtree, you can print this information.

1099 Settings

On the 1099 Settings tab, you can, if necessary, change the way that Peachtree calculates 1099 payments. For each account on the Chart of Accounts, you can identify whether and how Peachtree should calculate 1099 income. By default, Peachtree assumes that you will establish the correct 1099 type for each vendor when you create the vendor, so each account is set up to look at the vendor's record. You can, however, specify that a particular account should be used to calculate 1099 miscellaneous income, 1099 interest income, or you can specify that the account should not be used when calculating 1099 income. In most cases, you don't need to change the default settings.

Setting Sales Preferences

"What kind of information do you supply for customers?" you ask. Well, you set up standard terms for customers like you do for vendors. Only this time, *you're* the one establishing when payment is due and whether you offer customers a discount for paying early. Customer terms also tell Peachtree how to respond if customers pay early. You also identify the default sales account and discount account where you want Peachtree to assign most customer invoices. You specify how you want Peachtree to age invoices that you prepare. As with vendors, you can set up custom fields for customers to track specific information that may help you increase sales or offer perks. You also can decide whether to charge your customers finance charges for overdue invoices, and you can set their Pay Methods — cash, check, credit card, or anything green.

The concept of aging applies also to invoices you send to your customers. In this instance, aging refers to the specified period of time you allow before you pay an invoice — and potentially charge the customer finance charges for late payment.

As with vendors, Peachtree applies these preferences to all customers you create and all invoices you enter. If a customer or a transaction is unusual in some way, you can make a change to the specific customer or transaction.

Establishing default payment terms and accounts

When customers don't pay you in a timely fashion, you may experience *cash flow* problems. That is, you have money going out of your business for expenses but not enough money coming in to cover those expenses. To encourage your customers to pay on time, you establish payment terms similar to the ones your vendors set for you.

Using Peachtree's Customer Defaults dialog box, you can establish a typical set of terms to use for most customers. In Chapter 7, when you create customers, you'll see that Peachtree automatically assigns these default terms to each customer. Change preferences for only those customers who *don't* use the typical terms.

To set default payment terms and accounts for most customers, follow these steps:

1. **Choose Maintain⇨Default Information⇨Customers to display the Customer Defaults dialog box (see Figure 4-4).**

Figure 4-4:
Use the
Customer
Defaults
dialog box
to define
typical
settings for
customers.

Customer Defaults

| Terms and Credit | Account Aging | Custom Fields | Finance Charges | Pay Methods |

Standard Terms — Sets Default Terms, Credit Limit, and Credit Status

- C.O.D.
- Prepaid
- Due in number of days
- Due on day of next month
- Due at end of month

Net due in [30] days

Discount in [10] days

Discount Percent: [2.00]

Credit Limit: [50,000.00]

Credit Status: [Notify Over Limit ▼]

OK
Cancel
Help

GL Link Accounts   —   Sets Default Accounts for new Customer Records, the Sales Account can also be changed in each Customer Record

GL Sales Account [40000-00 🔍]   Sales

Discount GL Account [49000-00 🔍]   Sales Discounts

2. **From among the Standard Terms option buttons, choose the option that best describes the terms you offer most of your customers.**

   The terms shown in Figure 4-4 are 2% 10 Net EOM, which means your customers can discount the invoice by 2 percent if they pay it within 10 days; otherwise, the entire amount of the invoice is due at the end of the month. (EOM stands for *end of month*.)

3. **Fill in the appropriate boxes to the right of the terms you selected in Step 2.**

   The options for customer terms work like the options for vendor terms. As you select an option button on the left, the boxes on the right change. For example, if you choose C.O.D. or Prepaid, only the Credit Limit box on the right remains available because none of the other boxes apply.

   You can use the Credit Status list to control Peachtree's behavior in relation to the customer's credit limit when you enter an invoice. The list contains five choices. On one end of the spectrum, you can record invoices without seeing any messages, regardless of the relationship between the customer's balance and credit limit. On the other end of the spectrum, Peachtree will not allow you to enter an invoice for a customer regardless of the relationship between the customer's balance and credit limit. In between these choices, you can have Peachtree display a warning or an error message when a transaction will cause a customer's balance to exceed the credit limit. And you can have Peachtree display a warning whenever you record a transaction for a customer who owes you money even if the customer's balance doesn't exceed his or her credit limit.

4. **Select the GL Sales Account that you use most often when you sell goods or services to customers.**

To select the account, type the account number or click the Lookup list identifier (the magnifying glass) to the right of the account number to display and select from a lookup list. If you don't select an account, Peachtree will prompt you for an account each time you create a new customer.

5. **Select the Discount GL Account you use to track discounts taken by customers.**

6. **When you've finished setting payment preferences, click OK to save those preferences.**

Even if you never offer discounts to your customers, Peachtree expects you to set up the account anyhow. (If you haven't set up a discount general ledger account, see Chapter 3 for information on creating accounts.)

Aging customer invoices

We talk about aging a lot in our society, and now you're getting a whole new picture of wrinkled bills and invoices. Just as you can control the aging process for vendor bills, you can age customer invoices from either the invoice date or the due date.

Accounts receivable aging works the same as accounts payable aging — that is, you can choose to age by due date or by invoice date. Suppose that you post an invoice as of February 20, 2007, with terms of 2% 10, Net 30 Days.

If you set up accounts receivable aging to age by due date, the invoice is due 30 days from the invoice date of February 20, which is March 22. On the Accounts Receivable Aging report, the invoice appears to be somewhere between 0 and 30 days old — that is, on March 31, 2007, the invoice is somewhere between 0 and 30 days *past the due date* of the invoice.

Alternatively, if you set up accounts receivable aging to age by invoice date, the same invoice appears on the Accounts Receivable Aging report to be somewhere between 31 and 60 days old. That is, on March 31, 2007, the invoice is somewhere between 31 and 60 days *past the invoice date* of the invoice.

This report is *not* showing you what is past due; it is showing you the age of invoices based on the number of days *past* either the due date or the invoice date.

Many people choose to age customer invoices by invoice date because the aging report then reflects how old the invoice is. Others prefer to age invoices by due date so that they can see how many days the invoice is overdue.

Creating custom fields for customers

In the Custom Fields tab of the Customer Defaults dialog box, you can enter labels for up to five fields for each customer. Use these fields to store extra information about customers, such as noting new customers who found your business on the Web. Simply place a check in any Enabled box, and type the descriptive text in the Field Labels box. When you set up customers, you can fill in this information for each customer. On some reports in Peachtree, you can print this information.

Suppose that you've established a label and filled in information for customers. If you reopen the Customer Defaults dialog box and change the labels, you *won't* affect the information you stored for each customer; you must edit each customer's record and make a change to match the new label you've established. If you simply don't want to show the information you've already entered, you can hide the stored information by removing the check mark from the Enabled check box in the Customer Defaults dialog box. However, the information reappears if you enable the custom field once again.

Setting up finance charges

Finance charges are fees you charge customers who pay late. Many businesses don't charge finance charges; others believe that finance charges encourage customers to pay on time and therefore improve cash flow. Still others believe that charging these fees is necessary if customers continuously ignore payment terms.

If you want to be able to charge finance charges, follow these steps:

1. **Choose Maintain⇨Default Information⇨Customers and click the Finance Charges tab of the Customer Defaults box.**

2. **Place a check mark in the Charge Finance Charges box.**

3. **Complete the remaining information to tell Peachtree how to calculate finance charges.**

   Peachtree charges an interest rate that you specify on invoices that are overdue by the number of days you specify. You can charge a higher rate on balances that exceed an amount you specify, specify a minimum finance charge amount.

4. **Optionally, check the Charge Interest On Finance Charges box.**

5. **Use the Lookup list indicator to select a G/L account for finance charges.**

6. **From the Appears On Invoices and Statements As list box, select the description for the finance charge (either Late Charge or Finance Charge).**

7. **Optionally, provide a warning message that Peachtree can print on invoices.**

8. **Click OK.**

This information becomes part of your standard terms.

Placing a check mark in the Charge Interest on Finance Charges check box tells Peachtree to calculate interest on any unpaid balance as well as unpaid finance charges. Check with your accountant before you check this box; in some states, it is illegal to charge interest on interest. Also, enabling finance charges does *not* make Peachtree automatically assess finance charges. And you don't need to assign finance charges to *all* of your customers. See Chapter 8 for information on assessing finance charges.

The Finance Charge Warning message at the bottom of the Finance Charges tab is printed on the bottom of invoices you send to customers. If you're not charging finance charges, you may want to change the message to something like "Happy Holidays" or "See our exhibit at the Business Expo March 16–19."

Establishing payment methods

Pay methods are exactly what they sound like — the various methods of payment that your company accepts. You establish these default settings on the Pay Methods tab of the Customer Defaults dialog box. Choose Maintain➪ Default Information➪Customers and click the Pay Methods tab. Then, in the boxes provided, type the names of the payment methods your company accepts.

These payment methods are available when you record payments you receive from customers. You can include the Payment Method field on reports. For example, you can add this field to the Cash Receipts journal and filter the journal to see *only* transactions of a particular pay method.

Adding a new payment method after you've already recorded transactions in Peachtree doesn't affect previously recorded transactions. The new payment method is simply available for new transactions.

On the Pay Methods tab, you also can tell Peachtree to automatically assign Deposit Ticket IDs in either the Receipts window or in the Select for Deposit window. Deposit Ticket IDs help you group payments you receive from customers. To help you reconcile your bank statement, you typically use the same Deposit Ticket ID for all customer payments that you plan to deposit in the bank at the same time. See Chapter 8 for more information on recording receipts and using Deposit Ticket IDs.

Setting Payroll Preferences

To correctly set up and use payroll in Peachtree, you need to identify some basic information, such as the state where your company operates. But understanding payroll is difficult even when you aren't worried about setting up payroll in an accounting program. On the "good news" front, Peachtree uses a wizard to walk you through establishing the defaults for preparing payroll checks and tax-related forms (W-2s, Federal Form 940, and Federal Form 941). Peachtree doesn't prepare most state tax forms, but Chapter 9 shows you how to use Peachtree payroll reports to find the information you need to complete the forms.

Using the Payroll Setup Wizard

The Payroll Setup Wizard helps you set up basic information about payroll, including payroll fields that Peachtree then uses to calculate payroll checks. *Payroll fields* are things such as gross wages and federal income tax (FIT) — one of those many mysterious abbreviations that appear on your payroll check stub. Chapter 19 describes how to set up a payroll field for some common payroll deductions (or additions — for those lucky enough to get a bonus) that you want to include on a paycheck.

Peachtree Software Company does *not* ship tax tables that calculate federal taxes with the software. To subscribe to Peachtree's Payroll Tax Table Update service, call 1-800-336-1420 Monday through Friday, 8:30 a.m. to 5:30 p.m. eastern standard time. You can use the Payroll Setup Wizard to help you set up payroll when you first create a company or later, after you've been using Peachtree for awhile. No problem — take your choice. In the paragraphs that follow, we show you how to use the wizard to set up basic payroll information.

The Payroll Setup Wizard also can be useful after you've set up payroll. For example, suppose that your company didn't have a 401(k) plan when you originally set up payroll but later decided to add one. The Payroll Setup Wizard makes implementing this change easy. Similarly, you can set up payroll and then decide to track vacation and sick leave. See Chapter 19 for information on setting up a 401(k) plan and tracking both vacation and sick leave.

To start the Payroll Setup Wizard, follow these steps:

1. **Choose Maintain⇨Default Information⇨Payroll Setup Wizard.**

   The first screen of the Payroll Setup Wizard lists the options you're going to set: general ledger accounts, standard payroll fields (taxes and so on), and optional payroll fields.

2. **Click Next.**

   You see the version number of the current global tax table installed on your computer. Peachtree uses tax tables to make calculations related to payroll. The most obvious tax tables calculate the amount of tax to deduct for FIT, FICA, Medicare, and Federal Unemployment Taxes (FUTA).

   To determine whether your tax tables are up-to-date, visit Peachtree's Web site at www.peachtree.com. Click the link for Tax Service, select the Peachtree product you're using, and then click the View Tax Update Version History link. Look through this Web page and compare your tax table version to the latest available.

3. **Click Next.**

   A screen appears for specifying the primary state to receive your payroll taxes, the applicable percentage in the Unemployment Percent for Your Company, and whether you want to record meals and tips for employees.

   When you enter rates into Peachtree, you must express them as percentages, but many state forms express rates in decimals. For example, suppose the state form shows that your unemployment rate is 0.008. That's a decimal. To express it as a percentage (0.8%), you'd type 0.8 into Peachtree. Yeah, entering these numbers requires that high school math stuff, where you have to divide a decimal by 100 to get the percentage equivalent. Yeah, yeah, yeah. . . .

   Depending on the state you select, Peachtree may ask you for a Locality and Locality Rate.

   If you choose to record meals and tips, Peachtree tracks the amounts for reporting and tax calculation, but it won't post any entries to the general ledger. For more information on recording meals and tips, refer to IRS Publication 15, Circular E, Employer's Tax Guide. You can download a copy of Circular E at the Web site of the IRS:

   www.irs.gov/formspubs/index.html

   See Chapter 21 to find out about more stuff you can find on the Web.

4. **Click Next to select general ledger accounts to use for payroll (see Figure 4-5).**

   If you based the Chart Of Accounts on one of the standard companies when you created your company, Peachtree suggests payroll accounts.

   If you don't have payroll accounts set up, you can define them on the fly. Click the lookup list button next to each account box to display a list of existing accounts. Click the New button to create new accounts while still using the Payroll Setup Wizard. Refer to Chapter 3 for information on setting up accounts.

Some people create separate payroll liability accounts for each payroll tax liability. To make your life easier using Peachtree, we recommend that you create payroll liability accounts that correspond to the taxing authority you pay. For example, you pay FIT, FICA, and Medicare to the same taxing authority, so set up only one payroll liability account for all three taxes. If you pay state and local taxes to the same taxing authority, set up only one liability account for both taxes. Check with your accountant if you are unsure. We recommend this approach because it makes writing your payroll tax liability checks easier.

5. **Click Next four times to skip setting up the optional payroll fields and see the payroll fields you created.**

   At this point, you've finished the basic setup for payroll; the remaining choices in the Payroll Setup Wizard enable you to set up payroll fields for a 401(k) Plan, vacation tracking, and sick leave tracking.

6. **Click Finish.**

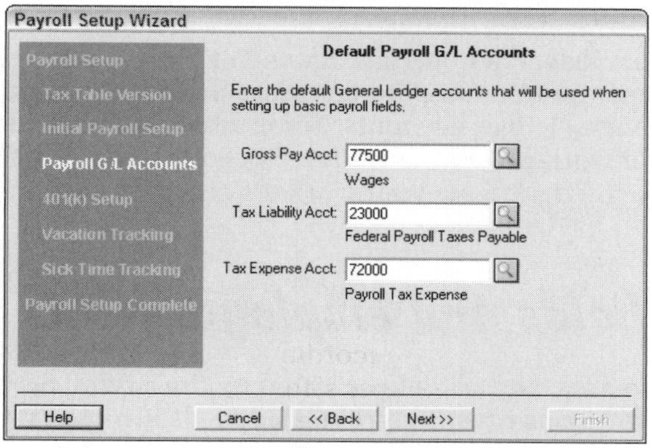

Figure 4-5:
Identify your
payroll
accounts.

Establishing general employee defaults
=======================================

Once you run the Payroll Setup Wizard, you can change the payroll settings from the Employee Defaults dialog box (choose Maintain➪Default Information➪Employees). You can use the General tab to change your state or set a locality if necessary and to establish custom fields for storing miscellaneous information about each employee. To make a custom field available, place a check mark in the Enabled box next to the field.

Peachtree automatically assigns payroll fields to the various boxes on the W-2 form, employee-paid taxes, or employer-paid taxes. You can, however, edit the assignments by clicking the appropriate button in the Assign Payroll Fields For section.

Setting pay levels

Pay levels are names you set for various types of hourly and salary pay. Choose Maintain⇨Default Information⇨Employees and click the Pay Levels tab. By default, Peachtree automatically establishes the pay levels that appear on the tab. Hourly wage pay levels appear on the left, and salary pay levels appear on the right.

You can create up to 20 hourly pay levels and 20 salary pay levels, and you can assign different pay levels to different general ledger accounts. Just type the name for the pay level in the Field Name list and assign the pay level to a G/L account.

You can override these defaults as necessary when you set up your employees. For example, suppose that you need to keep track of wages by department. You can set the default G/L account to the department with the largest number of employees and then, on individual employee records, change it to the appropriate department G/L account as necessary.

To make your general ledger and income statement more meaningful, your accountant may want you to use a different set of pay levels, pointing some or all to different general ledger accounts. For example, you can use pay levels based on your worker's compensation categories as one method of letting Peachtree help you determine your worker's compensation liability.

Employee fields and employer fields

Peachtree categorizes the payroll fields created by the Payroll Setup Wizard into employee-related fields or employer-related fields. On the EmployEE Fields tab (see Figure 4-6), you see payroll fields belonging to employees. These include gross wages, FIT, and the employee's share of FICA and Medicare. On the EmployER Fields tab, you can view payroll fields paid by the company, including FUTA, state unemployment taxes, and the employer's share of FICA and Medicare. You can see the general ledger account and payroll tax table Peachtree associated with each of the fields.

On the EmployEE Fields tab, you can do the following:

- Change the G/L account for a payroll field.

- Change the tax table Peachtree uses to calculate a particular payroll field. Click in the Tax Name column to display a Lookup list indicator that enables you to choose from a list of available tax tables.

- Place a check in the Memo column next to a field, such as Tips, to tell Peachtree to calculate that field without updating your general ledger or including the amounts in employees' pay; note that Peachtree can use fields marked as memos to calculate taxes.

✔ Place a check in the Run column next to a field to tell Peachtree *not* to set the balance for this field to zero at the end of the payroll year. For example, if you allow your employees to retain unused vacation from year to year, set up your Vacation field with a check in the Run box.

✔ For fields Peachtree calculates, you can click the Adjust button to identify the fields you want Peachtree to add when calculating Adjusted Gross Wages for the field. For example, you may want Adjusted Gross Wages to include gross wages, FICA, and Medicare, but *not* FIT when calculating an auto expense deduction.

✔ For fields Peachtree doesn't calculate using a tax table, you can supply a default amount. For example, if most employees pay the same amount for medical insurance, you can type that amount in the Amount column, and on the individual employee's records, supply the appropriate amount for employees who don't pay the standard amount.

If you're entering an amount you want deducted, enter it as a negative amount.

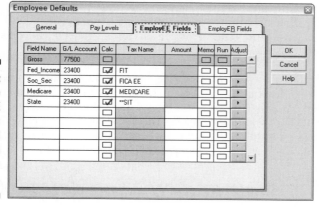

Figure 4-6:
On the
EmployEE
tab, you
see payroll
fields
belonging to
employees.

Although you are allowed to edit the names of payroll fields, *don't* change the name of a payroll field and *don't* change the order of the payroll fields after you've entered payroll transactions. You'll get inaccurate information on the payroll earnings reports and W-2 forms. We recommend that you retain the names of payroll fields Peachtree creates for you because they are often used in payroll tax tables.

On the EmployER Fields tab, you can set these preferences:

✔ Change the general ledger liability and expense accounts for a payroll field.

✔ Change the tax table Peachtree uses to calculate a particular payroll field. Click in the Tax Name column to display the Lookup list indicator and then select from a list of available tax tables.

> ✔ For fields Peachtree calculates, you can click the Adjust button to iden-
> tify the fields you want Peachtree to include when determining Adjusted
> Gross Wages for the field.

The same warning applies to EmployER field names that applied to EmployEE field names. *Don't* change the name of a payroll field and *don't* change the order of the payroll fields after you've entered payroll transactions. These alterations create inaccurate information on the payroll earnings reports and W-2 forms. And the names of payroll fields are often used in payroll tax tables.

Setting Inventory Preferences

Before you start filling your virtual shelves in Peachtree, you need to set up the preferences that help track all those wonderful items as they come and go. *Inventory items* in Peachtree terms are typically anything that you buy from vendors or sell to customers. It's important to understand that Peachtree inventory items do not necessarily have to be things that you keep on hand or that add value to the balance sheet; the item class of the inventory item determines whether it adds value to your balance sheet. In the section "Inventory items and general ledger accounts," later in this chapter, you read about item classes.

You can set preferences for inventory items using the Inventory Item Defaults dialog box, which you open by choosing Maintain⇨Default Information⇨ Inventory Items. The dialog box contains six tabs. On the General tab, you can specify whether to permit duplicate values in the UPC/SKU field of inventory items. Read on to find out about the other defaults you can set.

Inventory items and ordering defaults

The Ordering tab of the Inventory Item Defaults dialog box, shown in Figure 4-7, helps you control issues related to, well, ordering inventory items. For example, you can choose to have Peachtree include items on purchase orders when it calculates the quantity available.

You can have Peachtree warn you when you're entering a sales order, an invoice, or a receipt for an inventory item that is out of stock based on the quantity on hand or the quantity available.

In the last section of the Ordering tab, you can enable the auto-creation of purchase orders for drop-ship transactions and non-drop-ship transactions.

When you enable real-time posting and assign a preferred vendor to each inventory item, Peachtree will automatically create purchase orders for you when you convert a drop-ship quote to a sales order, a drop-ship quote to an invoice, or when you enter a drop-ship sales order or a drop-ship invoice containing inventory items.

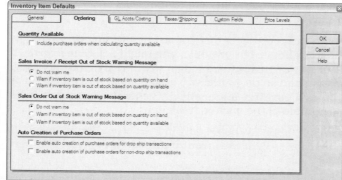

Figure 4-7:
Use the
Ordering
tab to set
ordering
defaults.

If your transactions are not drop-ship transactions, you can have Peachtree automatically create purchase orders for you when the quantity of an item you specify causes the quantity available as of the transaction date to fall below the minimum stock levels you set for the item. Again, for this feature to work, you must enable real-time posting and assign a preferred vendor to each inventory item.

Inventory items and general ledger accounts

Peachtree uses *item classes* to organize inventory items. You assign each inventory item to a class when you create the item. And you can choose the various accounts affected by inventory items in each of these item classes. For stock, master stock, and assembly items, you can also choose an inventory method. Chapter 11 includes information on how to create inventory items.

For the purpose of setting defaults, remember that an item's class determines how Peachtree records the cost of the item.

Peachtree Premium supports 11 item classes, Peachtree Complete supports 9 item classes, and the other versions support 7 item classes. These item classes follow:

- ✔ **Stock:** For inventory items that you track for quantities, average costs, vendors, low stock points, and so on.

   When you've assigned an item to the Stock class, you can't change the item's class.

- ✔ **Master Stock:** For items that consist of information shared by a number of substock items. For example, you might sell blue jeans, which consist of a number of attributes, such as size and style (straight leg, relaxed fit, classic fit, and so on.) After you create a master stock item and define its attributes, Peachtree automatically generates substock items based on the attributes of the master stock item.

- ✔ **Serialized Stock:** Available only in Peachtree Premium accounting, use this item class when the inventory items have serial numbers that you plan to track.

- ✔ **Nonstock:** For items that you sell but do not put into your inventory, such as service contracts. Peachtree prints quantities, descriptions, and unit prices on invoices but doesn't track quantities on hand. You can assign a cost of sales G/L account, but it is not affected by a costing method.

- ✔ **Description only:** When you track nothing but the description. For example, you can add comments to sales or purchase transactions using description-only items.

- ✔ **Service:** For services you can apply to your G/L salary and wages account to bill a customer for services provided by your employees.

- ✔ **Labor:** For third-party labor costs that you pass on to a customer. You can apply these costs to your G/L salary and wages account.

- ✔ **Assembly:** For items that consist of components that must be built or dismantled.

- ✔ **Serialized Assembly:** Available only in Peachtree Premium, use this item class for assembly items that also have serial numbers.

- ✔ **Activity:** Available only in Peachtree Premium and Peachtree Complete, for recording, using Peachtree's Time & Billing feature, how time is spent when performing services for a customer or job.

- ✔ **Charge:** Available only in Peachtree Premium and Peachtree Complete, for recording, using Peachtree's Time & Billing feature, the expenses of an employee or vendor when working for a customer or job.

See Chapter 10 for more information on Peachtree's Time & Billing feature.

Follow these steps to set or review the account assignments for the inventory item classes:

1. **Choose Maintain⇨Default Information⇨Inventory Items to display the Inventory Item Defaults dialog box.**

2. **Click the GL Accts/Costing tab.**

3. **Move the mouse pointer over any white box to see the Lookup list mouse pointer (arrow + ?), and then click to display the Lookup list button, as shown in Figure 4-8.**

4. **Click the Lookup list indicator (the magnifying glass) to display a list of your available accounts.**

5. **Highlight the account you want to use and then click OK.**

6. **Repeat Steps 3 through 5 as necessary in any white box on this screen to change an Item Class assignment.**

   For the Costing column, choose FIFO, LIFO, or Average as your costing method.

   Check with your accountant to help choose the correct method for your business. Just so you know what we're talking about, turn to the sidebar in Chapter 11.

7. **If necessary, change the GL Freight Account using Steps 3,4, and 5.**

   You use the GL Freight Account to assign freight charges to an invoice.

8. **When you are finished, click OK or click another tab and read the related information in the next section.**

Figure 4-8:
Set the default accounts for your inventory items.

Taxes and shipping

Ah, taxes. The government needs to get its cut when you sell something — and so, when appropriate, you must collect sales tax and pass it on to your state's taxing agency. As you would expect with anything connected with then government, sales taxes are not straightforward. The government requires that you charge tax on some things but not other things. To take that concept a step further, some organizations (notably governmental and charitable agencies) don't pay taxes. And, of course, it's up to you, the seller, to keep straight who pays tax and for what.

If necessary, choose Maintain⇨Default Information⇨Inventory Items to display the Inventory Item Defaults dialog box. Click the Taxes/Shipping tab. On the left side of the Taxes/Shipping tab, you can define up to 25 tax types (you have our sympathy if you need all of them). You use tax types to organize the sales taxes that you remit and report to your state sales tax agency. Typically, you want to set up tax types that match the categories you must report on your state's sales tax return.

After you establish tax types, you assign a tax type to each inventory item you create — see Chapter 11 for more information. When you sell the item, Peachtree will note the tax type, and when you pay your sales tax, you use a report that segregates your sales by tax type. So that's why you want to set up tax types that match the categories you report on your state sales tax return. See Chapter 7 for information on setting up sales taxes and Chapter 6 for information on paying sales taxes.

You also can use the right side of the Taxes/Shipping tab to create up to 10 shipping methods. Remember that shipping methods don't have anything to do with inventory items; you assign shipping methods to customers and vendors. The shipping methods you assign will appear on quotes, sales orders, invoices, purchases, and purchase orders. Find out more about setting up vendors in Chapter 5 and setting up customers in Chapter 7.

Custom fields

Although you don't assign shipping methods to inventory items, you may assign custom fields to inventory items — notes, alternate vendors, and weight are a few examples of the type of information you might store in custom fields. Choose Maintain⇨Default Information⇨Inventory and click the Custom Fields tab. Place a check mark in the Enabled box next to each custom field that you want to use and then type the name of the custom field in the Field Labels box.

Price levels

Peachtree Premium and Peachtree Complete support multiple prices — price levels, so to speak — for inventory items. You can set up to 10 price levels for each inventory item, assigning an easy-to-remember level name such as Retail, Wholesale, and Discount5 (for Discounted 5%), and then use the various price levels to establish pricing schemes. For example, you might establish Price Level 1 as your full retail price, Price Level 2 as a 5% discount off the retail price, and Price Level 3 as a 10% discount off the retail price. You start by identifying which of the 10 price levels you want to use on the Price Levels tab of the Inventory Item Defaults dialog box, shown in Figure 4-9. To use a price level, place a check mark in the Enabled column next to the price level.

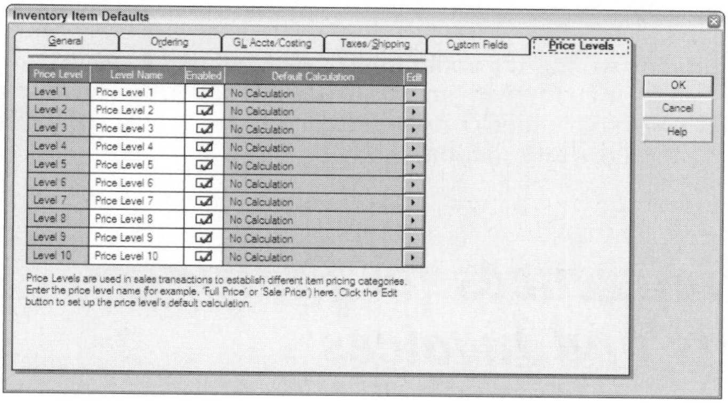

Figure 4-9: Identify the price levels you want to use by checking the Enabled box.

You also can set default price calculations for each price level. The calculation can be based on the last cost of an item or on Price Level 1. After selecting the basis for the calculation, you can increase or decrease the price by either a percentage or an amount. You set default price calculations by clicking the button in the Edit column next to the appropriate price level. Peachtree displays the Default Price Level Calculation dialog box, shown in Figure 4-10.

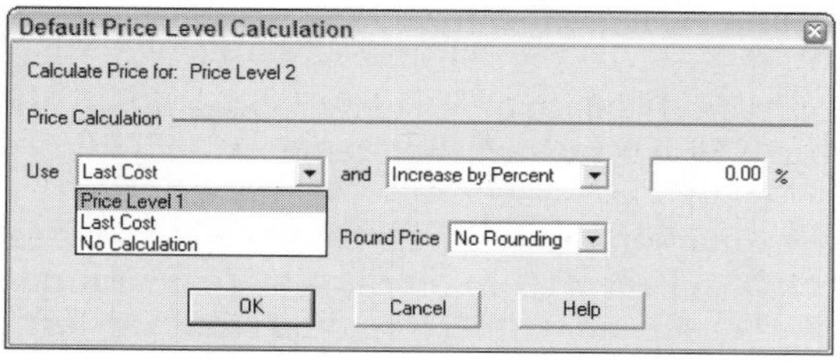

Figure 4-10: Use this dialog box to establish a calculation for a price level.

The calculations you establish in the Inventory Item Defaults dialog box are defaults for all items. You also can establish selling prices for each individual item by using the Maintain Inventory Items window. Any prices you establish for an individual item override prices you set in the Inventory Item Defaults box. See Chapter 11 for details.

The Price level feature in Peachtree is powerful. Even after you establish defaults and then override them by setting price levels for individual items, you can override individual item price levels on invoices as you create them. See Chapter 7 for more information.

Peachtree also enables you to assign price levels directly to customers; suppose, for example, that you always discount all merchandise for a particular customer to Price Level 3. In the Maintain Customers/Prospects window, you can assign a customer to Price Level 3 so that all items on all invoices for the customer default to Price Level 3. Again, see Chapter 7 for more information.

You're probably wondering about how to change prices — after all, nothing stays the same price forever (unfortunately). Yes, you can easily raise (or lower, if you are so inclined) prices without editing individual items. See Chapter 11 for more information.

Setting Preferences for Printing Statements and Invoices

Just as you can set defaults for the way you want Peachtree to handle your customers, vendors, and employees, you also can control the information printed on statements and invoices. You set these preferences by choosing Maintain➪Default Information➪Statement/Invoices.

Suppose, for example, that you don't use preprinted invoices or statements but that you want your company's name, address, and phone numbers to appear on the top of the invoice or statement. In the Statement/Invoices Defaults box, shown in Figure 4-11, simply place a check mark in the last check box to print your company's name, address, and phone numbers, as they appear in the Maintain Company Information window.

Use the rest of the boxes on the Statement Print Options tab to control the customers selected when Peachtree prints statements:

 ✔ If you place a check mark in the Any activity since the last statement was printed check box, Peachtree will print a statement for any customer who has purchased something from you since the last time you printed statements.

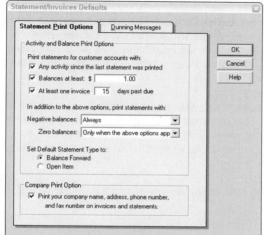

Figure 4-11:
Use this
box to
control the
information
that prints
on invoices
and
statements.

✔ If you place a check mark in the Balances at least check box and supply a minimum balance number, Peachtree will print statements for customers with balances equal to or greater than the minimum balance.

✔ If you place a check mark in the At least one invoice X days past due check box and then type a number of days overdue, Peachtree will print statements for any customers who have an invoice overdue by at least the number of days you entered.

✔ Place a check mark in the Negative balances box to specify whether Peachtree should print statements for customers with credit balances — the people to whom you owe money. You can choose Always, Never, or Only when the above options apply.

✔ Place a check mark in the Zero balance box to specify whether Peachtree should print statements for customers whose balance is 0. You can choose Always, Never, or Only when the preceding options apply.

Strangely enough, each of these check boxes is a yes-or-no question, but the check boxes in this section of the dialog box work together. If a customer meets *any* condition that you have checked, Peachtree will print a statement. For example, suppose that you place a check mark in the Any Activity Since The Last Statement Was Printed box and also in the Balances At Least check box and you supply $1.00 as the minimum balance. Peachtree will print statements for all customers who have bought something from you *and* all customers whose balance is greater than $1.00. So, even if you did not want customers with 0 balances, Peachtree will print statements for those customers if they have bought something and paid for it. Be sure to examine the logic of all the boxes you choose to check.

Peachtree can print *balance forward* statements, similar to the way information appears on a MasterCard or Visa credit card bill, where an invoice appears only once on a statement and its balance subsequently becomes part of the Previous Balance line. Or Peachtree can print open item statements, where all outstanding invoices — the ones that aren't paid in full — appear on the statement.

Using the Dunning Messages tab, you can specify four messages that may appear on statements. The message that appears on a particular statement depends on the length of time a customer's account is overdue. In addition to entering the message, you also can enter the number of days the account is overdue.

Visit this book's Web site for more information on Peachtree.

Part II
The Daily Drudge

The 5th Wave   By Rich Tennant

"MY GIRLFRIEND RAN A SPREADSHEET OF MY LIFE, AND GENERATED THIS CHART. MY BEST HOPE IS THAT SHE'LL CHANGE HER MAJOR FROM 'COMPUTER SCIENCES' TO 'REHABILITATIVE SERVICES.'"

In this part . . .

Data entry. It's a dirty job . . . but somebody has to do it. Whether you handle the day–to–day accounting responsibilities associated with your business or have someone in your office do them for you, you'll find this part valuable.

In this part, we show you how to keep up with tasks including billing your customers and collecting money from them, purchasing and paying for goods and services used in your business, and paying employees. We also cover job costing and time and billing tasks.

Chapter 5

Buying Goods

- -

In This Chapter

▶ Setting up vendors

▶ Tracking goods with purchase orders

▶ Entering a vendor bill

▶ Receiving inventory

▶ Getting credit for returns

- -

*B*uying things is part of the business of doing business. Some businesses buy goods from vendors and keep them in inventory to resell to customers. Some businesses buy goods to use in the manufacturing of a product to sell to customers. And all businesses buy the goods and services that they use to stay in business, such as office supplies and utilities.

So, no matter how you look at it, you can expect to receive bills in the mail. And, of course, paying bills isn't fun, but at least Peachtree can make the process easier and save you time — time you can spend earning more money.

This chapter describes the typical actions you take to record and track vendors' bills.

Terminology alert: Peachtree tends to switch back and forth between two different terms when referring to bills that vendors send you: a *purchase* and an *invoice*. For the sake of clarity, we call it a purchase unless the screen calls it an invoice. For our purposes, invoices are things you send to customers so that *you* can get paid.

Working with Vendors

If you buy goods or services from a particular vendor on a regular basis, you can save time in the long run if you set up that vendor in Peachtree. In fact, if you *don't* set up the vendor, you'll find it difficult to track how much you've spent with that vendor. There . . . you have two good reasons to set up vendors with whom you do business on a regular basis.

Adding vendors

When you set up a vendor, you supply name and address information, a purchase account to use each time you post a purchase from the vendor, and custom field information. You also can view historical information about your purchases from the vendor for the previous 12 months.

To add a new vendor, follow these steps:

1. Choose Maintain⇨Vendors to display the Maintain Vendors window, as shown in Figure 5-1.

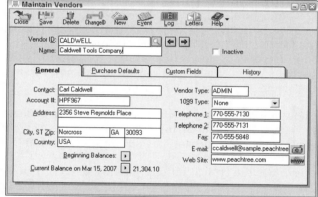

Figure 5-1:
Use this
window to
add, edit, or
delete
vendors.

2. Fill in the Vendor ID and the Name text boxes.

The ID is the number you use to select the vendor when you want to post a purchase or payment, so try to make it meaningful. The ID can be up to 20 characters and numbers long, and it is case sensitive. We suggest that you use lowercase letters so that you can type the ID quickly. By default, Peachtree sorts the vendor list and reports using the Vendor ID. To get Peachtree to sort the vendor list in alphabetical order by default, use characters from the vendor's name as the ID.

3. On the General tab, fill in contact information — your account number with the vendor and the vendor's address and phone numbers.

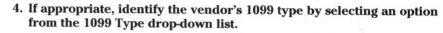

The account number you supply appears by default on checks you print from the Payment window. Find out more about the Payment window in Chapter 6.

4. **If appropriate, identify the vendor's 1099 type by selecting an option from the 1099 Type drop-down list.**

According to IRS rules, you must issue a 1099 to a vendor who is an independent contractor if the contractor is not incorporated and you pay $600 or more per year to that vendor. Peachtree can print 1099s at the end of the year for vendors you designate as 1099 vendors. Sales representatives might be considered 1099 vendors, based on the IRS definition of employees and independent contractors. If you have Peachtree Complete or Premium, you can filter several of Peachtree's reports by 1099 Type; see Chapter 14 for more information on printing and filtering reports. See Chapter 9 for more discussion on paying sales representatives who are also employees.

5. **Use the Vendor Type text box to group similar vendors together.**

For example, you may want to distinguish between vendors who supply you with inventory and vendors who provide overhead services such as telephone. The text you enter in the Vendor Type text box can be up to eight characters long; note that this field is case sensitive. Entering a vendor type is useful because you can limit some reports to specific vendor types.

6. **If appropriate, supply an e-mail and a Web address for the vendor.**

Both e-mail and Web addresses are interactive. So, if you supply an e-mail address and click the icon next to the E-mail text box, Peachtree opens your e-mail program and starts a message to the vendor. Similarly, clicking the button next to the Web Site text box launches your browser and directs it to the vendor's Web site.

To generate e-mail messages from within Peachtree, you must have a MAPI-compliant, default e-mail application installed on your computer. If your default e-mail system is AOL, you will not be able to send e-mail alerts from Peachtree because AOL is not a fully MAPI-compliant e-mail application.

7. **Click the Beginning Balances button to display the Vendor Beginning Balances window, where you can enter unpaid bills you received from vendors before you started using Peachtree.**

Technically, you can enter as many beginning balance bills as you want for an individual vendor; however, if you exceed 100 bills, you can enter but not edit or delete any information for the 101st bill and subsequent bills.

If you click the Current Balance button, Peachtree displays the Vendor Ledger report for the current vendor, showing you the bills and checks that comprise the vendor's balance as of the specified date.

8. **Click the Purchase Defaults tab to select a default purchase rep, account, terms, and form delivery options for the vendor.**

   An employee can serve as a purchase representative.

   You need to select a default Purchase Account and terms only if they differ for the vendor you're creating from the default account and terms you established in the Vendor Defaults dialog box. (See Chapter 4 for details on global default purchase settings.)

   In the Form Delivery Options area, you can choose to e-mail forms (such as purchase orders) to vendors or print them and mail them. If you select the E-mail option, you can choose to e-mail a copy of the form to the purchase representative at the same time that you e-mail the form to the vendor.

9. **If the vendor is a 1099 vendor, supply the vendor's Tax ID number, which eventually appears on the 1099.**

10. **Select a shipping method from the Ship Via drop-down list.**

    Peachtree creates most of the shipping methods that appear in the Ship Via drop-down list when you create your company; you can add to or change these methods when you set up defaults for inventory. You can find information on setting up inventory defaults in Chapter 4.

11. **To change the terms for the vendor, click the Terms button.**

    Peachtree displays the Vendor Terms dialog box (see Figure 5-2). Deselect the Use Standard Terms check box and set up the vendor's terms.

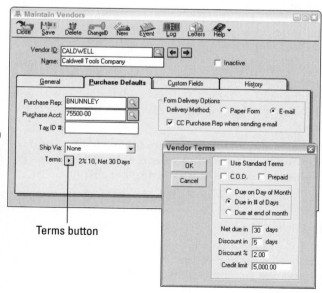

Figure 5-2:
To change the terms for a vendor, deselect the Use Standard Terms check box.

Terms button

12. **On the Custom Fields tab, fill in the information you established in the Vendor Default dialog box.**

13. **Click the Save button to save the vendor information.**

Changing vendor information

You can change any information you have entered about a vendor, including the vendor ID. If you need to make a change to a vendor's information, follow these steps:

1. **Choose Maintain⇨Vendors.**

2. **Type a few letters of the vendor's ID — remember, ID's are case-sensitive — or click the lookup list box indicator next to the Vendor ID text box to display a list of vendors.**

3. **Highlight the vendor you want to change and click OK.**

   The information you saved previously for the vendor appears.

4. **If you need to change the vendor ID, display the vendor's information in the Maintain Vendors window and then click the Change ID toolbar button.**

   Peachtree displays the Change Vendor ID dialog box. Type a new ID in the New Vendor ID text box and click OK. Peachtree changes the vendor's ID.

5. **Click the tab containing any additional information you want to change.**

6. **Make the change(s).**

7. **Click the Save button.**

Viewing vendor history

After you have recorded purchases and payments for vendors, Peachtree tracks these transactions by month. Choose Maintain⇨Vendors to open the Maintain Vendors window. Type the Vendor ID or highlight your choice from the lookup list and then click the History tab to view a history of your activity with the vendor.

"De-activating" a vendor

If a vendor has gone out of business or you've decided that you just don't want to do business with a particular vendor, you can change the vendor's status to inactive. After you make a vendor record inactive, Peachtree displays a warning if you try to buy something from the vendor.

Although you see a Delete button in the Maintain Vendor window, you can't delete a vendor unless no transactions exist for the vendor. You know, you put somebody in and then realized you didn't want them after all — and you didn't record any transactions. *Then* you can display that vendor on-screen and click Delete. Otherwise, to get rid of a vendor, you must first make the vendor inactive. After closing a fiscal year, you can purge inactive vendors so that they don't appear in lookup lists. See Chapter 17 for information on closing a fiscal year and purging.

To make a vendor inactive, follow these steps.

1. **Choose Maintain⇨Vendors to open the Maintain Vendors window.**
2. **In the Vendor ID text box, select the vendor you want to make inactive.**
3. **When the vendor appears on-screen, select the Inactive check box and then click the Save button. The vendor is now inactive.**

When you need to reactivate the vendor, deselect the Inactive check box.

An inactive vendor won't appear in the lookup lists if you decided to hide inactive records when you set Peachtree's global options. You can find out how to hide inactive records in Bonus Chapter 1 on this book's Web site.

Working with Purchase Orders

A *purchase order* is a document you use to request merchandise from a vendor. When you enter a purchase order, Peachtree doesn't actually affect any of your accounts — that doesn't happen until you either receive the merchandise or, if you're using cash basis accounting, when you pay the vendor.

Peachtree takes note of the transactions — that is, you can print reports that show you the accounts that the purchase orders *will* affect when they are filled. But the purchase orders don't actually update the accounts when you save the purchase orders.

Entering purchase orders

"If a purchase order doesn't affect any of my accounts, why use it?" you ask. Well, first, you don't *need* to use purchase orders; Peachtree operates correctly if you don't use them. But most people use purchase orders as reminders, particularly when ordering inventory, because the purchase order shows the items they've ordered but not yet received. Others use purchase orders for non-inventory items such as office supplies or contract labor to help track expected expenses.

Purchase orders provide you with a great way of remaining organized so that nothing slips through the cracks. You can use the Purchase Order report to help you stay on top of things.

You can't enter purchase orders in Peachtree unless you have set up a vendor, but you can set up a vendor while working in the Purchase Orders window.

To enter a purchase order, follow these steps:

1. **Choose Tasks⇨Purchase Orders to display the Purchase Orders window, as shown in Figure 5-3.**

   You can customize the appearance of the Purchase Order window to better suit your needs; if you have changed these settings, your window won't look exactly the same as the window you see in Figure 5-3.

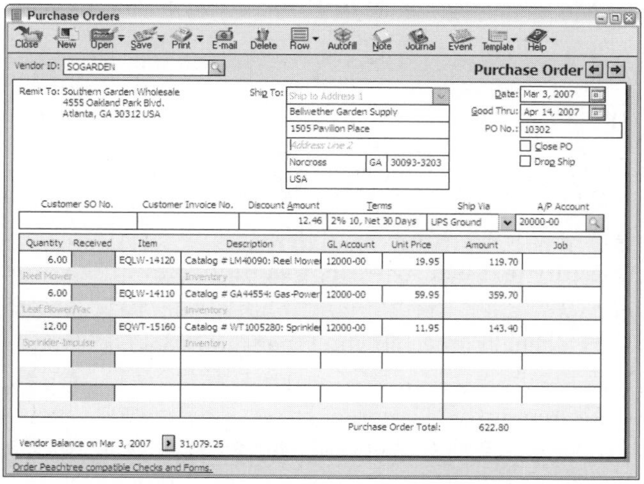

Figure 5-3:
A typical purchase order.

2. **Type the vendor's ID in the Vendor ID text box or click the lookup list box selector to display the list of vendors.**

   If the vendor exists, Peachtree fills in the vendor's name and the Remit To address. Your company's name also appears in the Ship To address box. You can see the vendor's current balance as of the system date, and you can click the button next to the balance to display a Vendor Ledger report of the purchases and payments that comprise the balance.

   If you need to add a vendor, click the lookup list selector and then click the New button on the toolbar. Peachtree displays the Maintain Vendors window. Refer to the earlier section in this chapter, "Adding vendors." Close the Maintain Vendors window to return to the Purchase Orders window.

3. **In the PO No. text box, type a number for the purchase order if you don't intend to print it but just want to save it or if you intend to print it later.**

   If you intend to print the purchase order, leave the PO No. box blank, and Peachtree supplies a sequential purchase order number when you print the purchase order.

   You can't use the same purchase order number more than once for a particular vendor. You can reuse a purchase order number as long as you assign it to a different vendor.

4. **If necessary, change the date of the purchase order.**

5. **Enter a date in the Good Thru text box — the date after which the purchase order should not be filled.**

6. **If necessary, change the shipping method in the Ship Via drop-down list.**

   While you can change the A/P account, typically, you don't. Although Peachtree doesn't affect any of your accounts when you post the purchase order, later, when you receive merchandise against the purchase order, Peachtree uses the account information on the purchase order to update your company's books.

7. **In the Quantity text box, type the quantity you want to order.**

   For a whole number such as three, type **3.0**. If you set global options to Automatic Decimal Entry and you type simply **3**, Peachtree assumes you want .03.

8. **Click in the Item box.**

   The Lookup list box appears so that you can select the item you want to order from the existing inventory items. Peachtree fills in the item description, the general ledger account associated with the item, the item's unit price, and the amount (unit price times quantity).

Read about setting up inventory items in Chapter 11. If you want to order something that you haven't set up as an inventory item, skip the Item box and fill in the Description, GL Account, and Unit Price text boxes. Peach-tree calculates the amount. If you enabled Peachtree's spell-checking options (see Bonus Chapter 1 on this book's Web site for more information), Peachtree flags any spelling mistakes as they happen.

9. **Click in the Job box to display the Lookup list box selector and choose a job from the list.**

   If you're purchasing a Stock item or an Assembly item, you cannot assign it to a job; however, if you're purchasing any other type of item, you can assign it to a job. You also can assign the line to a job if you don't select any item from the Item list. Chapter 12 covers setting up and assigning types of jobs.

10. **Repeat Steps 7 through 9 for each item you want to order from this vendor.**

11. **Click either the Save button or the Print button.**

    If you want to continue entering purchase orders and print them later in a group, click the Save button. Otherwise, click the Print button. To print your purchase orders in a group, see the section about printing forms in Chapter 14.

You can preview the purchase order before you print it by clicking the drop-down arrow on the Print button and selecting Preview.

But there's an easier way . . .

This feature is available only in Peachtree Premium and Peachtree Complete.

In Chapter 4, where we discuss setting up inventory options, you have the choice to enable auto-creation of purchase orders for drop ship and non-drop ship transactions. If you enable these options and enable real-time posting, you can let Peachtree generate purchase orders for you, based on information you supplied when you defined your inventory items (see Chapter 11 for details on inventory items).

To make this feature work, you need to assign a preferred vendor to each inventory item and, to make the feature work well, you need to supply a minimum stock quantity and a reorder quantity for each inventory item.

Assuming that you've done these things, choose Tasks⇨Select for Purchase Orders. The Select for Purchase Orders dialog box appears, as shown in Figure 5-4.

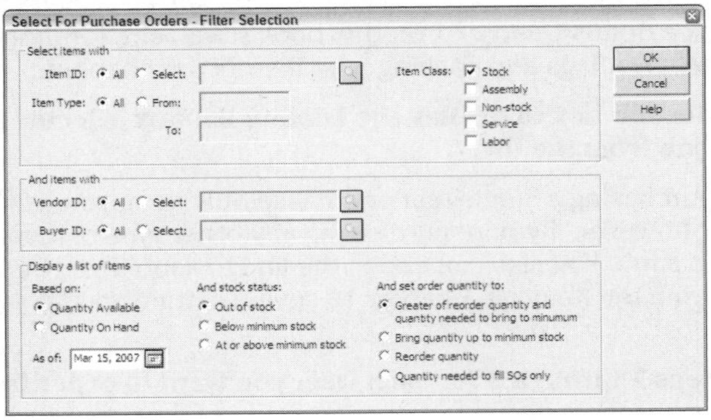

Figure 5-4:
Use the
Select For
Purchase
Orders
dialog box to
identify the
purchase
orders
you want
Peachtree
to create
for you.

Figure 5-4: Use the Select For Purchase Orders dialog box to identify the purchase orders you want Peachtree to create for you.

In the Select For Purchase Orders dialog box, you set up the selection criteria that Peachtree should use to display a list of potential purchase orders to create.

In the Select Items With section of the dialog box, you can choose which items to include using the Item ID, Item Type, and Item Class options. For example, in the sample company, you can select the All option for the Item ID, the SUPPLY option for the Item Type, and the Stock option of the Item Class.

In the And Items With section, you can narrow the selection by choosing only certain vendors or buyers (buyers are set up as employees and you identified buyers as well as vendors when you created inventory items).

In the Display a List of Items section, you can indicate that you want Peachtree to select items to order based on the how many items are available or on hand by selecting the Quantity Available or the Quantity On Hand options as of a particular date; you can also order based on as the item's minimum stock level. In the And Set Order Quantity To section, you can identify the quantity you want Peachtree to place on the purchase order(s) it suggests.

When you click OK, Peachtree displays the Select For Purchase Orders window shown in Figure 5-5, where you can review the proposed purchase orders and, if necessary, exclude any you don't want Peachtree to create by deselecting the check box in the Order column of the proposed purchase order.

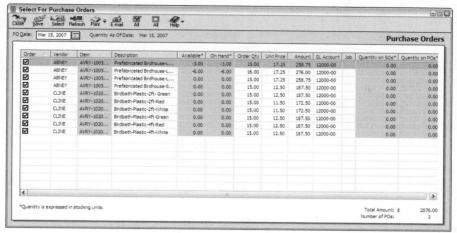

You can make changes to the purchase orders before Peachtree creates them; click in the appropriate column and make your change. For example, you can select a different vendor or change the Order Qty or GL Account.

After you identify the purchases you want to create, you can preview them as they will appear to the vendor by clicking the drop-down arrow on the Print button and selecting Preview. If you want a hard copy of the Select For Purchase Orders window, click the drop-down arrow on the Print button and select Report.

To create a purchase, click the Save button; if you prefer, you can click the Print button or the E-mail button. If you click the Print button, Peachtree prints the purchase order and asks you to confirm that it printed properly. If you click Yes, Peachtree saves the purchase order. If you click the E-mail button, Peachtree displays a dialog box where you can assign a purchase order number; when you click OK, Peachtree displays the e-mail message it will send to the vendor (see Figure 5-6), including the purchase order in PDF format. After you review the message, Peachtree again displays a dialog box that asks you to confirm that the purchase e-mailed properly. If you click Yes, Peachtree saves the purchase order.

After you produce a purchase from the Select For Purchase Orders window, you can click the Refresh button on the toolbar; Peachtree updates the information in the Quantity on POs column.

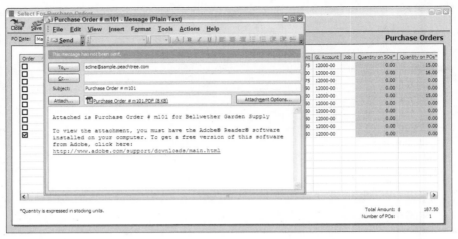

Figure 5-6:
When you
e-mail a
purchase
order,
Peachtree
attaches the
purchase
order in
PDF format.

Editing and erasing purchase orders

You can change purchase orders, and you can delete purchase orders. Although good accounting practices say you shouldn't ever delete anything, because a purchase order doesn't affect your accounts, the offense doesn't seem quite so serious.

You can change or remove items from purchase orders if you have not yet received the items. If you know you'll never receive the items, you can close the purchase order. If the purchase order was simply a mistake and you have not received any items listed on it, why not just erase it? To edit or delete a purchase order, choose Tasks➪Purchase Orders to display the Purchase Orders window. Then click the Open button to display the Select Purchase Order dialog box, as shown in Figure 5-7.

The Select Purchase Order dialog box shows, by default, the period in which you are working. In Figure 5-7, you see the purchase orders entered with March (Period 3) dates. If you don't see the purchase order you want to edit or delete, open the Show list box and select an earlier period.

You can edit any purchase order, whether it is open or closed. Look for the Y in the Open? Column of the Select Purchase Order dialog box. If the Open? column is blank, the purchase order is closed, meaning all the goods have been received and entered, or you got tired of waiting and canceled it.

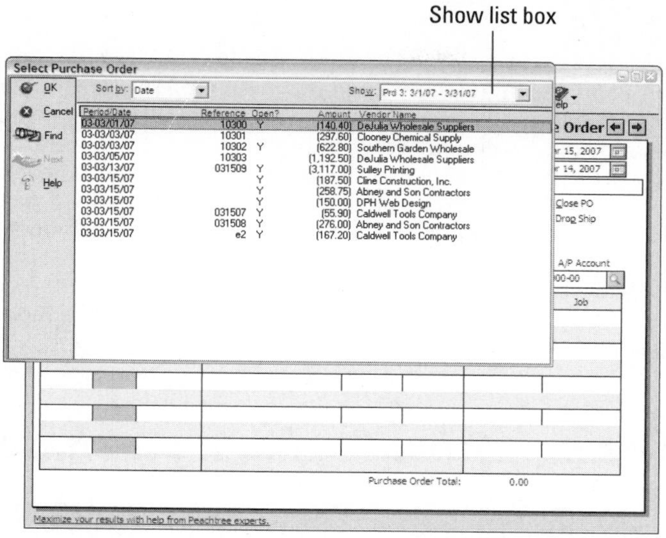

Show list box

Figure 5-7:
Select a
purchase
order to
view in the
Select
Purchase
Orders
dialog box.

Select a purchase order to view and click OK to display the purchase order in the Purchase Orders window. You can make any of the following modifications to the purchase order:

- ✔ Change the date entered in the Date or the Good Thru text boxes.

- ✔ Select a different shipping method from the Ship Via drop-down list, enter a new amount in the Discount Amount text box, change displayed terms in the Terms text box, or change the account number in the A/P Account text box.

- ✔ Adjust the quantity you ordered on any line of the purchase order — even a line you've already received. Find out how to receive items you order in the section, "Receiving goods against a purchase order," later in this chapter.

- ✔ Remove any line if you have not received those items. Click anywhere in the line you want to delete and click the Remove button.

- ✔ Close the purchase order by selecting the Close PO check box that appears immediately below the PO No. text box.

You cannot delete a purchase order if you have received any of the items listed on the purchase order; the Delete button appears grayed out (unavailable). If you know you'll *never* receive items remaining on a purchase order, close the purchase order.

Entering Bills

Scenario: A vendor with whom you do business on a regular basis sends you a bill. (Peachtree uses the terms *purchase* and *invoice* interchangeably to represent a vendor bill.) You don't want to pay the bill immediately, but you *do* want to pay the bill in a timely manner. So, enter the bill into Peachtree as a purchase, and Peachtree tracks the bill's age so that you pay it A) when it's still eligible for a discount and B) before the vendor charges you a late fee.

Do you receive a bill on a regular basis from a vendor? Chapter 6 shows you how to create a recurring purchase or payment for things like monthly utility bills or lease payments.

Purchasing without using a purchase order

Unlike purchase orders, purchases update your company's accounts. Whenever any transaction updates your company's books, at least two accounts are affected because of the double-entry bookkeeping concept.

Every purchase you enter automatically updates Accounts Payable. The other account Peachtree updates depends on whether you record a bill for an inventory item. If you select inventory items in the Purchases/Receive Inventory window, you tell Peachtree to update inventory for the other side of the transaction. If you don't select an inventory item, then you probably select an expense account, such as your telephone expense account. In that case, Peachtree updates Accounts Payable and the expense account.

Peachtree assumes that you wouldn't enter a bill from a vendor for merchandise without having first received the merchandise—and entering a bill for merchandise does update quantities on hand, so, don't enter a bill until you receive the goods. You might, however, receive the goods without yet receiving the bill. In this second case, you enter a purchase and make sure that you check the Waiting on Bill box.

If you're curious about the accounts Peachtree is updating (yes, *debiting* and *crediting*), Chapter 17 shows you a neat way to find out what Peachtree is doing.

Peachtree assumes that you wouldn't bother to enter a bill from a vendor you use only occasionally; instead, you'd just pay that bill. Therefore, you can't enter purchases in Peachtree unless you have set up a vendor. For one-time or occasional purchases from vendors you don't expect to use often, use the Payments window to pay the bill directly. See Chapter 6 for more information on paying bills.

To enter a purchase (a vendor's bill) that doesn't reference a purchase order, follow these steps:

1. **Choose Tasks⇨Purchases/Receive Inventory to display the Purchases/ Receive Inventory window (see Figure 5-8).**

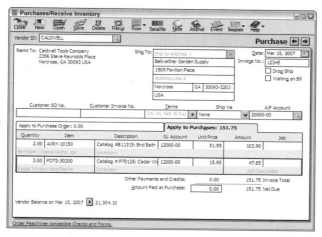

Figure 5-8: Use this window to record a bill from a vendor.

You can customize the appearance of the Purchases/Receive Inventory window to better suit your needs; if you do, the window won't look the same as the window you see in Figure 5-8.

2. **Enter the vendor's ID in the Vendor ID text box or click the lookup list box and select a vendor from the list.**

After you select a vendor, Peachtree fills in the vendor's name and Remit To address. Your company's name also appears in the Ship To address box. You can see the vendor's current balance as of the system date, and you can click the button next to the balance to display a Vendor Ledger report of the purchases and payment that comprise the balance.

If you have previously entered purchase orders for this vendor, Peachtree displays the Apply to Purchase Order tab. If you want to receive goods against one of these POs, skip to the next section.

3. **In the Invoice No. text box, type a number for the vendor's bill.**

You can't use an invoice number more than once for a particular vendor. You can reuse an invoice number as long as you assign it to a different vendor.

4. **If necessary, change the date of the purchase.**

   Yes, you can change the A/P account, but typically, you don't.

5. **In the Quantity text box, type the quantity for which you're being billed.**

   For a whole number such as three, type **3.0**. If you set global options to Automatic Decimal Entry and you type simply **3**, Peachtree assumes you want .03.

6. **You have two options for entering items that appear on the bill:**

   • If you are recording a bill for an item that you haven't set up as an inventory item, skip the Item text box and just fill in the Description, a GL Account, and Unit Price boxes. If you enabled Peachtree's spell-checking options (see Bonus Chapter 1 on this book's Web site for more information), Peachtree flags any spelling mistakes as they happen.

   • If you are recording a bill for an inventory item, select the item in the Item list box. Peachtree fills in the Description, GL Account, the Unit Price, and the Amount (unit price times quantity) boxes.

7. **If you are purchasing a serialized item, click the Serial No. button to display the Serial Number Entry dialog box shown in Figure 5-9, where you can add the serial numbers you are purchasing.**

   Type the serial number for the first item and click Add. Repeat the process for each serialized item you are purchasing. If the serial numbers are consecutive, select the Add consecutive serial numbers check box and specify the number of items you are purchasing. When you finish, click OK.

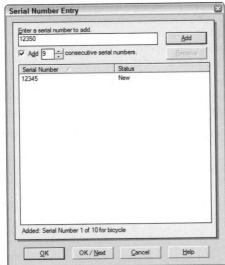

Figure 5-9:
Use this window to record serial numbers when you purchase serialized inventory items.

8. **Click in the Job text box to display the lookup list button and choose a job from the list.**

   If you're purchasing a stock item or an assembly item (serialized or unserialized for Peachtree Premium users), you cannot assign it to a job. However, if you're purchasing any other type of item, you can assign it to a job. You can also assign the line to a job if you don't select an item from the Item list. You can read about setting up jobs in Chapter 12.

   If you assign a line to a job, Peachtree allows you to include it on a customer's bill as a reimbursable expense. Chapter 12 covers information about including reimbursable expenses on customer invoices.

9. **Repeat Steps 5 through 8 for each item you want to order or that appears by the bill you're recording.**

10. **Click the Save button to save the transaction.**

Receiving goods against a purchase order

Scenario: You ordered merchandise using a purchase order, and the merchandise arrives. *Maybe* the bill comes with the merchandise, and *maybe* it doesn't. Either way, you need to update your company's accounts to reflect the receipt of the merchandise so that you know they're available to sell.

You use the Purchases/Receive Inventory window to receive goods against a purchase order. You can, simultaneously, indicate whether you received the bill. Follow these steps:

1. **Choose Tasks⇨Purchases/Receive Inventory to display the Purchases/Receive Inventory window.**

2. **Type the vendor ID in the Vendor ID text box or click that handy magnifying glass to display the list of vendors.**

   After you select a vendor, Peachtree fills in the vendor's and Remit To address. Your company's name also appears in the Ship To address box. You can see the vendor's current balance as of the system date, and you can click the button next to the balance to display a Vendor Ledger report of the purchases and payment that comprise the balance.

   If you have previously entered purchase orders for this vendor, Peachtree displays the Apply to Purchase Order tab, and the window looks like the one shown in Figure 5-10.

3. **In the Invoice No. text box, type a number for the vendor's bill.**

   You can't use an invoice number more than once for a particular vendor, so if you get stopped by this, be sure you haven't got an old invoice.

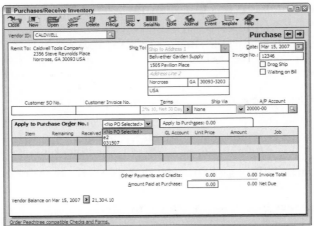

Figure 5-10:
The
Purchases/
Receive
Inventory
window
when you've
entered
POs for the
vendor.

If you have vendors who don't provide you with an invoice number, your company might have a standard solution for this problem like entering a combination of the vendor ID plus the date or the primary PO number. This usually helps avoid duplications (but not always).

4. **If necessary, change the date of the purchase.**

5. **If only the merchandise arrived but you have no bill from the vendor, select the Waiting on Bill check box.**

   If you received both goods and a bill, leave the box deselected.

   As with other transactions, you can change the A/P account, but typically, you don't.

6. **On the Apply to Purchase Order No. tab, click the Apply to Purchase Order No. drop-down list, select the PO number that lists the goods you ordered.**

   Peachtree fills in the lines that appear on the purchase order.

7. **On each line of the Apply to Purchase Order tab, in the Received text box, type the quantity you received.**

   If you are purchasing a serialized item, click the Serial No. button to add the serial numbers you are purchasing. In the Serial Number Entry box that appears, type the serial number for the first item and click Add. Repeat the process for each serialized item you are purchasing. If the serial numbers are consecutive, select the Add consecutive serial numbers check box and specify the number of items you are purchasing. When you finish, click OK.

Remember that you have to put the decimal-zero after the whole number, or Peachtree adds the leading decimal: To get 6, type **6.0**. Peachtree fills in the Amount text box by multiplying the unit price by the quantity.

8. **Click the Save button to save your work.**

When the bill arrives . . . finally

If you have entered vendor receipts against a purchase order but didn't have a bill at the time you entered the vendor receipts, you should have selected the Waiting on Bill check box in the Purchases/Receive Inventory window. When the waiting is over and you've got the vendor's bill, follow these steps to tie up the loose ends:

1. **Choose Tasks⇨Purchases/Receive Inventory to open the Purchases/ Receive Inventory window.**

2. **Click the Open button to display the Select Purchase dialog box.**

   If you select the vendor first, Peachtree alerts you that a bill already exists for this vendor.

3. **From the Sort By drop-down list, select ID to sort the list by vendor name.**

4. **Find the vendor's name in the Vendor Name column, and then look for a Y in the Waiting? column and Unpaid in the Status column.**

   Use the Reference column to further help you identify the correct purchase.

5. **Highlight the correct purchase and click OK.**

   Peachtree displays the purchase in the Purchases/Receive Inventory window.

6. **Deselect the Waiting on Bill check box.**

7. **Click the Save button.**

By making this status change, you indicate to Peachtree that you now consider the bill eligible for payment. See Chapter 6 for information on paying bills.

Shipping Directly to Customers

Suppose that you need to buy something, maybe a special order for a customer, and you want to ship it directly to the customer. No problem. You can specify a customer's address in the Ship To box on either a purchase order or a purchase. Choose Tasks➪Purchase Orders to display the Purchase Orders window or Tasks➪Purchases/Receive Inventory to make a purchase. In either window, follow these steps:

1. **Type the vendor ID in the Vendor ID text box or click the lookup list box selector to display the list of vendors.**

2. **Select the Drop Ship check box.**

   Peachtree displays a Customer ID field next to the Vendor ID field.

3. **Select the customer from the Customer ID list.**

   Peachtree supplies the customer's address and enables you to select a different shipping address if you click the Ship To drop-down list arrow.

   You can type the recipient's name and address if you haven't set the recipient up in the Customer List.

4. **If you have already entered an invoice to the customer, you can enter the invoice number in the Customer Invoice No. text box. If you've entered a sales order but not an invoice, enter the sales order number in the Customer SO No. text box.**

   Both of these text boxes are informational only; they don't tie to invoice or sales order transactions. You'll find them most useful, however, if you enter numbers that represent real transactions because they can help you track drop shipments on reports.

   You don't need to create the invoice before you set up the drop shipment, but don't forget to bill your customer. For more information about creating invoices for customers, see Chapter 7.

5. **Click the Save button.**

To help you track drop shipments, you can add the Drop Shipment, Customer ID, Customer SO No., and Customer Invoice No. fields to the Purchase Journal, the Purchase Order Journal, and the Purchase Order report. You also can filter the Purchase Order report so that it displays only drop shipments created in the Purchase Orders window.

Entering Credits

Suppose that you have a purchase that you no longer need. Should you just erase it? If you want to practice good accounting, the answer is a definite *no*. Deleting purchases removes the *audit trail* — that thing accountants mean when they talk about the list of transactions you enter because your business does business. When accountants can trace transactions from beginning to end, they're really happy campers.

Having said that, you need to understand that Peachtree allows you to delete any *unpaid* purchase, even though your accountant won't like it. Display the purchase in the Purchases/Receive Inventory window and click the Delete button.

But Peachtree *won't* allow you to delete a purchase if you've applied any transactions to it. Suppose, for example, that you accidentally paid a purchase that you later determined you should not have paid. If you try to delete the purchase, the Delete button in the Purchase window is unavailable. In this case, you need to void the check you wrote that paid the purchase, and then you need to enter a vendor credit memo in Peachtree to cancel the effects of the purchase. (See Chapter 6 to find out how to void a check.) After you've voided the check, follow the steps in this section to finish canceling the purchase.

Besides fixing errors in purchases, don't forget about the times when a vendor issues a credit memo to you for merchandise you return. You need to enter the vendor credit memo into Peachtree to reduce the balance you owe the vendor and match it to the original purchase. To record the vendor credit memo, use the Vendor Credit Memos window. While you can enter a vendor credit memo without having previously entered a purchase (you use the Apply to Purchases tab of the Vendor Credit Memos window), typically you enter vendor credit memos for existing purchases. In the following steps, we assume that you are returning any merchandise for which you received a credit:

1. **Choose Tasks⇨Vendor Credit Memos to display the Vendor Credit Memos window.**

2. **Enter the vendor's ID in the Vendor ID text box.**

   After you select a vendor, Peachtree fills in the vendor's name and Remit To address. You can see the vendor's current balance as of the system date, and you can click the button next to the balance to display a Vendor Ledger report of the purchases and payment that comprise the balance.

3. **Enter a date in the Date text box, and then enter a credit number in the Credit No. text box.**

   For the Credit No. text box, we suggest that you enter the original invoice number followed by **CM** to indicate credit memo. This numbering scheme helps you tie the credit memo to a particular purchase.

4. **On the Apply to Invoice No. tab, click the Apply to Invoice No. drop-down list, select the invoice number of the purchase for which you are recording a credit memo.**

   Peachtree fills in the lines that appear on the purchase.

5. **On each line of the Apply to Invoice No. tab, in the Returned text box, type the quantity you want to return (see Figure 5-11).**

TIP

If you plan to return everything, you can click drop-down list arrow on the Return button and select All to have Peachtree fill in all the amounts for you.

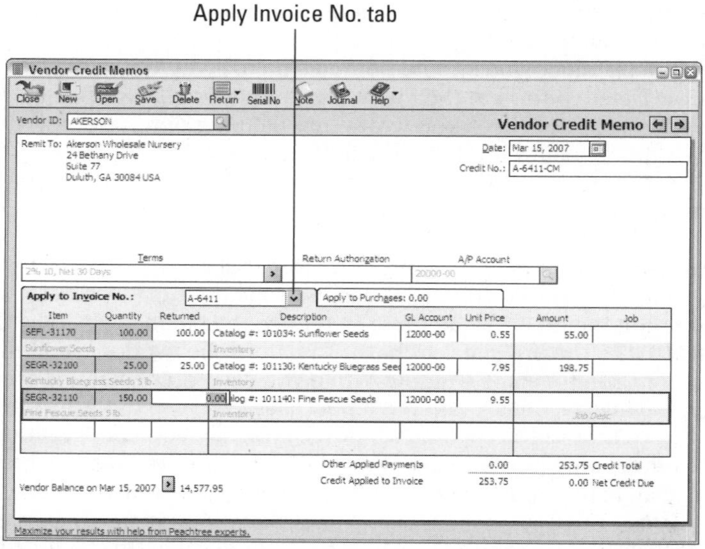

Apply Invoice No. tab

Figure 5-11:
Applying a vendor credit memo to a purchase.

If you are returning a serialized item, click the Serial No. button to display the Serial Number Selection dialog box and identify the serial numbers you are returning. Select the check box next to the number(s) you are returning and click OK.

If you are using Automatic Decimal Entry, remember that you have to put the decimal-zero after the whole number, or Peachtree adds the leading decimal: To get 9, type **9.0**. Peachtree fills in the amount (unit price times quantity).

6. Click the Save button to save the transaction.

Peachtree records the transaction; if you print your Aged Payables report, you'll see that the purchase no longer appears on the report.

REMEMBER

If you aren't applying the credit memo to an existing purchase, make sure that the credit memo you enter on the Apply to Purchases tab of the Vendor Credit Memos window mirrors the purchase you entered originally; that is, the credit memo should affect the same things (vendor, general ledger accounts, and inventory items) that the original purchase affected.

Reporting on Purchasing

To keep things short and sweet, Table 5-1 provides you with a description of the reports that pertain to buying goods. Chapter 15 covers the details on how to print reports.

Table 5-1	Reports Related to Buying Goods
Report Name	*What It Does*
Vendor List	For each vendor, lists the ID, name, contact name, telephone number, and tax ID.
Vendor Master File List	Similar to the Vendor List report, but also includes address information and terms.
Vendor Ledgers	Shows the transactions and a running balance for each vendor.
Purchase Order	Lists the details of all purchase orders by purchase order number.
Purchase Order Register	Lists purchase order numbers, dates, vendor IDs, and amounts; optionally use the PO State on the Filter tab to display only open purchase orders.
Aged Payables	Lists outstanding invoices by vendor and the age of each outstanding invoice.
Purchase Journal	Shows the accounts Peachtree updated for each purchase in the period.
Purchase Order Journal	Listing only purchase orders, this report closely resembles the Purchase Journal.
Items Purchased from Vendors	Lists, by vendor, the item ID, description, quantity, and amount of each item purchased from each vendor. If you sort the report by vendor name or ID, you can drill down to view the transactions in the transaction window.

Visit this book's Web site for more information on Peachtree.

Chapter 6

Paying Bills

In This Chapter

▶ Paying a group of bills

▶ Generating checks and reports

▶ Paying one bill at a time

▶ Creating recurring transactions

▶ Tracking payments and voided checks

▶ Remitting sales tax

Although we wish things were different, the facts are simple: You can't hold those bills indefinitely . . . eventually, you have to pay them. If you prefer to let the bills pile up awhile, you can enter them gradually and pay all bills due by a certain date on your bill-paying day. Occasionally, you may need to pay only one or two bills or write a check to cover an unexpected expense — you know, the UPS person is standing there waiting for a check to cover the COD package in your hand.

Peachtree helps you pay groups of bills all at once or pay individual bills on the spur of the moment. You can make repetitive payments easily. And when you have to void checks or pay sales tax on all those goods you've sold, Peachtree helps you keep all the amounts in the right accounts.

Terminology alert: Peachtree tends to switch back and forth between two different terms when referring to bills that vendors send you: a purchase and an invoice. For the sake of clarity, we use the term purchase (or bill) unless the screen uses the term invoice. For our purposes, invoices are things you send to customers so that *you* can get paid.

Paying a Group of Bills

Most people sit down on a regular basis — say every two weeks — and pay all bills due by a certain date. They hold the bills that are due later until the next bill-paying day. In Peachtree, you can select all bills due by a certain date, or you can select bills for certain vendors or greater than an amount you specify. Then you can simply tell Peachtree to write the checks and bid your bundle good-bye.

Before you start paying your bills, you may want to print the Aged Payables report and the Cash Requirements report to get a handle on the outstanding purchases you've entered into Peachtree. (See Chapter 15 for information on printing reports.) By reviewing these reports, you can determine whether you need to pay a group of bills or just a few bills. To pay a group of bills, you use Peachtree's Select for Payment window. (To pay just a few bills or to pay a bill from an occasional vendor that you don't want to set up in Peachtree, see "Paying One Bill at a Time," later in this chapter.)

Using the Select for Payment window, Peachtree looks for purchases you've entered that are eligible for payment based on criteria you provide. You can use this window *only* to pay bills you've entered previously as purchases. (See Chapter 5 for help entering bills.) To pay a group of bills, follow these steps:

1. **Choose Tasks➪Select for Payment.**

   The Select for Payment – Filter Selection dialog box appears, shown in Figure 6-1.

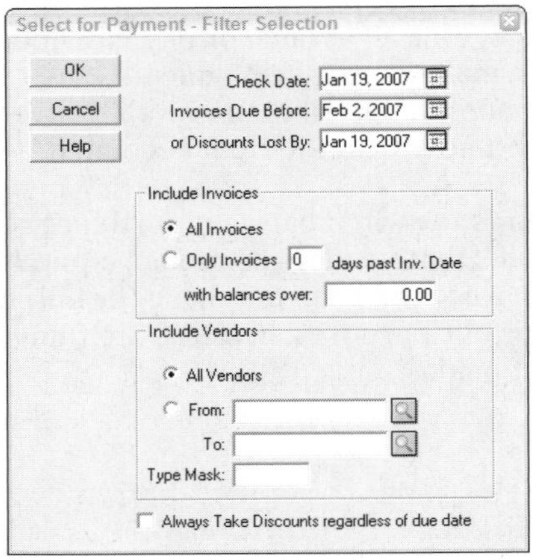

Figure 6-1:
Select bills to pay in the Select for Payment – Filter Selection dialog box.

Select for Payment - Filter Selection	
OK	Check Date: Jan 19, 2007
Cancel	Invoices Due Before: Feb 2, 2007
Help	or Discounts Lost By: Jan 19, 2007

Include Invoices
- All Invoices
- Only Invoices 0 days past Inv. Date
  with balances over: 0.00

Include Vendors
- All Vendors
- From:
- To:

Type Mask:

☐ Always Take Discounts regardless of due date

2. **Set the Check Date.**

   Most people use today's date.

   You can enter just the month and the day; Peachtree automatically uses the current year established by your computer's clock. If you enter only the day, Peachtree automatically uses the month and year established by your computer's clock.

3. **Use the Invoices Due Before date to set a cut-off date for purchases that you want to pay.**

   Peachtree does not select any purchases due after the date you enter in this box.

   Peachtree calculates the due date when you enter the bill by using the terms you established for the vendor. So the due date typically is *not* the same as the date you entered the bill and usually is 30 days later. We suggest that you set the Invoices Due Before date equal to a date that falls just before your next bill paying date. That way, you won't be late paying bills.

4. **Set a date for the Or Discounts Lost By box if your vendors offer you discounts for paying by a specified date.**

   If you don't get vendor discounts, this date doesn't matter.

5. **In the Include Invoices section, select the range of invoices to include.**

   If you set dates in the preceding steps, you typically click the All Invoices option. However, you can click the Only Invoices . . . Days Past Inv. Date option and specify a number of days. In the With Balances Over box, you can also filter the invoices to only those more than a specified amount.

6. **In the Include Vendors section, make your choices regarding payees.**

   You may want to simply include All Vendors, but you can choose to include a range of vendors by entering the Vendor ID in the From and To boxes, or the Vendor Type in the Type Mask box, or both the ID and Type.

7. **If you always take discounts offered by vendors — even if you're paying later than the discount date — place a check mark in the Always Take Discounts Regardless of Due Date check box.**

8. **Click OK.**

   Peachtree displays the Select for Payment window you see in Figure 6-2, displaying purchases that meet the criteria you just specified.

Peachtree initially displays the bills in Invoice Date order, but you can change to Due Date order or Vendor order using the Sort By list box. Peachtree also selects a cash account to use to pay the bills and a discount account to use for any discounts you take, but you can select different accounts using the Lookup list indicator (magnifying glass) next to the appropriate fields.

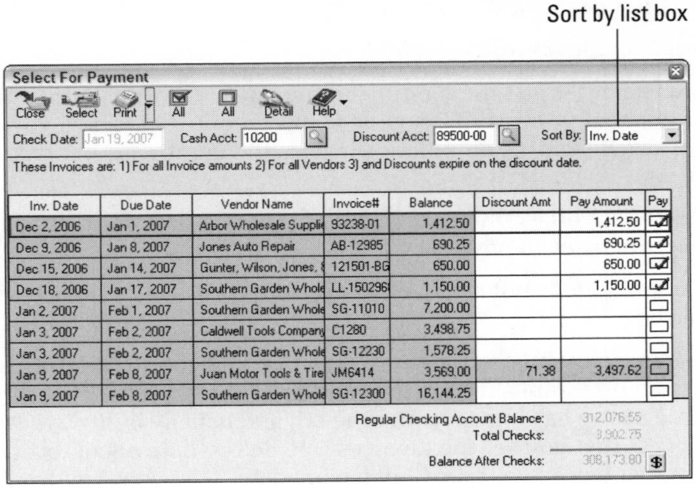

Sort by list box

Figure 6-2:
This
window
shows the
bills that are
eligible for
payment
based on
the choices
you made
in the
preceding
dialog box.

Select For Payment

| Close | Select | Print | All | All | Detail | Help |

Check Date: Jan 19, 2007   Cash Acct: 10200 🔍   Discount Acct: 89500-00 🔍   Sort By: Inv. Date ▼

These Invoices are: 1) For all Invoice amounts 2) For all Vendors 3) and Discounts expire on the discount date.

Inv. Date	Due Date	Vendor Name	Invoice#	Balance	Discount Amt	Pay Amount	Pay
Dec 2, 2006	Jan 1, 2007	Arbor Wholesale Supplie	93238-01	1,412.50		1,412.50	☑
Dec 9, 2006	Jan 8, 2007	Jones Auto Repair	AB-12985	690.25		690.25	☑
Dec 15, 2006	Jan 14, 2007	Gunter, Wilson, Jones,	121501-8G	650.00		650.00	☑
Dec 18, 2006	Jan 17, 2007	Southern Garden Whole	LL-150296	1,150.00		1,150.00	☑
Jan 2, 2007	Feb 1, 2007	Southern Garden Whole	SG-11010	7,200.00			☐
Jan 3, 2007	Feb 2, 2007	Caldwell Tools Company	C1280	3,498.75			☐
Jan 3, 2007	Feb 2, 2007	Southern Garden Whole	SG-12230	1,578.25			☐
Jan 9, 2007	Feb 8, 2007	Juan Motor Tools & Tire	JM6414	3,569.00	71.38	3,497.62	☐
Jan 9, 2007	Feb 8, 2007	Southern Garden Whole	SG-12300	16,144.25			☐

Regular Checking Account Balance: 312,076.55
Total Checks: 3,902.75

Balance After Checks: 308,173.80 💲

When the entire line for a bill appears gray, that entry is a purchase for which you have not yet received a bill (the check mark remains in the Waiting for Bill check box on the purchase). Peachtree won't let you pay these purchases. If you think the entry should be eligible for payment, close the Select for Payment window and edit the purchase to remove the check mark from the Waiting for Bill box. See Chapter 5 for more information.

Peachtree assumes that you want to pay all the bills it displays, but you can choose not to pay any bill by removing the check mark in the Pay column, as we did in Figure 6-2. If you allow Peachtree to calculate balances automatically, it updates the numbers that appear at the lower-right corner of the window.

If you don't allow Peachtree to recalculate balances automatically, you see Uncalculated in the lower-right corner of the window. You can recalculate balances in this window only by clicking the Recalc button ($). If you want to recalculate balances in all windows, go to Bonus Chapter 1 on this book's Web site.

On the toolbar at the top of the window, you can click the drop-down arrow on the Print button and click Report to print a report of the bills you've selected to pay. The report sorts the bills by vendor, as shown in Figure 6-3.

You also can preview the checks as they will look when they print if you click the drop-down arrow on the Print button and select Preview.

4/9/04 at 12:46:27.90   Page: 1

Bellwether Garden Supply
Select For Payment Preview Report
As of Mar 15, 2007

Filter Criteria includes: 1) For all Invoice amounts 2) For all Vendors 3) and Discounts expire on the discount date 4) Bank Account: 10200 5) Invoices Due Before: 2/2/07 6) Discounts Lost By: 1/19/07.
Report order is by Vendor ID.

Vendor ID Vendor	Invoice#	Inv. Date	Due Date	Balance	Disc. Date	Discount Amt	Pay Amount	Pay Method
DEJULIA Arbor Wholesale Suppliers	93238-01	12/2/06	1/1/07	1,412.50	12/12/06		1,412.50	
				1,412.50			1,412.50	
GARY Gunter, Wilson, Jones, & Smit	121501-BGS	12/15/06	1/14/07	650.00	12/25/06		650.00	
				650.00			650.00	
JUAN Jones Auto Repair	AB-12965	12/9/06	1/8/07	690.25	12/19/06		690.25	
				690.25			690.25	
SOGARDEN Southern Garden Wholesale	LL-15029684	12/18/06	1/17/07	1,150.00	12/28/06		1,150.00	
				1,150.00			1,150.00	
Report Totals:				3,902.75			3,902.75	

Number of Checks: 4

Beginning Account Balance: 312,076.55

Total Amount of Payments: 3,902.75

Ending Account Balance: 308,173.80

Figure 6-3: Printing a report of the bills you're about to pay.

The Print button also has a Postage option that you can use to buy postage online at Stamps.com. Using Stamps.com requires software available on the Peachtree CD-ROM or from Stamps.com. Stamps.com is a fee-based service you can use to print postage from your computer.

If you highlight any line in the window and double-click or click the Detail button, you can see but not edit the details for that line. Click the Select button to change the bills you selected, and Peachtree redisplays the dialog box your saw in Figure 6-1.

Printing Checks

As you would expect, Peachtree supports printing checks on your computer's printer. You must order check stock with the correct bank information on it. You can order checks from Peachtree. Look for the check ordering information inside the box with your Peachtree software, in Help (click the Contents tab and open the Peachtree Products and Services book), or on Peachtree's Web site at www.peachtree.com.

You can also ask your local forms supplier if they have purchase check forms that work with Peachtree and your printer.

Whoever supplies your checks can also supply window envelopes. Using these envelopes will save you time when paying bills because you won't need to use labels or address envelopes.

When you click the Print button in the Select for Payment window (see the preceding section for details on displaying this window), Peachtree starts the printing process. Follow these steps to complete the process:

1. **Establish the starting check number.**

   Peachtree suggests a starting check number that you can change if Peachtree suggests an incorrect starting number. Peachtree assigns the starting number to the first check you print and subsequent numbers to subsequent checks when Peachtree posts your checks. If you had numbers preprinted on your check stock, make sure that the check(s) you print and the check(s) Peachtree posts both use the same check numbers.

2. **Select a check form from the Print dialog box.**

   The form should match the type of check form you purchased. You can customize Peachtree's forms; see Chapter 13.

   On the check stub, most of Peachtree's check forms print purchase information such as the invoice number, date, and amount, but you can print the details of the items you bought (each line item that appears on the purchase) instead if you choose the OCR – MultiP AP 1 Stub Detail or OCR – MultiP AP 2 Stub Detail form.

3. **Choose the number of copies you want to print.**

4. **Click Print.**

   You can click the Practice button to print a practice check. On practice checks, Peachtree prints a check filled with Xs and 9s that you can use to determine if the form alignment is correct.

   Peachtree prints the checks and a message appears on-screen asking if the checks printed correctly. If you choose Yes, Peachtree assigns the check numbers and posts the checks. If you choose No, Peachtree doesn't assign the check numbers or post the checks; you can print them again.

Paying One Bill at a Time

Occasionally, you need to write only one or two checks. You know, you went to the office supply store and bought a box of copy paper, and you paid for it with a check. Now you need to record the check. You certainly don't want to enter a purchase and then pay the purchase using the Select for Payment window. To print or record a single check, use the Payments window. Essentially, you use the Payments window in three situations:

✔ You don't need to print a check — you just need to record that it was written.

✔ You don't have many checks to write.

✔ You need to write a miscellaneous check, like a refund check to a customer or a loan check to an employee.

From the Payments window, you can print checks that pay bills, print checks without first recording bills, or simply record checks you wrote manually. For example, suppose that it's bill-paying day and you have only two bills to pay. Use the Payments window to print checks to pay the bills. Or, suppose that the UPS guy is waiting for a check for a COD purchase. You can print the check from the Payments window without first recording a purchase. Or, suppose that you enter the telephone bill in the Purchases/Receive Inventory window, intending to pay it on bill-paying day. Then you change your mind because you're going to be at the phone store anyhow, and you want to bring a check to pay the bill. Use the Payments window to record the check you wrote manually.

You can use the Write Checks window to produce a single check, but *do not* use this window to write a check that pays a bill. If you entered a bill for a vendor, pay the bill by using either the Select to Pay window or the Payments window. We're not overly fond of the Write Checks window, because you won't see any warning if you select a vendor for whom a purchase exists, enabling you to accidentally write a check to pay a bill without applying the check to the bill. For this reason, we strongly recommend that you use either the Select to Pay window to pay a group of bills or the Payments window to pay a few bills or write miscellaneous checks, and just ignore the existence of the Write Checks window.

From the Payments window, you can pay vendors you've set up, or you can write a check to someone you haven't set up in Peachtree. You also can use this window to issue an employee loan or (heaven forbid) write a refund check to a customer. Follow these steps:

1. **Choose Tasks⇨Payments to display the Payments window.**

2. **Select a vendor or type a name in the Pay to the Order of box.**

   If the vendor doesn't have any unpaid purchases, or if you don't select a vendor but instead type a name in the Pay to the Order of box, Peachtree displays the Apply to Expenses tab shown in Figure 6-4. Fill in the quantity and, if appropriate, select an item. If you don't select an item, fill in the description, supply the GL account if necessary, and type a unit price. Peachtree calculates the amount. If appropriate, assign the line to a job.

   You can include payments that you assign to jobs as reimbursable expenses on customers' bills. See Chapter 7 for more information.

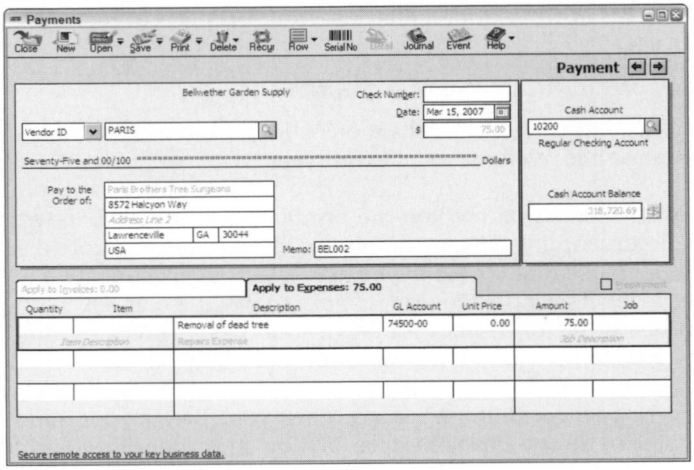

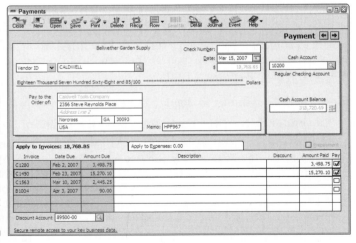

Figure 6-4:
Use the
Payments
window to
post (and
optionally
print) a
single
check.

If you select a vendor and the vendor has outstanding purchases, Peachtree displays the Apply to Invoices tab, listing all unpaid purchases for the vendor (see Figure 6-5). Place a check mark in the Pay column next to all purchases you want to pay. Peachtree displays the dollar amount on the check face.

You can partially pay the purchase by typing an amount in the Amount Paid column on the line of the purchase you want to pay.

Figure 6-5:
If the
vendor has
outstanding
bills, check
the ones
you want
to pay.

You can display the purchase shown on any line. Double-click the purchase, and Peachtree displays it in the Purchases/Receive Inventory window where you can edit it.

3. **If you *don't* intend to print the check, type the Check Number.**

For example, if you're recording that check you wrote at the office supply store for the box of copy paper, you have no reason to print the check, but you must enter it. For this situation, enter the check number.

By default, Peachtree supplies a check number for any check you *print*. If you enter a check number in the Payments window for a check you intend to print, Peachtree prints the word *Duplicate* on the check face — and you don't want that to happen. Therefore, leave the check number blank if you intend to print the check.

If you're a Type A personality who insists on completing all empty boxes on a screen, you can suppress the printing of the word *Duplicate* by customizing the check form. See Chapter 13 for details.

4. **At the top of the screen, supply a date for the check.**

5. **In the right column, select the Cash Account from which you want to write the check.**

6. **Depending on whether you enter a check number in Step 4, continue by clicking Save or Print.**

If you included a number in the Check Number box, click the Save button to save the check.

If you didn't include a number in the Check Number box, click the Print button to print the check immediately. Peachtree displays the Print Forms dialog box, which we cover in the "Printing Checks" section earlier in this chapter. Select Print; when you finish printing checks, Peachtree assigns the check numbers and posts the checks.

If you prefer to keep working and print a batch of checks later, click Save to post your checks without assigning check numbers to them. See Chapter 13 for details on printing checks in batches.

Editing Payments

From an accounting perspective, there's little reason to edit a payment. In the real world, however, you'll come up with a reason — such as, you recorded that check for office supplies and typed the wrong amount, which you noticed when you were about to file the receipt. You edit payments the same way you edit purchase orders and purchases, which we describe in Chapter 5. In the

Payments window, click the Open button to display the Select Payment window, which lists all payments you recorded. Highlight the transaction you want to edit and click OK. You also can erase checks. We talk more about that in the section on voiding checks later in this chapter.

Handling Repeat Bills and Payments

Suppose that you pay a bill — such as your rent or your health insurance — every month for the same amount. Peachtree lets you set up recurring purchases or payments. You enter the purchase or payment once and tell Peachtree how often to record the transaction. Recurring transactions save you data-entry time.

You set up recurring purchases and recurring payments in the same way; the only difference is the window you use. To set up a recurring payment, start in the Payments window.

Recurring transactions affect the general ledger. In accrual-basis companies, both recurring purchases and recurring payments affect the general ledger. In cash-basis companies, only recurring payments affect the general ledger. Therefore, if you enter a recurring transaction, Peachtree updates the general ledger in the appropriate period; if you print future period reports, you will see the effects of the transactions in those future period reports. As you would expect, though, Peachtree displays each period's balances accurately for that period.

Use recurring purchases when you expect to print a check to pay a bill. If you *don't* expect to print a check — perhaps your health insurance company automatically deducts its payment from your checking account — use recurring payments.

To set up a recurring purchase, follow these steps:

1. **Choose Tasks⇨Purchases/Receive Inventory to open the Purchases/ Receive Inventory window.**

2. **Set up the purchase (select the vendor, and so on), but don't assign an invoice number.**

   You may want to click the Waiting on Bill box so that you don't accidentally pay a future bill before it becomes due.

3. **Click the Recur button on the toolbar.**

   Peachtree displays the Create Recurring Journal Entries dialog box (see Figure 6-6). Don't let the name scare you.

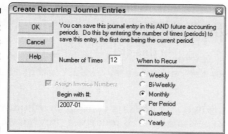

Figure 6-6:
Use this
dialog box
to set up
transactions
that happen
repeatedly.

4. **In the When to Recur list, select the frequency you want.**

5. **In the Number of Times box, type the number of transactions you want to enter for the time frame you chose in Step 4.**

   For example, if you're going to make a payment every week for 7 weeks, choose Weekly from the When to Recur list and type 7 in the Number of Times box. If you're going to make the payment every month for one year, choose Monthly in the When to Recur list and type 12 in the Number of Times box.

   You can create recurring purchases and payments that extend to the end of the last open period, but not beyond. Peachtree allows you to have two years open (usually 24 months).

6. **In the Begin with # box, assign a starting number for the recurring purchase.**

   If you want, set up a prefix for the bill. In Figure 6-6, we added the year and a dash to the number to make Peachtree start each purchase it creates for this recurring transaction with 2007-. Peachtree adds an incremental number, starting with 01. Because we created 12 transactions, Peachtree numbers the last recurring purchase as 2007-12.

7. **Click OK.**

   You can hear some activity on your hard disk while Peachtree creates the transactions. Then Peachtree redisplays the Purchases/Receive Inventory window, ready for you to enter your next purchase.

If you open a recurring purchase, take a minute to notice a couple of interesting things:

✔ You can see multiple entries for the recurring transaction in the Select Purchase window. For example, if on April 1 you set up the payment to recur weekly for seven weeks, look for at least four or possibly five entries in April. If you set up the purchase to recur monthly, you need to use the Show list box in the Select Purchases window to display All Transactions or a future period.

✔ When you display the recurring purchase in the Purchases/Receive Inventory window, look at the bottom of the window for an entry telling you how many more entries exist.

✔ When you save an edit to any recurring transaction, Peachtree prompts you to save the change for the current entry or the current entry and all remaining entries.

✔ In the Payments window, when you select a vendor for whom you set up a recurring purchase, you see lines for all recurring purchases, regardless of the period. Remember, you can double-click any line and view or edit the purchase in the Purchases/Receive Inventory window.

✔ When you click the Edit button in the Payments window to display the Select Payment window, recurring payments don't have reference numbers like recurring purchases do. The Reference number for a payment is the check number. Peachtree leaves the number blank so that you can print a check for the payment. If you write the check by hand, edit the payment and assign a check number.

Voiding Checks

If you write a check and then discover a problem with the check, you can void it. When you void a check, Peachtree creates a negative check for the same amount as the check you void, but the value of the voided check *increases* your cash account — remember, the original check reduced your cash account. In other words, if you add the two transactions, you get 0 (accountants say the transactions "Net to 0"), and a $0 transaction causes no change in your cash balance. The voided check transaction that Peachtree creates has the same number as the original check, but Peachtree adds a *V* to the number; that is, if you void check 101, Peachtree creates check 101V. You can view (and edit) the voided check in the Payments window the same way you can view and edit any other payment.

To void a check, follow these steps:

1. **Choose Tasks⇨Void Checks to display the Void Existing Checks window shown in Figure 6-7.**

2. **If necessary, click the lookup list indicator to choose the cash account from which you wrote the check that you now want to void.**

3. **Enter the Void Date for the check.**

   Be sure this date falls in the period that you want the cash account increased, which is not necessarily the same period that the check was written.

Figure 6-7:
Use this
window
to identify
the check
you want
to void.

Number	Date	Source	Amount	Payee
10201	3/12/07	AP	124.68	Clooney Chemical Supply
10202	3/12/07	AP	360.00	Gary, Wilson, Jones, & Smith
10203	3/12/07	AP	550.00	Mills Leasing Corp.
10204	3/12/07	AP	335.50	Daniel Lawn Pro, Inc.
10205	3/14/07	AP	147.00	Gwinnett County License Board
10206	3/14/07	AP	274.56	Juan Motor Tools & Tires
10207	3/14/07	AP	550.00	Mills Leasing Corp.
10208	3/14/07	AP	250.54	Southern Garden Wholesale
10209	3/14/07	AP	500.00	Jackson Advertising Company
10210	3/15/07	AP	530.64	Safe State Insurance Company

Void Existing Checks

Account ID: 10200   Void Date: Mar 15, 2007

Void   Close   Help

4. **Highlight the check you want to void and then click the Void button.**

   Peachtree displays a message asking whether you're sure you want to void the check.

5. **Click OK, and Peachtree creates a voided check transaction.**

You can sort the checks in the Void Existing Checks window in different ways to help you find the check you want to void. Click any of the column headings in the window to sort checks by that column heading.

If you accidentally void the wrong check, open the Payments window and click the Edit button. You can find the voided check in the window — the check number ends with a *V* for *Void*. Highlight that transaction and click OK to display it in the Payments window. Then delete it by clicking the Delete button.

After you void a check, you can see both the original check and the voided check transaction in the Account Reconciliation window when you balance your checkbook, and Peachtree has already marked them both as cleared. For more information on balancing your checkbook, see Chapter 16.

When you void a check that paid a vendor bill, Peachtree reopens the vendor bill. That is, Peachtree assumes you still want to pay the bill. If you do want to pay the bill, simply use the Payments or the Select for Payment window. If, however, you *don't* want to pay the bill, enter a vendor credit memo for the bill. Chapter 5 has more information on creating vendor credit memos.

pg. 93-94

Paying Sales Tax

Most states expect customers to pay a sales tax on goods they purchase; in some states, customers also pay tax on services. In addition, the county or local government may also assess a tax on customer's purchases. If your business sells taxable goods, you collect the sales tax for at least one taxing authority. Then, of course, you're expected to remit the sales tax to the taxing authority — along with a sales tax return (so that they can make sure that you're not cheating them out of any of the sales taxes you collect).

Paying sales tax in Peachtree is no different than paying any other bill; you can enter a purchase to remind yourself that you owe the money or you can simply write the check. The tricky part? Finding out *how much* to pay because not all sales are taxable in every state. And when the sales are taxable, local taxes might apply as well. To complicate the issue further, if you operate your business close to a border between jurisdictions, your business may be collecting taxes for more than one jurisdiction — and at different rates.

If you set up your sales taxes correctly (see Chapter 7 for more information), you can use the Taxable/Exempt Sales report (see Figure 6-8) to help you prepare the sales tax return and remit your sales taxes. Select Reports⇨Accounts Receivable to print this report, which breaks down the taxes you owe by taxing authority.

If you set up multiple exempt categories as described in the Inventory Preferences section Chapter 4, customize this report to add a column for the Tax Type, as we did in Figure 6-8 so that the report lists and identifies the totals for each exempt category that you need for the sales tax return. See Chapter 14 for help customizing reports.

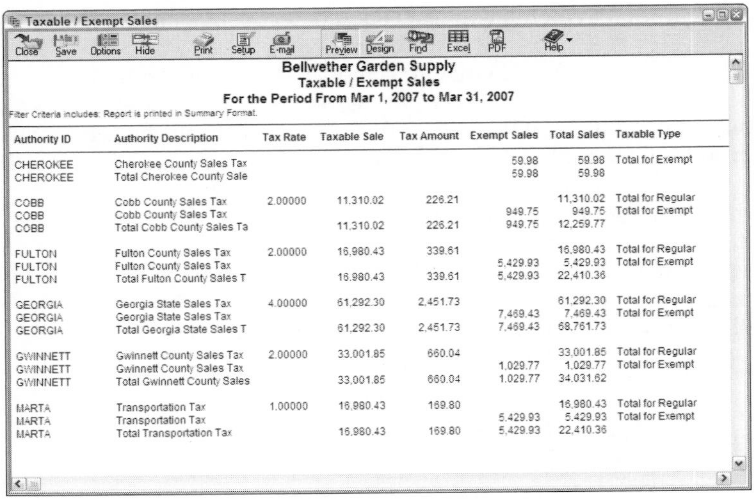

Authority ID	Authority Description	Tax Rate	Taxable Sale	Tax Amount	Exempt Sales	Total Sales	Taxable Type
CHEROKEE	Cherokee County Sales Tax				59.98	59.98	Total for Exempt
CHEROKEE	Total Cherokee County Sale				59.98	59.98	
COBB	Cobb County Sales Tax	2.00000	11,310.02	226.21		11,310.02	Total for Regular
COBB	Cobb County Sales Tax				949.75	949.75	Total for Exempt
COBB	Total Cobb County Sales Ta		11,310.02	226.21	949.75	12,259.77	
FULTON	Fulton County Sales Tax	2.00000	16,980.43	339.61		16,980.43	Total for Regular
FULTON	Fulton County Sales Tax				5,429.93	5,429.93	Total for Exempt
FULTON	Total Fulton County Sales T		16,980.43	339.61	5,429.93	22,410.36	
GEORGIA	Georgia State Sales Tax	4.00000	61,292.30	2,451.73		61,292.30	Total for Regular
GEORGIA	Georgia State Sales Tax				7,469.43	7,469.43	Total for Exempt
GEORGIA	Total Georgia State Sales T		61,292.30	2,451.73	7,469.43	68,761.73	
GWINNETT	Gwinnett County Sales Tax	2.00000	33,001.85	660.04		33,001.85	Total for Regular
GWINNETT	Gwinnett County Sales Tax				1,029.77	1,029.77	Total for Exempt
GWINNETT	Total Gwinnett County Sales		33,001.85	660.04	1,029.77	34,031.62	
MARTA	Transportation Tax	1.00000	16,980.43	169.80		16,980.43	Total for Regular
MARTA	Transportation Tax				5,429.93	5,429.93	Total for Exempt
MARTA	Total Transportation Tax		16,980.43	169.80	5,429.93	22,410.36	

Figure 6-8: Use this report to fill out the sales tax return that you must include when you make your sales tax payment.

Using Reports to Track Money You've Paid

When you need to track the outflow of money, Peachtree offers some reports that help you. Table 6-1 provides you with a description of the reports that pertain to paying bills. See Chapter 14 to find out how to print reports.

Table 6-1	Reports Related to Paying Bills
Report Name	**What It Does**
Check Register	Lists each check with the check number, payee, the amount, and the cash account from which the check was written.
Cash Requirements	Lists all unpaid purchases and their due dates for the date range you specify.
Cash Disbursements Journal	Shows the accounts that Peachtree updated for each check you wrote in the period. You can filter this report for 1099 vendors.

Visit this book's Web site for more information on Peachtree.

Chapter 7

Selling Products and Services

*W*hat incredible assets we have in our customers! (Well, most of them anyway.) After all, we wouldn't be in business without them, would we?

Peachtree operates under the assumption that you might generate a quote to a customer, convert that quote into a sales order, and then turn that sales order into an invoice when you produce the goods or service. You do not, however, have to use quotes or sales orders to use Peachtree's invoicing feature.

Even if you don't use quotes or sales orders, we suggest that you read this entire chapter. Peachtree's steps for creating and editing quotes, sales orders, and invoices are almost identical. Therefore, to eliminate redundancy, we explain most of the details in one place (see the section, "Bidding with Quotes"). We show you the differences between entering quotes, sales orders, and invoices in the individual sections of this chapter.

In addition to talking about the forms you use to sell things to your customers, we're going to start by talking about another important selling issue — sales taxes.

Working with Sales Taxes

Everyone hates to pay sales tax; taxes make us feel like we're paying more for our purchase than we should. Like it or not, though, most states expect customers to pay sales tax, usually on goods, but occasionally on services or freight as well. If you run your business in a locality that charges sales taxes, you, as the seller, are obligated to collect the sales tax from your customer.

Yielding to the authorities

If your business sells taxable goods or services, you collect the sales tax for the *taxing authority* — that's the term Peachtree uses to identify the agency that has the right to tell you to collect sales tax from your customers. That authority could be only your state government but frequently other local agencies are involved as well.

For example, suppose that your state along with several counties in your state charge a sales tax. In this case, you need to set up Sales Tax Authorities for your state and for each county as well.

Most states base the tax amount on the total invoice amount, but some states base their sales tax on the individual line item amount. Peachtree provides the ability to calculate sales taxes using a variety of methods. Table 7-1 illustrates the different scenarios in which your state might calculate sales tax. (Of course, if your state doesn't have sales taxes . . . feel free to avoid this table completely.)

Table 7-1	Sales Tax Scenarios
Scenario	**What It Does**
Single tax rate	Applies the standard tax rate on all sales regardless of amount.
Maximum dollar sales	Applies the standard tax rate up to a ceiling amount. After that, no more tax is calculated. For example, if the tax is 3% on the first $4000 of a sale and the sale is $5000, only $4000 is taxed at the 3% amount. The remaining $1000 is untaxed.
Minimum dollar sales	Applies the standard tax rate only when sales reach a specified amount. For example, if the minimum taxable sale amount is $500, a sale of $450 it is not taxed.
Maximum dollar tax	Applies the standard tax rate until the tax reaches a maximum amount, and then no more tax is calculated on that sale. For example, if the tax rate is 2%, with a maximum dollar tax of $20, sales up to $1000 are taxed at the 2% amount, but sales of $1000 and more are taxed a flat $20.
Maximum percent sales amount	Applies the standard tax rate to a specific maximum percentage, less than 100%. For example, the tax rate might be 3% but it applies only to 75% of the sales price.
Each taxable line item	Calculates the tax rates on each line item, instead of applying the previous tax rates to the grand total of the order.

Suppose that your business is located in the state of Georgia and that the state charges 4 percent sales tax for goods up to $999.99 and 3.5 percent sales tax for sales $1000.00 and over. You pay the tax to the Georgia Department of Revenue. If you have a branch of your business located in Brown County, Georgia, which has its own local tax, you have to charge those customers the additional local tax — say, 2 percent — which, in turn you pay to the Brown County Treasurer's office. If another branch is located in Green County, Georgia, another locality with a tax, the customers at that store have to pay an additional, say, 2.5 percent, which you turn over to the Green County Treasurer's office. In this situation, you have three taxing authorities: the State of Georgia, Brown County, and Green County.

What if you pay two or more of your taxes to the same payee? What authorities should you create? In that situation, you still should set up three different authorities. Doing so allows you to determine the exact amount of tax collected for each locality tax on Peachtree's Sales Tax report.

Before you set up the Sales Tax Authorities codes, you must set up a vendor to whom you remit the sales tax. You can find out how to set up a vendor in Chapter 5.

To follow this exercise, you must have a vendor set up; we will use Georgia Department of Revenue as the vendor name in this example. To set up Sales Tax Authorities, follow these steps:

1. **Choose Maintain⇨Sales Taxes⇨Sales Tax Authorities to display the Maintain Sales Tax Authorities window.**

2. **Type an ID for the authority.**

   You can use up to eight letters or numbers (alphanumeric characters). For our example, use GEORGIA.

3. **Type a description of the authority.**

   You can type up to 30 characters. We typed **Georgia State Sales Tax** for our example.

4. **In the Tax Payable To box, type or select the vendor ID to which you remit this sales tax.**

   This step assumes that you have set up the tax payee as a vendor, as mentioned at the beginning of these steps. For our example, we chose the Georgia Department of Revenue.

5. **Enter the G/L liability account to which you want to post the sales tax you collect.**

6. **Enter the tax rate, or select the Formula option and enter your sales tax calculation method.**

   If your state charges 4 percent, type 4.00; if it charges 5.5 percent, type it as 5.50. Peachtree automatically converts this value to a percentage.

7. **Click Save.**

8. **Repeat Steps 2 through 7 for each authority you need.**

   Figure 7-1 shows the three authorities for our example.

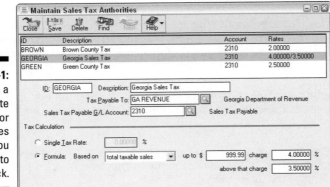

Figure 7-1:
Create a separate authority for each sales tax you want to track.

Creating sales tax codes

After you determine the sales tax authorities, you need to set up the Sales Tax Codes. The Sales Tax Codes are made up of combinations of Sales Tax Authorities. Following along with the example we used in the preceding section, because your customers in Brown County have to pay a Georgia State and Brown County tax, those two taxes together make up one Sales Tax Code for your Brown County branch. The customers in Green County pay Georgia State tax and Green County tax, so that combination generates the need for a second Sales Tax Code. You also need a third Sales Tax Code for those customers who simply pay the Georgia State tax with no county tax included.

Follow these steps to set up a Sales Tax Code:

1. **Choose Maintain⇨Sales Taxes⇨Sales Tax Codes to display the Maintain Sales Tax Codes window.**

2. **In the Sales Tax Code box, type an ID. In the Description box, you may type a description.**

Use a maximum of eight alphanumeric characters for the ID. We suggest you use some type of description, perhaps using **GABrown** as an ID with the description **Georgia, Brown County**.

3. **Click the box in the ID column and enter the first taxing authority ID for this tax code.**

   Peachtree fills in the description, tax rate, and G/L account you assigned to the selected authority.

   This ID text box reveals a little quirk in Peachtree. Generally, if a field has a lookup list available, the field displays a magnifying glass for you to click. This one doesn't. We don't know why . . . but it doesn't. So, if you don't remember the taxing authority ID, you can right-click the ID field to display the Sales Tax Authority lookup list. If you double-click the ID field, the Maintain Sales Tax Authority window opens, allowing you to create new sales tax authorities.

4. **If your state requires you to charge sales tax on the freight you charge to your customers, place a check mark in the Tax Freight box.**

   If you add a freight amount in the invoice freight box when you create an invoice to your customer, Peachtree calculates tax on the freight.

5. **Enter any remaining tax authorities for this sales tax ID and then click Save.**

   See Figure 7-2 for an example.

6. **Repeat Steps 2 through 5 for each Sales Tax Code you need.**

7. **Click Close.**

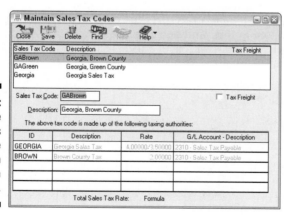

Figure 7-2:
Create
a Sales
Tax Code
for each
combination
of tax.

Working with Customers

Before you can generate quotes, sales orders, or invoices, you need to set up your customer defaults and enter the individual customers. In Chapter 4, we show you how to create the defaults you use here. Peachtree identifies each customer by a unique ID that allows Peachtree to track any transactions related to the customer.

Adding customers

When you set up a customer, you supply the customer's name and address, a sales account to use each time you post a sale to the customer, credit information, and any custom field information you set up in your defaults. You also can view historical data about your sales to and receipts from your customers over the previous 12 months.

To add or modify customer information, choose Maintain⇨Customers/Prospects. Peachtree displays the Maintain Customers/Prospects window, as shown in Figure 7-3. The following sections examine what you can do with each tab in this dialog box.

The General tab

Peachtree supplies the General tab for basic customer identification information, such as ID, name, address, and phone numbers. You use the ID as the identification to select the customer when you create a customer transaction. You can enter up to 20 alphanumeric characters (except the characters *, ?, and +) for a customer's ID. Peachtree sorts the customer reports by customer ID. Numbers sort before letters, and because the field is case sensitive, uppercase letters sort before lowercase letters.

Figure 7-3:
Use this window to add, edit, or delete customers.

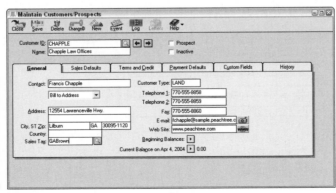

To make data entry easier, we suggest that you use either all uppercase or all lowercase letters so that you don't need to bother with the Shift key. Peachtree sorts the Customer List report and many other reports using the Customer ID by default. To get Peachtree to sort the customer list in alphabetical order by default, use characters from the customer's name as the ID.

Choose Maintain⇨Customers/Prospects. Peachtree displays the Maintain Customers/Prospects window. Fill in the General tab by following these steps:

1. **Type a Customer ID and the customer's Name.**

   You may enter up to 30 alphanumeric characters for the customer's name. IDs are case sensitive, so the IDs Baker, BAKER, and baker, for example, are treated as three different customer IDs.

   If you determine that you want a different ID, click the ChangeID button, type the new ID in the Enter New Customer ID box, click OK, and then click Save.

2. **If you do *not* want this customer ID included on any customer reports, click the Prospect check box.**

   A *prospect* is a potential customer, one who has not actually bought any goods or services from you. If you generate an invoice for the prospect or clear the check box, the prospect becomes a regular customer, and Peachtree includes the ID on customer reports.

3. **Fill in the contact information and phone numbers and, if appropriate, the E-mail and Web Site addresses.**

   If you enter an e-mail address and click the icon next to it, Peachtree opens your e-mail program and generates a message to your customer. Clicking the button next to the Web address launches your Web browser and directs it to the customer's Web site. If you plan to e-mail forms (quotes, sales orders, or invoices) to your customers, fill in the e-mail address.

4. **Click the drop-down arrow for the Bill to Address box, choose the shipping address you want to enter, and enter the shipping information.**

   You can store up to nine shipping addresses for each customer. Whenever you create a quote, sales order, or invoice, you can choose from the stored shipping addresses, thereby saving data entry time.

We need to discuss two additional fields in this window: the Customer Type field and the Sales Tax field.

✔ **Customer Type:** Use the Customer Type field to group similar customers together. You can then limit the information on most A/R reports to a specific customer type. For example, you may want to distinguish between commercial customers and retail customers. Being consistent when entering the customer type is the secret to using the Customer Type field effectively. The Customer Type field is case sensitive.

✔ **Sales Tax:** You need to choose the Sales Tax Code that applies to this customer. To do so, type the applicable Sales Tax Code or click the lookup list button.

If you no longer do business with this customer, place a check mark in the Inactive box.

The Sales Defaults tab

On the Sales Defaults tab, you can define several additional pieces of customer information. Peachtree relates many of the fields on this window to the inventory and payroll modules:

1. **Choose Maintain⇨Customers/Prospects and click the Sales Defaults tab.**

2. **If applicable, select a default Sales Rep for this customer and type the Sales Rep ID or select one from the lookup list.**

   See Chapter 9 for information on creating sales reps.

3. **Define a GL Sales Account for the customer if it's different from the default account established in Customer Defaults.**

   For more information about Customer Defaults, see Chapter 4.

   When you create an inventory item, you specify a sales account for the item. When you generate an invoice, the sales account associated with inventory items overrides the customer sales account. You can find out how to set up inventory items in Chapter 11.

4. **In the Open P.O. # box, enter a purchase order number if your customer has given you a standing purchase order number to use for all purchases from you.**

   This purchase order number appears by default in the Customer Purchase Order field on the Quotes, Sales Orders, and Sales/Invoicing windows.

5. **In the Ship Via box, choose a preferred shipping method.**

   Determine shipping methods in the Maintain Inventory Item Defaults window. If necessary, you can override the preferred method when you generate a customer invoice. You set up shipping methods in Chapter 4.

6. **If the customer does not have to pay sales tax, enter the Resale number.**

   Most states require a customer to provide you with their resale number for tax-exempt purchases.

7. **Choose the pricing level most often associated with this customer.**

   Pricing levels are tied to inventory items. See Chapter 11 for details on how to assign up to ten prices to each inventory item. Peachtree then automatically charges the customer the price shown in the pricing level you specify here.

8. **Select a form delivery method.**

   Forms include Sales Orders, Packing Slips, Invoices, and Statements.

To use the e-mail delivery method in Peachtree, you must have a MAPI-compliant, default e-mail application installed on your computer. If your default e-mail system is AOL, you will not be able to send e-mail from Peachtree because AOL is not a fully MAPI-compliant e-mail application.

Terms and Credit tab

All things not being equal, Peachtree provides the ability to assign different credit terms to different customers. You use the Terms and Credit tab to establish the specific terms for the current customer.

Choose Maintain⇨Customers/Prospects and click the Terms and Credit tab. Peachtree assumes that each customer uses the default terms you established when you set up Customer Defaults. To make any changes from the Terms and Credit defaults, you must first remove the check mark from the Use Standard Terms and Credit check box. You can then edit the terms, indicating whether to charge finance charges, change the customer's credit limit, or determine whether or how Peachtree should notify you about the customer's credit limit status.

Use the Credit Status box to place a customer on credit hold. If a customer's status is Always Hold, Peachtree displays a warning message and will not allow you to save an invoice for that customer.

Payment Defaults tab

The information stored on the Payment Defaults tab is optional. If you accept credit cards from your clients, this tab provides a place to store the customer's credit card number and expiration date.

Options in the Receipt Settings area are time-savers. If the Use Receipts window settings box is checked, Peachtree uses the payment method and cash account you selected on the last saved receipt. You might want to change this setting if, for example, the selected customer always pays by credit card but the majority of your other customers pay by check.

Custom Fields tab

When you set up default customer information, (see Chapter 4), you created the custom fields for the Maintain Customers/Prospects window. To enter custom information, choose Maintain⇨Customers/Prospects. Click the Custom Fields tab and enter the available information for the customer in each custom field box. Click the Save button to save this information.

History tab

When you first set up a customer, the History tab doesn't have any information. However, after you've recorded customer sales transactions, the History tab gives you a month-by-month summary of both sales and receipts.

To view a customer's history, choose Maintain⇨Customers/Prospects and then click the History tab. You can't edit any information on the History screen; Peachtree provides it for a quick overview of the customer's history.

Customers move around, so you may find that the information you've stored about a customer is outdated. You can change any information you entered in the Maintain Customers/Prospects window. Display the customer's ID, change any desired information, and then click Save.

Where to begin? Beginning balances

Chances are, you've been selling your goods and services for a while. And . . . you probably haven't been paid yet for all the work you've done. You've probably given your customers a specified amount of time to pay their invoices to you. You specify your terms when you set up your default customer information in Chapter 4.

Although some invoices aren't due yet, others may be past due. Either way, the customer owes you money. When you begin using Peachtree, you need to tell Peachtree about those unpaid invoices, especially if your business is accrual based. Enter these as customer beginning balances.

Entering invoices as beginning balances does not affect the general ledger. In an *accrual-based* business, sales are applied to your general ledger at the time that you create the invoices.

To enter customer beginning balances, follow these steps:

1. **Choose Maintain⇨Customers/Prospects.**

2. **Click the Beginning Balances button to display the Customer Beginning Balances dialog box.**

3. **Double-click the first customer for which you need to enter a beginning balance invoice.**

   Did you think you'd have to recreate your invoices? You don't. Simply provide Peachtree with a few key pieces of information.

4. **Enter the invoice number and the date of the original invoice.**

   The date is needed so that Peachtree can age the invoice properly.

5. **Optionally, enter the customer's purchase order number for the invoice.**

6. **Enter the invoice amount.**

7. **Enter A/R Account number.**

   The A/R Account is the Accounts Receivable account. Notice, we say *Accounts Receivable.* We're not talking about the sales account. It's a common mistake to enter the sales account number.

8. **Repeat Steps 4 through 7 for each outstanding invoice for the selected customer.**

   Figure 7-4 shows a sample list of outstanding invoices.

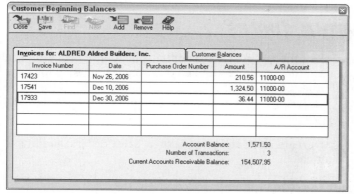

Figure 7-4:
Enter
invoices
dated prior
to the
usage of
Peachtree.

Technically, Peachtree has no limit to the number of beginning balance invoices you can enter for an individual customer. However, if you exceed 100 invoices, you can enter but not edit or delete the 101st invoice and subsequent invoices.

9. **Click Save.**

10. **Click the Customer Balances tab and select the next customer for whom you want to enter beginning balances.**

11. **When you finish entering beginning balances, click the Close button. Click it again to close the Maintain Customers/Prospects window.**

We recommend that you print an Aged Receivables report to verify the invoice information and dates and a Trial Balance report to make sure that the Aged Receivables balance matches the GL balance.

Bidding with Quotes

Many businesses let their customers know how much a product or service costs by producing a *quote* before the customer decides to buy. Peachtree allows you to create a quote; when the customer determines he or she *does* want to make the purchase, you can convert that quote to a sales order or an invoice.

Quotes are optional in the Peachtree sales process.

Entering quotes

The top part of the quote window contains header information such as customer name, address, quote number, date, and other such information. Enter the actual products or services you supply in the body of the quote. In Bonus Chapter 1 on this book's Web site, you can find out how to modify the appearance of the Quotes window by using templates.

The steps to create, edit, and print quotes, sales orders, and invoices are almost identical.

To create a quote in Peachtree, follow these steps:

1. **Choose Tasks➪Quotes/Sales Orders➪Quotes to display the Quotes window, as shown in Figure 7-5.**

2. **Type or select the Customer ID.**

   You can't enter a quote in Peachtree unless you have set up a customer. Peachtree displays the customer's current balance and credit limit in the lower-left corner.

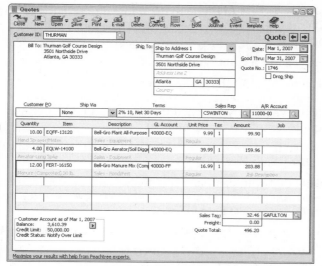

Figure 7-5:
Quotes
inform your
customer in
advance of
the price of
a product or
service.

If you begin typing the Customer ID, only to find you haven't yet entered the customer into Peachtree, press the plus (+) key while the insertion point is in the ID box. Peachtree displays the Maintain Customers/ Prospects window, allowing you to create the customer record. When you close the Maintain Customers/Prospects window, Peachtree redisplays the Quote window. This procedure works for any lookup list you open in Peachtree. Pressing the plus (+) key opens the appropriate Maintain window: Vendors, Customers/Prospects, Inventory, Employees/Sales Reps, or Chart of Accounts.

3. **Type the recipient Ship To address, or click the Ship To arrow and choose the Bill To address or one of the Ship To addresses you entered when first setting up the customer.**

   Peachtree doesn't store a manually entered ship to address permanently in the customer record. However, Peachtree *does* store the custom address with the current quote and transfers the address to the resulting sales order or invoice or both.

4. **Enter the Date you want printed on the quote and an Expiration Date for the quote.**

   Peachtree assumes that the quote is valid for a period of 30 days and prints the ending date on the quote form. If you're giving your customer a longer or shorter period of time, choose a different date in the Good Thru date box.

Peachtree doesn't do anything to the quote if the customer doesn't respond in the specified number of days. The date is simply printed on the quote form.

5. Optionally, enter a Quote Number.

If you're going to print the quote (and usually you do), don't enter a quote number because Peachtree assigns the number when it prints the quote. If you've already assigned the quote a number, perhaps from a verbal quote, enter the quote number.

If you plan to have your vendor ship the item directly to your customer, click the Drop Ship box.

It's unlikely that your customer has given you a purchase order number for a quote. After all, if you're quoting it, it's not yet a purchase. You can leave the Customer PO field blank.

6. Optionally, type a shipping method or choose a shipping method from the Ship Via list box.

7. Optionally, change the Terms for this order.

By default, Peachtree displays the terms you chose when you set up this customer in Maintain Customers/Prospects.

8. Optionally, select a Sales Rep ID.

Take a look at Chapter 9 for information on how to set up a sales representative.

If your business is accrual-based, you can select the A/R Account option for this potential sale, although typically you shouldn't change the default. If your company is cash-based, this field displays `<Cash Basis>` and you can't access the account box. If you have elected to hide general ledger accounts in A/R, you won't even see an A/R Account box.

9. In the body of the quote, enter the Quantity for the first item on the quote.

If you're quoting a service or product that doesn't have a quantity, you can leave the quantity blank.

10. If you're selling an inventory item, select the Item ID.

Peachtree fills in the item description, the G/L sales account, the item's unit price, and the tax status. Then Peachtree multiplies the quantity times the unit price for the amount. Read about setting up inventory items in Chapter 11.

11. If you're quoting or selling a nonstock item or you don't use inventory, leave the Item box blank and fill in the Description, GL (Income) Account and Unit Price.

Peachtree calculates the amount. If you did not enter a quantity in Step 9, you must enter an amount instead of a unit price. If you enabled Peach-tree's spell-checking options, Peachtree flags any typing mistakes as they happen.

Quotes do not affect the general ledger, but whenever the quote becomes a sale, Peachtree uses the G/L account numbers to update your financial information.

If you have globally hidden general ledger accounts, Peachtree does not display G/L Account fields in the Quotes window. To modify G/L accounts used for this transaction, you must click the Journal button in the window toolbar.

12. **If you're quoting a noninventory item, select the Tax status.**

    The Tax box refers to the tax types you determine when setting inven-tory defaults. Peachtree uses default tax types of 1 for Taxable and 2 for Exempt. If you're using inventory items, Peachtree determines the tax type from the inventory item.

13. **You probably won't have a job number assigned yet because this is still a quote, so skip the job box.**

14. **Repeat Steps 9 through 13 for each item you want to quote.**

15. **If you're going to charge shipping charges, enter the estimated amount in the Freight box.**

16. **Optionally, click the Note button to store one of three different notes. Choose from a customer note, which prints on the actual Quote form, a statement note, which prints on the customer statement, or an inter-nal note, for internal reference only.**

    If you later convert the quote to a sales order or invoice, the notes con-vert also.

We're assuming that you need to print the quote; however, if don't need to print the quote, click the Save button. Peachtree saves the quote for future reference. To print or e-mail your quote, click the Print or E-mail button. See Printing Forms in Chapter 13.

Converting a quote to a sales order or an invoice

Congratulations! You got the sale! Now you're ready to generate a sales order or an invoice from the original quote.

To convert a quote to make the sale, follow these steps:

1. **Choose Tasks⇨Quotes/Sales Orders⇨Quotes to display the Quotes window.**

2. **Click the Open button to display a list of previously created quotes.**

3. **Choose the quote you want to convert and then click OK.**

   You may have to click in the Show list to display quotes from a different time period.

   If you don't remember what month you created the quote, try this: In the Show list, choose All Transactions (it's at the top of the list). Then click Find and enter a few characters of your customer's name. Click OK, and Peachtree locates the first quote for the customer you specify. If this isn't the one you're searching for, click Next. Peachtree locates the next occurrence.

4. **Change the date on the quote to the sales order or invoice date you want to use.**

   The date you choose must fall within or be later than the current accounting period.

5. **Click the Convert button to display the Convert Quote dialog box.**

6. **Select a conversion option.**

   The options that appear depend on your selection are as follows:

   • If you choose Sale/Invoice, you get a text box prompting you for an invoice number. If you elect not to enter an invoice number, the quote still converts to an invoice, but you need to print it at a later time.

   • If you choose Sale/Invoice and Print Now, you're prompted for a beginning invoice number and other print options after you click OK.

   • If you choose Sales Order, a text box appears with the next sales order number displayed. You can change this sales order number if desired.

7. **Click OK.**

After you convert a quote, it no longer exists as a quote if you click the Open button in the Quote window. You can, however, see it as a sales order or invoice in the Sales Order window or the Sales/Invoicing window.

Working with Sales Orders

Why should you use sales orders? Why not just create an invoice? Well, this choice is really a matter of timing. If your business receives a customer order and ships the product or provides the service within a day or two, you could skip the sales order step and wait to enter the invoice. If a lapse exists between the time you take the order and the time you provide the product or service, however, you may find the sales order feature helpful. The sales order feature lets you enter items for a customer and then invoice and ship the items as they become available, tracking the backorders in the system.

By viewing inventory and sales order reports, you know the number of items backordered for your customers, which can help you plan purchases from your vendors.

Even though you reference G/L accounts when you create a sales order, Peachtree doesn't update the general ledger until you create an invoice from a sales order.

You may find entering data in the Sales Order window similar to creating a quote. To create a sales order, follow these steps:

1. **Choose Tasks⇨Quotes/Sales Orders⇨Sales Orders to display the Sales Orders window.**

2. **Fill in the Customer information or select the customer ID from the lookup list.**

   The lower-left corner displays the customer's current balance, credit limit, and credit status. Click the arrow to display the customer ledger.

   If the customer ID is not setup in Peachtree, the ID box flashes and when you later save or print the transactions, Peachtree will prompt you to save the customer information.

3. **Type the Ship To address, or click the Ship To arrow and choose the Bill To address or one of the Ship To addresses you entered when first setting up the customer.**

   Peachtree doesn't store a manually entered ship to address permanently in the customer record. However, Peachtree *does* store the custom address with the sales order and later transfers the address to the resulting invoice.

4. **Enter the date you want for the sales order and a ship by date.**

   The ship-by date can appear on several sales order reports to help you better track your customer orders.

Peachtree automatically assigns the next sales order number, but you can change it if you want.

5. **If you want your vendor to ship the item directly to your customer, click the Drop Ship box.**

If you activated the default inventory option in Peachtree Premium to create purchases orders automatically, Peachtree creates a purchase order for the item. See Chapter 4.

Refer to the previous section, "Entering quotes," to review entering line items

6. **Fill in the body of the sales order, keeping the following variations in mind:**

   • A sales order does not have a good through field.

   • Your customer may or may not supply you with a customer purchase order number.

   • If you do not enter a quantity, enter an amount.

   • If you're using Peachtree's job costing, you may have already assigned a job number to the customer order. If so, be sure to indicate the job ID and optionally the phase code and cost code to each sales order line item.

Peachtree can play a visual trick on you here. When you click the Job box, it expands backwards and covers up part of the Amount box (see Figure 7-6). At first glance, it may appear that the amount has disappeared, but it's only hidden. When you move the insertion point past the Job box, Peachtree redisplays the Amount box. Read about setting up jobs in Chapter 12.

   • If you're going to charge shipping charges and you know the amount, enter it in the Freight Amount box.

   • The Shipped quantity box is unavailable for you to edit. When you ship the ordered goods, whether partially or completely, and bill them on an invoice, Peachtree tracks the quantity shipped and enters it in this column of the sales order.

7. **Optionally, click the Note button to store one of three different notes: a customer note, which prints on the actual Sales Order form, a statement note, which prints on the customer statement, and an internal note, for internal reference only.**

8. **When you've finished entering the sales order, click the Save button to save the transaction or the Print button to print it.**

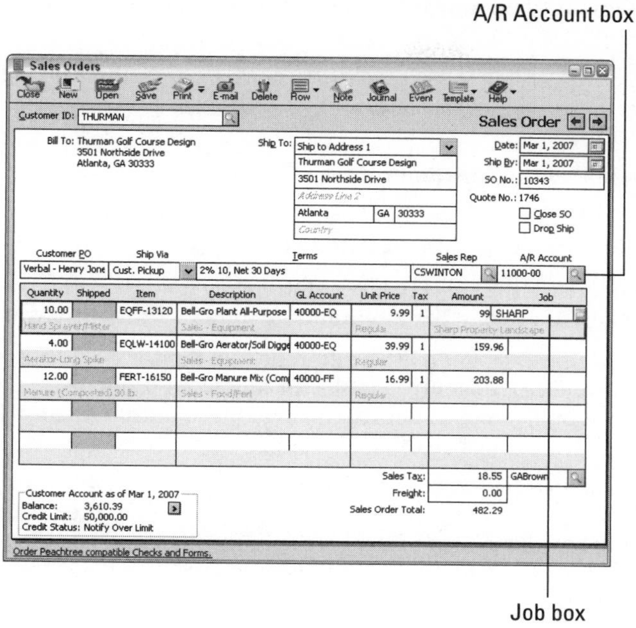

A/R Account box

Figure 7-6:
The amount
is not
gone, just
temporarily
hidden.

Job box

Generating an Invoice

Finally! Your company has produced the product or performed the service, and you are now ready to collect your money. Most businesses generate an invoice as proof of the sale to give or send to their customers.

If you read the previous sections on creating quotes or creating sales orders, you know quite a bit about creating an invoice. As with quotes and sales orders, you enter the invoice header and body information. The difference is that when you *do* use sales orders, you enter the information a little differently from the way you enter data if you *don't* use sales orders.

Invoicing against a sales order

Only one sales order can apply to an invoice. However, you can create multiple invoices from a single sales order.

To create an invoice and apply it to a sales order, follow these steps:

1. **Choose Tasks⇨Sales/Invoicing to display the Sales/Invoicing window.**

   The Sales/Invoicing window is similar to the Quotes and Sales Order windows.

2. **Type or select the Customer ID.**

   You can't create an invoice in Peachtree unless you have set up a customer through Maintain Customers/Prospects.

   Remember, with the insertion point in the ID field, you can press the plus (+) key to display the Maintain Customers/Prospects window.

   Here's where things get a little different. See Figure 7-7. When you select your customer ID, Peachtree looks for any open sales order for that customer. If an open sales order exists, Peachtree automatically displays the Apply to Sales Order No. tab.

   If the invoice you want to enter does not apply to a sales order, click the Apply to Sales tab and proceed to the information in the next section, "Invoicing against sales."

Sales order selection box

Ship button

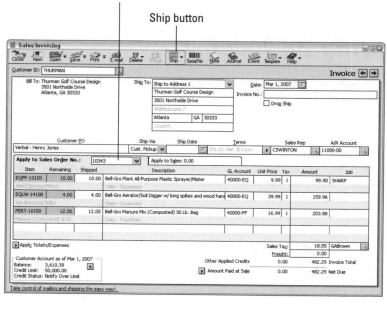

Figure 7-7: When the sales order is filled, Peachtree automatically marks the sales order closed.

3. **On the Apply to Sales Order No. tab, click the arrow to display a list of open sales orders.**

4. **Choose the sales order you want to invoice.**

   Peachtree fills in the information you supplied when you created the sales order, including Ship To, Purchase Order Number, Sales Rep, and the items ordered.

5. **Enter the invoice Date and change any header information.**

   Leave the invoice number blank if you want Peachtree to assign an invoice number when you print the invoice.

   Inventory item numbers on a sales order can't be edited from an invoice. To change item numbers, you must edit the original sales order. You can, however, change the quantities or item description. To add additional items or charges to the invoice, click the Apply to Sales tab and add the items there.

6. **In the Shipped column, enter the quantities shipped. Or if the entire order has been filled, click the Ship toolbar button and choose All.**

   If you clicked the All button, Peachtree fills in the remaining quantities of the order.

7. **Enter the Freight amount.**

   If you entered freight information when you created the sales order, Peachtree displays it on the invoice only if you use the Ship All feature. If you make a partial shipment and need to charge freight, enter the freight amount manually.

   If you're going to ship the product via UPS and plan to use the shipping feature available in Peachtree Complete and Peachtree Premium, click the <u>Freight</u> link. See "Shipping the UPS Way," later in this chapter, for information on the shipping feature.

8. **Optionally, click the Note button to store one of three notes:** a customer note, which prints on the actual invoice, a statement note, which prints on the customer statement, and an internal note, for internal reference only.

9. **Click Save or Print.**

   You probably want to print the invoice, but if you are not going to print it or if you want to continue entering invoices and print them later in a batch, click the Save button to save the invoice. To print your invoices, see "Printing Forms" in Chapter 13.

When you save or print the invoice, if the current invoice total plus any unpaid invoices for this customer exceed the credit limit determined when you set up the customer, depending on the credit status you selected, Peachtree will warn you and potentially stop you from proceeding with the invoice.

Invoicing against sales

Your business doesn't use sales orders? You can create an invoice without a sales order.

To create an invoice, follow these steps:

1. **Choose Tasks⇨Sales Invoicing to display the Sales/Invoicing window.**

2. **Enter the invoice header information.**

   To review how to enter the header information, see the "Creating quotes" section, earlier in this chapter. The header information includes the invoice date, shipping address, customer's purchase order number (if available), shipping method, terms, and sales rep ID.

3. **If you want your vendor to ship the item directly to your customer, click the Drop Ship box.**

   If you activated the default inventory option in Peachtree Premium to create purchase orders automatically, Peachtree creates a purchase order for the item. See Chapter 4.

4. **Fill in the line items for the invoice based on the following options:**

   • Enter a quantity for the first item on the invoice. You can leave the Quantity field blank when invoicing a service or product that doesn't have a quantity.

   • If the product is an inventory item, select the item ID. Peachtree fills in the item description, the G/L account, the item's unit price, and the tax status. Then Peachtree multiplies the quantity times the unit price for the amount.

You can tell Peachtree to warn you if you do not have enough stock to sell the item. See "Setting Inventory Defaults" in Chapter 4.

   • If your product is a non-inventory item or you don't use inventory, leave the Item box blank and enter a description, G/L account, and unit price.

   • The Tax box refers to the tax types you determine when setting inventory defaults. If you're using inventory items, Peachtree determines the tax type from the inventory item.

- If you do not enter a quantity, enter an amount.

- Optionally, if you're using Peachtree's job costing feature, click in the Job box to display the magnifying glass and then choose a job from the list.

- If you're going to charge shipping charges and you know the amount, enter it in the Freight Amount box.

If you are going to ship the product via UPS and plan to use the shipping feature available in Peachtree Complete or Peachtree Premium, click the <u>Freight</u> link which saves the invoice and opens the Shipping window with the customer information already entered. See "Shipping the UPS Way," later in this chapter, for information on the shipping feature.

5. **Optionally, click the Note button to store one of three different notes.**

   You can choose from a customer note, which prints on the actual invoice, a statement note, which prints on the customer statement, and an internal note, for internal reference only.

6. **Click Save or Print.**

   You probably want to print the invoice but, if you are not going to print it or if you want to continue entering invoices and print them later in a batch, click the Save button to save the invoice. To print your invoices, see "Printing Forms" in Chapter 13.

As with sales orders, if the current invoice total plus any unpaid invoices for this customer exceed the credit limit you established when you set up the customer, depending on the credit status you selected, Peachtree will warn you and potentially stop you from proceeding with the invoice.

Shipping the UPS Way

This feature is available only in Peachtree Complete and Peachtree Premium.

What happens when you mix brown and peach? No . . . we're not referring to disintegrating fruit. You get UPS (brown) integration with your Peachtree (peach) software! You might deliver your goods to your clients in many different ways. You might hand deliver them, the customer might pick them up from your warehouse, or you might ship them using a common carrier such as a freight line or a parcel delivery service. If you ship your goods through UPS, you can generate and track the shipment information directly through Peachtree's Shipments feature.

You must have an Internet connection for the Shipments feature to work.

A shipment generated through the Shipments feature doesn't have to be for goods you sell. It could be for any document or package you want to ship to anyone, anywhere.

Before you can use the Shipments feature, you must have an account number registered through UPS. Contact UPS at 1-800-PICK-UPS (1-800-742-5877) to initiate an account. Don't lose the account number, because you'll need it to register through Peachtree's Shipping Registration Wizard.

After you have an account number assigned but before you can ship your first package, you must use the Shipping Registration Wizard to activate the link between UPS and Peachtree. Choose Tasks⇨Shipments⇨Shipping Registration Wizard. Follow the steps, which include entering your shipping address, a contact person, your UPS account number, and the billing method you want UPS to use.

The contact person entered in the Shipping Registration Wizard *must* be set up as an employee in Maintain Employees even if you don't use Peachtree to process payroll.

Now when you have UPS packages to ship, follow these easy steps:

1. **Choose Tasks⇨Shipments⇨Shipments.**

   Peachtree opens a Shipping window like the one you see in Figure 7-8.

Ship to Type drop-down list

Estimate button

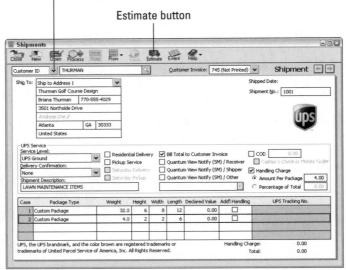

Figure 7-8: Choose your shipping options for this shipment.

2. **Optionally, in the Ship to Type list, choose whether you're shipping to a customer, a vendor, or an employee.**

3. **Select the ID. If you're not shipping to a customer, a vendor, or an employee, leave this field blank.**

   If you clicked the Freight hyperlink in the Sales/Invoicing window, you see the shipping window with the customer information and invoice number already entered.

4. **Enter a shipment number.**

   This is a required data entry field. After you create a shipment number, such as 101, Peachtree remembers the sequence for the next shipment and numbers it 102. Optionally, you could use the customer invoice number as the shipment reference number.

5. **Select the level of UPS service you want.**

   You can select the service level as well as any extras, such as delivery confirmation or COD charges.

6. **Optionally, in the Shipment Description box, enter a brief description of the contents of the shipment.**

7. **Enter the package information, including package type and weight.**

8. **Optionally enter the package value and select whether you want the package to have special handling.**

   Each package going to this recipient must be listed with its own package type, weight, and dimensions. Peachtree lists the standard UPS provided packages as well as a custom box, where you enter your own dimensions. The length should be the longest dimension in the package.

9. **If you want a cost estimate before shipping this order, click the Estimate button and follow the on-screen instructions.**

   The UPS Estimate Settings box prompts you for the method you plan on using to get the package to UPS and then displays a list of the UPS service level options and their published rates.

10. **Click the Process button.**

    Peachtree registers the shipment with UPS and assigns a UPS tracking number.

    If you are billing the total to the customer invoice and the customer invoice already has an invoice number assigned, Peachtree thinks the invoice is already printed and warns you that proceeding will change the invoice's total amount due.

A confirmation message appears, stating the total estimated charges, and prompts you to print the shipping labels. Print the shipping label on plain paper and attach it to the package, usually in a special UPS window envelope.

11. Click OK twice and then click Yes after the label prints.

Your UPS account does not get billed until the actual package is scanned by a UPS representative. If you decide to not ship the package, you can void the shipment by locating it through the Open button and clicking the Void button.

You can track the status of your shipment by choosing Tasks➪Shipments➪ Track a Package and entering the UPS tracking number.

Editing a Sales Transaction

Like most transactions you enter in Peachtree, quotes, sales orders, and invoices are not written in stone. Peachtree makes it easy for you to modify anything on the transaction — even after it has been printed. Click the Tasks menu and choose the type of document you want to edit: Quote, Sales Order, or Sales/Invoicing. Next, click the Open button and choose the transaction you want to edit and then click OK. Make any desired changes to the transaction and then click Print to reprint the transaction or click Save to save the transaction without reprinting it.

The Select Sales Orders, Select Quote and Select Invoice windows displays sales orders generated in the current period. If you don't see the transaction you want to edit, open the Show list box and select a different period.

Voiding an Invoice

If you generate an invoice and then discover that the invoice needs to be canceled, use the Void Invoice feature. See Chapter 8 if you need to issue a credit memo to the customer.

Although technically you could delete an invoice to get rid of it, deleting an invoice is not good accounting practice. When you delete transactions, you lose your audit trail of the actions you've taken. And, if the original invoice occurred in a previous month, you could hurt the integrity of your reports. Your accountant would not be a happy camper.

When you void an invoice, Peachtree creates several transactions. First, Peachtree creates another invoice with the same invoice number as the original, except it adds a *V* to the invoice number. That invoice amount is a negative dollar amount equal to the amount of the original invoice. For example, if you generate invoice number 1234 for $150.00 that you must cancel, Peachtree generates another invoice 1234V for –$150.00 to void the original.

If the original transaction involves inventory items, Peachtree restores to inventory the items sold. In the general ledger, Peachtree creates a reversing entry, affecting sales and accounts receivable, and if applicable, cost of sales and inventory. If the original invoice does not come from a sales order, the reversing entry contains negative values for the quantities *sold*. However, if the original invoice does come from a sales order, the reversing entry contains negative values for the quantities *shipped*. Peachtree then reopens the sales order.

Next, Peachtree creates a zero-dollar receipt to pay both the original and voided invoices. This receipt clears both transactions from the Aged Receivable report. In other words, if you add the two transactions together, you get 0 and, a $0 transaction causes no change in your cash balance. You can view the zero-dollar receipt by clicking the Open button in the Tasks⇨ Receipts window and selecting the appropriate receipt.

To void an invoice, follow these steps:

1. **Choose Tasks⇨Sales/Invoicing.**

2. **Click the Open button and double-click the transaction you want to void.**

   The transaction must appear on the screen before you can void it.

   Optionally, choose a different period from the Show drop-down list to find the invoice you want.

3. **Click the Delete button and then choose Void.**

   Peachtree opens a Void Existing Invoice dialog box like the one in Figure 7-9.

Figure 7-9:
Peachtree displays the invoice number, date, amount, and customer.

4. **Type the date you want — usually the current date — in The Following Invoice Will Be Voided as Of box.**

5. **Click OK.**

   Peachtree lists the word *Void* beside both the original and reversing invoices and uses the invoice number as the receipt reference number.

Recurring Invoices

In some businesses, you have customers that you bill the same amount every month for the same products or services. By setting up recurring entries, you can save a great deal of time entering these invoices. Even if the amount differs next time, it's helpful to have all the other information filled out for you. Then, you have to change only the amount.

Recurring entries can't be created if you generate the invoice using a sales order.

You also can create recurring purchases, payments, and general journal entries. You can adapt the following steps for these other tasks.

To create recurring invoices, follow these steps:

1. **Choose Tasks⇨Sales/Invoicing to display the Sales/Invoicing window.**

2. **Enter the invoice information as you usually would, but do *not* enter an invoice number or click Save or Print.**

3. **Click the Recur button to display the Create Recurring Journal Entries dialog box, shown in Figure 7-10.**

4. **Enter the number of times to create the entry, including the current transaction.**

   The maximum number of times depends on the transaction's original date and the current accounting period. You can enter recurring transactions only within the two open fiscal years of Peachtree. For example, if you're creating a new invoice and are currently in period 3, the maximum number of monthly recurrences would be 22.

5. **Under When to Recur, select a time frame for the recurring invoice.**

   You can choose Weekly, Bi-Weekly, Monthly, Per Period, Quarterly, or Yearly.

6. **Optionally, assign a beginning invoice number by clicking the Assign Invoice Numbers check box.**

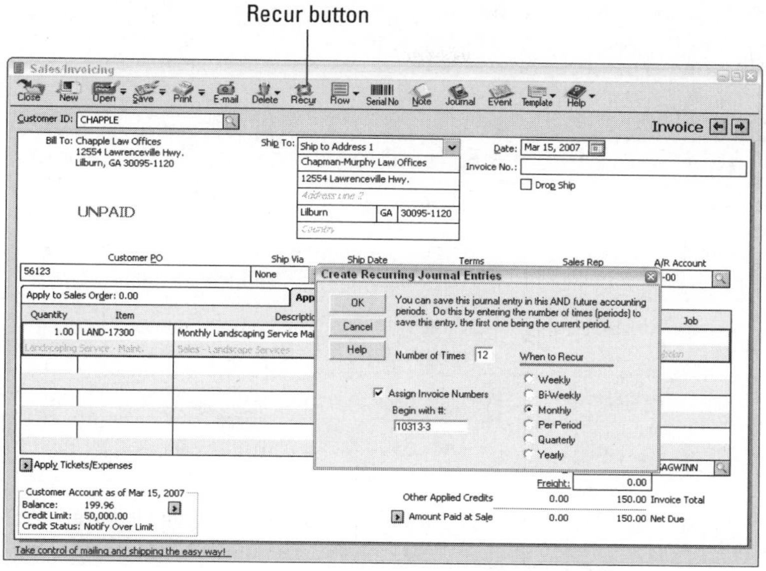

Recur button

Figure 7-10:
Save data
entry time
by creating
recurring
entries.

Peachtree displays a box to enter a beginning invoice number. All transactions are numbered incrementally. A number of our clients use a system that includes the current year as the first two or four digits of the number, followed by a dash and then the beginning invoice number.

Peachtree doesn't automatically print recurring invoices. If you leave the invoice number blank, you can print the recurring transactions when you use Peachtree's batch printing method or edit the transaction and click Print. Chapter 13 discusses how to print batches of forms.

7. **Click OK for Peachtree to save all transactions in the appropriate periods.**

If you need to edit or delete a recurring transaction, Peachtree prompts you with the Change Recurring Journal Entries dialog box. You can edit only the current invoice or the current invoice and all future occurrences. Editing a recurring transaction does not affect previous transactions.

Reviewing Customer Reports

Peachtree offers several useful reports that you can use for listing customer information, compiling tax information, and tracking quotes that you want to turn into sales. In Tables 7-2, 7-3, and 7-4, we provide you with a description of the reports that pertain to selling your goods and services. You can sort the report data in a variety of ways, and you can control how much and which information you want to display on the report. See Chapter 14 to find out how to print reports.

Table 7-2	Reports Related to Quotes and Customers in General
Report Name	*What It Does*
Customer List	For each customer, lists the ID, name, contact name, telephone number, and resale number
Customer Master File List	Similar to Customer List, but also includes address information, tax codes, and terms
Prospect List	Lists each prospect with contact and telephone number
Quote Register	Lists each quote with quote date, expiration date, customer name, and quote amount
Sales Tax Codes	Lists each Sales Tax Code with all corresponding authorities, tax rates, and vendor information

Table 7-3	Reports Related to Sales Orders
Report Name	*What It Does*
Picklist Report	Lists open sales order items such as item ID and description, quantity to ship, and warehouse location. Sort this report by sales order number, ship by date, location, customer ID, or item ID.
Sales Backorder Report	Lists open order items, such as item ID, description, and quantities on order, on hand and on purchase orders. Sort this report by sales order number, ship by date, location, customer ID, or item ID.
Sales Order Journal	Lists sales orders in journal entry format.
Sales Order Register	Lists each sales order and its status. Sort this report by customer ID, sales order date, or ship date.
Sales Order Report	Lists the details of all sales orders by sales order number, ship by date, customer ID, or item ID.

Table 7-4	Reports Related to Customer Invoicing
Report Name	*Description*
Customer Ledgers	Shows the transactions and a running balance for each customer for a specified date range.
Customer Sales History	Summarizes, by customer, how much each has purchased
Invoice Register	Lists each invoice number with date, quote number, customer name, and invoice amount. Sort this report by Invoice number, customer ID, or invoice date.
Items Sold to Customers	Lists for each customer, the quantity, amount, and profit of both inventoried and non-inventoried items sold.
Sales Journal	Lists transactions as reported to the general ledger.
Shipment Register	Lists shipments and to whom they were made. Sort this report by shipment number, shipment date, or ship to ID.
Sales Rep Report	Lists sales statistics by sales rep ID or customer.
Taxable/Exempt Sales	Lists all taxable and exempt sales per tax authority. See Chapter 6 for information on using this report to pay your sales tax.

Visit this book's Web site for more information on Peachtree.

Chapter 8

Collecting the Money

*O*ne of our favorite sayings is, "As much fun as I'm having doing what I'm doing . . . I'm still doing it for the money."

Most people *do* find that their preferred part of being in business is collecting the money. Peachtree not only provides you with an easy way to track the money your customers owe you, but also provides you with a few ways to encourage your customers to pay up.

Peachtree refers to the money you receive from your customers as *receipts*. That sounds logical enough, doesn't it?

Recording Receipts

Peachtree's Receipts feature allows you to enter all checks, cash, and credit card slips you receive and deposit them in your checking account. Peachtree provides two ways to account for receipts. The method you use is mostly determined by timing.

One method is used when you receive the customer's money *at the time of the sale*. You enter the receipt right on the invoice and when you print the invoice, it can also show the funds received.

The other and most commonly used method is to apply the receipt to an invoice through the Receipts window. You can use this method either if the customer pays you at the time of the sale or at a later date.

Applying receipts to an invoice

To apply a receipt to a customer invoice, begin by taking a look at the Receipts window:

1. **Choose Tasks ➪ Receipts to display the Receipts window.**

2. **If necessary, enter a deposit ticket ID.**

   What appears in the Deposit Ticket ID field of the Select for Deposit window depends on your choice of methods for generating these IDs in the Pay Methods tab in Customer Defaults. (See Chapter 4.) If you opted for the Receipts window, Peachtree displays the current date; otherwise this field is blank. If you leave the deposit ticket IDs blank, Peachtree can automatically suggest deposit ticket IDs in the Select for Deposit window.

   For more information about deposit ticket IDs, see, "Laughing All the Way to the Bank," later in this chapter.

   If you want this transaction to be reconciled as a separate item, enter a unique deposit ticket ID. You can find out more about account reconciliation in Chapter 17.

3. **Select the customer ID.**

   If this customer has unpaid invoices, Peachtree lists them on the Apply to Invoices tab (see Figure 8-1). If the customer has no outstanding balance, Peachtree displays the Apply to Revenues tab.

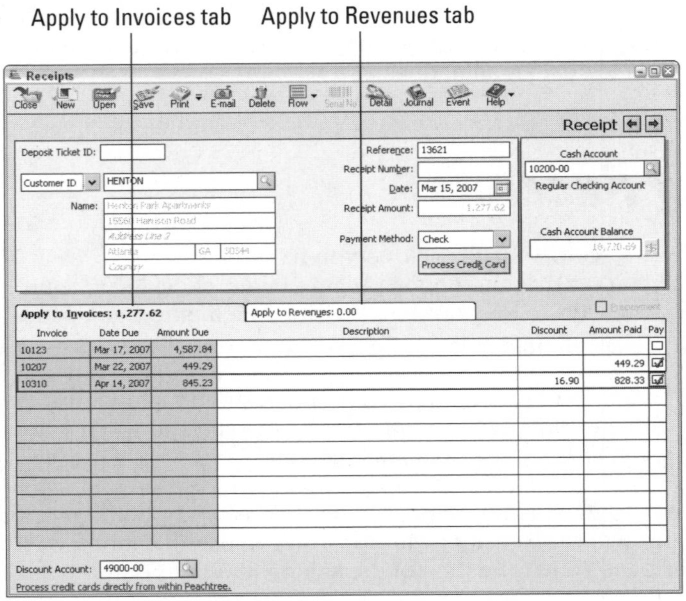

Apply to Invoices tab   Apply to Revenues tab

Figure 8-1: Peachtree lists the customer's unpaid invoices (and credits).

Double-click any unpaid invoice to see the transaction details.

4. **Enter a Reference number that helps identify the receipt.**

You must enter a Reference number, usually the customer's check number. If the receipt was transmitted electronically, you might enter the EFTS confirmation number or the date.

5. **Enter the Date of the receipt.**

Use this field to record the date you *received* the check, not the date on the check.

6. **Select a Payment Method: Cash, Check, Charge, and so on.**

You set up payment methods in the Customer Defaults dialog box. You can find out how to set customer defaults in Chapter 4. You can run some reports based on payment methods. Chapter 15 shows you how to filter reports.

If the customer is paying by credit card, you can store the credit card information or use Peachtree's service to process the credit card. See "Handling Credit Card Receipts," later in this chapter.

7. **In the Cash Account list, verify the bank account into which you're depositing the receipt.**

Always confirm the cash account. Peachtree remembers which account you last used in this window.

8. **Place a check mark in the Pay column beside each invoice being paid by this receipt.**

If the amount of the receipt doesn't match the invoice amount, enter the actual amount received in the Amount Paid column.

If, based on the customer terms, the invoice is eligible for a discount, Peachtree automatically displays the discount amount. You can accept that amount, delete it, or enter a different amount. If you have discounts, verify the discount account number at the bottom of the window.

If the amount paid is less than the amount due, Peachtree assumes that the customer still owes the difference. The next time you open the Receipts window for the customer, Peachtree displays the remainder due on the invoice.

If the amount paid is less than the amount due and you're going to write off the difference, enter the full amount of the invoice in the amount box and then click the Apply to Revenues tab and enter a negative amount for the amount you're writing off. (Make sure the amount you're writing off is not taxed.) Choose your write-off account for the G/L account. This process clears the invoice from A/R, posts the correct amount to cash, and charges the unpaid balance on the invoice to the write-off account.

If you do not see a box to select the G/L account, it means the boxes are hidden. You can click the Journal button at the top of the window and enter the account numbers you want to use.

If the amount paid is more than the invoice amount, Peachtree automatically creates a credit balance against the specified invoice. The next time you display the Receipts window for this customer, you see a credit balance. If you're going to absorb the overpayment (usually for small amounts), click the invoice as paid in full and then click the Apply to Revenues tab and enter the overpayment amount as a positive number. This clears the transaction from accounts receivable.

If you make a direct sale that doesn't require an invoice, click the Apply to Revenues tab and specify a sales account and an amount.

The amount Peachtree displays in the Receipt Amount box should match the total amount received from your customer.

9. **Click Save to record the receipt or click Print to print a receipt that you can give to your customer.**

Printing the receipt also saves the receipt.

The Receipts window also gives you a handy way to write off an entire invoice as a bad debt. In the Receipts window, enter a unique reference number that helps identify the receipt as a write-off. For example, we typically use the letters WO (for write-off) or BD (for bad debt) and the original invoice number as the reference number (BD12345). Click the Cash Account box to select the Bad Debt Expense account. Click the Pay check box for the invoice you want to write off as a bad debt and then click Save. Peachtree clears the transaction from account receivable and increases the bad debt expense account. Be sure to change the cash account back to the regular checking account before closing the window.

Entering receipts from nonestablished customers

Occasionally, you receive money from a customer you haven't invoiced. If the customer isn't set up in your customer list, you can still record a receipt.

The procedure is the same as applying receipts to an invoice, except you won't enter a Customer ID. Skip this field and enter the customer's name in the Name text box. Because you haven't entered an invoice for this customer, Peachtree displays the Apply to Revenues tab. Select the sales account, enter the receipt amount, and then click Save or Print.

Applying receipts at the time of sale

You can apply a receipt also by recording it at the time of sale as you create the invoice. (You see how to create an invoice in Chapter 7.) Using this method allows Peachtree to print the amount received on the invoice.

To apply a receipt at the time of the sale, follow these steps:

1. **Choose Tasks⇨Sales/Invoicing window to display the invoice window.**

2. **Click the Amount Paid at Sale button to display the Receive Payment dialog box, as shown in Figure 8-2.**

3. **Enter the payment information.**

   Also, be sure to verify the Cash Account into which you're depositing the money.

4. **Click OK to close the Receive Payment window.**

5. **Save or Print the transaction.**

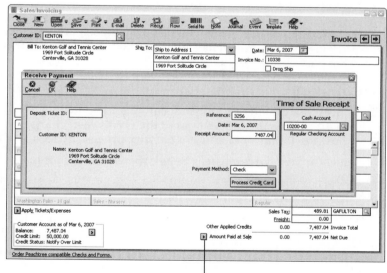

Figure 8-2: Enter receipt information in the Receive Payment window.

Amount Paid at Sale

Handling Credit Card Receipts

If your business accepts credit card payments from customers, you can enter and track these transactions in Peachtree. Assuming (we know, there we go assuming again) you have to wait for that time lapse before you receive the money from the credit card financial institution, you can begin recording credit card transactions in Peachtree, but you need the following first:

- ✔ A G/L account in your chart of accounts to use for the credit card receivable amount. Create an account in the Accounts Receivable area of your chart of accounts, giving it an ID and a description to identify it, such as VISA Receivable. Choose Accounts Receivable as the account type. If necessary, create additional accounts using the same method. (Chapter 3 shows you how to create accounts.)

- ✔ A vendor ID for the credit card financial institution that deposits money. This way, you can record and track processing fee expenses.

To record a credit card transaction, you must follow two sets of steps: one when the transaction occurs and another when you know that the credit card financial institution has deposited the money in your account:

1. **In the Receipts or Receive Payments window, record receipt information but do not Save or Print the transaction yet.**

   You can apply the customer credit card receipts to open invoices or to revenue.

   Use the techniques shown in the "Applying receipts to an invoice," "Entering receipts from nonestablished customers," or "Applying receipts at the time of sale" section, earlier in this chapter. *However,* you must use this exception: Enter the credit card receivable G/L account as the Cash account.

2. **To keep the customer's ledger accurate and up-to-date, record the amount paid as the full amount of the credit card charge, regardless of how the financial institution handles processing fees.**

   You enter the processing fees as an expense when your bank statement arrives.

3. **Click the Process Credit Card button.**

   The Credit Card Information window appears, displaying fields that are applicable to credit card transactions. (See Figure 8-3.)

4. **Enter the credit card number and other information pertaining to the customer's credit card, such as name and expiration date.**

   You can store default credit card information in the customer record. See Chapter 7 for more on storing customer information.

5. **If you subscribe to Peachtree's credit card service, click the Authorize button to connect with your online merchant account provider.**

   When authorized, the provider will automatically supply the authorization number. If you don't subscribe to this service, enter the authorization number manually.

6. Click OK and then click Save or Print.

After the credit card financial institution has notified you that the money has been deposited into your account, you need to create another receipt that transfers the funds from the credit card receivable account to your bank account.

Create a receipt in the Receipts window just like you create any other Peachtree receipt, with the following exceptions:

✔ Skip the Customer ID field and enter the credit card company name in the Name field. Because you're not using a Customer ID, Peachtree automatically displays the Apply to Revenues tab.

✔ On the line item GL Account field, enter the credit card receivable GL account number.

✔ Enter the amount actually transferred to your account.

Laughing All the Way to the Bank

When you enter receipts, you decide whether to assign a Deposit Ticket ID or let Peachtree assign one when you go to the bank. Peachtree lets you group deposited items together using the Select for Deposit window to greatly speed up the bank reconciliation process.

What's a Deposit Ticket ID, you ask? Well, Peachtree uses Deposit Ticket IDs to make account reconciliation easier to manage. You should assign the same Deposit Ticket ID to all transactions that you deposit on the same deposit ticket. All receipts that use the same Deposit Ticket ID appear as one lump sum in account reconciliation, making reconciliation a much easier process. (See Chapter 16 for steps to use account reconciliation in Peachtree.)

More often than not, you receive checks daily and enter them into Peachtree daily, but you do not go to the bank until you've accumulated several days' worth of checks. The following example lists five checks you receive on three different days but want to lump together into a single bank deposit:

Date	Check Amount
March 16	$125.75
March 16	$28.41
March 17	$722.01
March 18	$549.10
March 18	$100.05

When you go to the bank, you make one deposit of $1,525.32, and that amount appears on your bank statement. Although in Peachtree you have five different receipts, assigning a single Deposit Ticket ID to these transactions makes the total amount of $1,525.32 appear in the Account Reconciliation window. If each of the five transactions above has its own unique Deposit Ticket ID, the Account Reconciliation window would list all five of them independently, making bank account reconciliation extremely difficult. You'd have to sit and figure out which transactions add up to the ones listed on your bank statement. If you have lots of receipts with separate Deposit Ticket ID's, you'd spend lots of time trying to reconcile receipts to your bank statement.

The Select for Deposit window lets you combine multiple customer receipts into a single bank deposit. To select receipts to include in a bank deposit, follow these steps:

1. **Choose Tasks⇨Select for Deposit.**

   The Select for Deposit window appears, as shown in Figure 8-4.

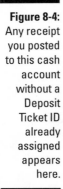

Figure 8-4:
Any receipt you posted to this cash account without a Deposit Ticket ID already assigned appears here.

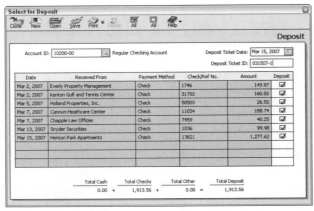

To review, modify, or print an existing deposit, click the Open button. Existing deposits include receipts that already have a Deposit Ticket ID associated with them. If you entered the receipt with a Deposit Ticket ID, that ID appears in the Deposit Ticket ID field.

2. **If needed, select a different cash account from the Account ID drop-down list.**

   If you don't see a receipt that you plan to deposit, you may have entered a Deposit Ticket ID on the receipt or you entered a different cash account when you recorded the receipt. Edit the receipt to make the correction so that you can include it with the deposit.

3. **Enter the Date on which you will make the deposit.**

4. **Enter or accept the currently suggested Deposit Ticket ID.**

   Peachtree maintains a numbering scheme based on the last Deposit Ticket ID entered. Deposit Ticket IDs can be alphanumeric and up to eight characters. We recommend using the deposit date and -1, -2, and so on. For example, 031507-1 would be the first deposit made on March 15th.

5. **Click the Deposit check box next to the receipts you want included in the current deposit.**

   To quickly select all Deposit check boxes, click the All toolbar button with the red check mark. To quickly clear all Deposit check boxes, click the All toolbar button without the red check mark.

6. **Click the Print button to print and save the deposit record or choose Save to save the deposit without printing it.**

   Peachtree calls the form a *deposit ticket*, but it does not contain the bank routing information needed to get the money into your account. You might ask your bank whether you can simply attach the report to an actual deposit slip to save you time and effort. It's also helpful to print a copy for your records and attach your bank receipt to it.

Boing! Handling Bounced Checks

One of those nasty facts of life, now and then, is that customers write bad checks, sometimes by accident and sometimes not. In Peachtree, you handle checks returned for nonsufficient funds (NSF) in two simple steps:

1. **Create a new invoice to charge the customer the NSF fees.**

2. **Create a receipt and apply a negative amount for the same amount as the original check.**

   For example, suppose the original (bounced) check is for $82.10. In the example you see in Figure 8-5, we created an NSF invoice number,

23501NSF, for $20.00. Then, on the receipt window, we apply a negative $82.10 (which represents the original returned check amount) against the open invoice.

3. **Click Save.**

Peachtree updates the customer balance to reflect the money that the customer once again owes against the original invoice and corrects your bank account balance.

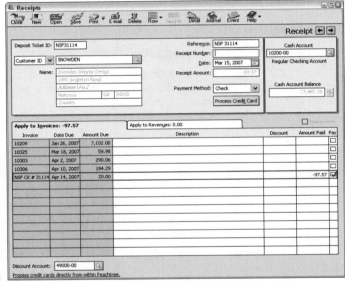

Figure 8-5: Create a negative receipt to adjust your bank balance.

Later, when your customer writes you a second check or instructs you to redeposit the original check, you will have a second receipt for audit trail purposes. If the customer writes a second check for the original amount plus the NSF fee, Peachtree clears the invoice in full. If, however, the customer instructs you to redeposit the original check, enter only the amount of the check. After all, the customer still owes you the NSF fee.

We *really* hope you don't have to use this section of our book.

Giving Credit Where Credit Is Due

Unfortunately, products are returned sometimes, or you need to make an adjustment to a customer invoice. In these situations, you need to create a credit memo to reduce the amount of money your customer owes.

If you owe money to a customer for overpayment or because you applied a credit memo to an invoice, you can write a check to the customer for the refund amount you owe.

Creating a credit memo

You can create a credit memo that refers to an unpaid original invoice, or you can create an open credit. Additionally, you can create credit memos for inventoried items or other goods or services. The following steps show you how to use Peachtree's Credit Memo feature:

1. **Choose Tasks⇨Credit Memos to display the Credit Memos window.**

2. **Enter the Customer ID.**

   After you select a customer, Peachtree fills in the customer name and address. In the lower-left corner of the window, you can see the customer's current balance as of the system date. You can click the button next to the balance to display a Customer Ledger report of the invoices and receipts that make up the balance.

3. **Select a Date and enter a Credit No.**

   For the Credit No., we suggest that you use the original invoice number preceded or followed by *CM* to indicate credit memo. This numbering scheme helps you tie the credit memo to a particular sale.

4. **If the credit memo is for an unpaid customer invoice, click the drop-down list on the Apply to Invoice No. tab and select the invoice number for which you are recording a credit memo.**

   Peachtree fills in the lines that appear on the original invoice.

   If you're creating a credit memo for which there is no existing invoice, click the Apply to Sales tab and enter the information for the items to be credited, including quantity, item, price, and if applicable, job.

5. **In the Returned box on each line of the Apply to Invoice tab, type the quantity the customer returned.**

   Enter the returned quantity as a positive number. Peachtree understands that this is a return. (See Figure 8-6.)

   To quickly fill in the original transaction quantities, click the Return button and select All.

   If the customer is returning inventory items, Peachtree automatically restores the item quantities to inventory. If the inventory items are damaged, you will need to enter an inventory adjustment to remove them. See Chapter 11 to make inventory adjustments.

   If the customer is returning serialized inventory items, click the Serial Number button and select the serial numbers being returned.

Return button

Serial Number button

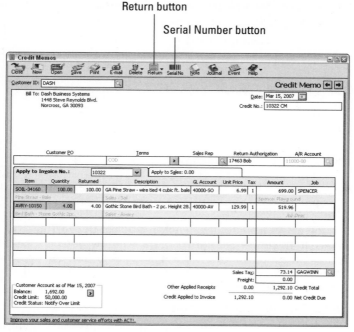

Figure 8-6:
If a line
item was
originally
assigned
to a job,
Peachtree
also assigns
the credit
to the
same job.

If you charge the customer a restocking fee, enter it on the Apply to Sales button with a negative dollar amount.

6. **Click the Save button to save the transaction, or click the Print button to print and save the credit memo.**

   Peachtree applies the credit memo to the open invoice and closes both transactions. If you created a credit memo without applying it to an invoice, the credit memo appears on the Aged Receivable report.

Issuing refund checks for a credit memo

If you owe money to a customer for an overpayment, an open credit, or some other reason, you can write a check to the customer for the refund amount owed.

Issuing a refund check is a two-part process. First, you write the check from the Payments window, and then you apply the check to the credit memo or overpayment in the Receipts window. This process is based on the assumption that you've already created a credit memo or applied the overpayment. See the preceding section for more information.

Follow these steps to issue a customer refund check:

1. **Choose Tasks➪Payments to display the Payments window.**

2. **Select Customer ID from the first drop-down list, indicating that the check goes to a customer rather than a vendor (see Figure 8-7).**

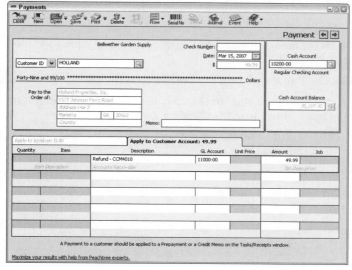

Figure 8-7:
After you select Customer ID from the drop-down list, Peachtree displays customer IDs in the lookup list box.

3. **Choose the Customer ID of the customer receiving the refund.**

   As with generating checks to vendors, don't enter a check number if Peachtree will be printing the check for you. Enter a check number only if you're writing checks by hand (heaven forbid).

4. **Verify the check Date and the Cash Account from which you are writing the check.**

5. **On the Apply to Customer Account tab, enter a description for the refund.**

   Entering a description helps you remember later, why you issued the refund.

6. **Enter or select the GL account to which you want to post the refund amount.**

   Typically, this is your Accounts Receivable account.

7. **Enter the amount of the refund.**

8. **Click Print or Save.**

   For details on printing checks, see Chapter 6. If you're not going to print the check or you plan to print a batch of checks later, click Save.

When you create a check to a customer, Peachtree applies it to the customer account, and it appears as a balance due from the customer. To complete the process, you need to apply the refund check to a credit memo or an overpayment.

1. **Choose Tasks⇨Receipts.**

2. **Select the Customer ID.**

   The credit memo appears in the invoice listing, along with the refund check.

3. **Click the Pay check box for both the credit memo and refund check.**

   The amount of the receipt displays zero (0.00). Therefore, no money is being applied to the general ledger. See Figure 8-8.

4. **Enter a receipt Reference number, such as the check number you wrote to the customer.**

5. **Click Save.**

   Both transactions are cleared from accounts receivable.

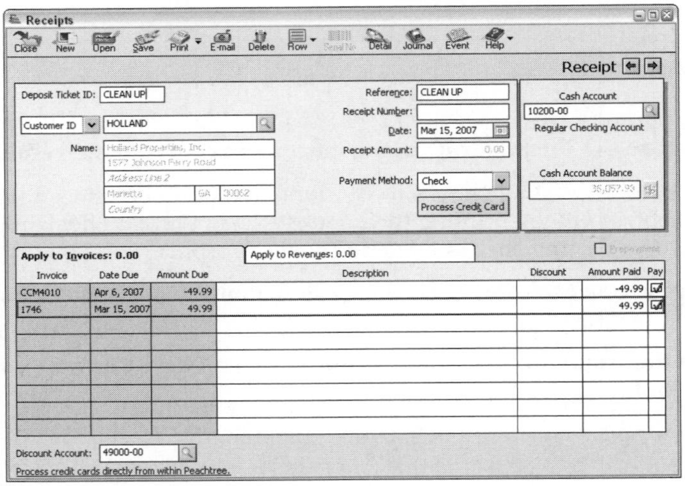

Figure 8-8:
Clear the credit memo and refund check from the customer record.

Entering Finance Charges

Sometimes you want to nudge your customers into paying their bills on time by charging them a late fee or a finance charge if they pay later than the due date. Peachtree can calculate finance charges for all customers who have not been excluded from finance charge calculations and who meet the filter criteria you determine when it's time to apply the finance charges. Chapter 4 shows you how to set up your default finance charge terms.

If you *don't* want to charge finance charges to certain customers, you must alter the default terms for those customers. In the Maintain Customers/ Prospects window, click the Terms and Credits tab. Then remove the check mark from the Use Standard Terms and Charge Finance Charge boxes.

How do finance charges work?

To whom does Peachtree charge finance charges? Well, only customers who have a check mark in the Charge Finance Charge box, mentioned in the preceding paragraph. Okay, that's obvious, but what other criteria does Peachtree use? After all, if a customer isn't late paying, you don't want to charge a finance charge.

Peachtree calculates finance charges using the following formula for *each* overdue invoice:

```
Finance Charge = Number of Days Past Due multiplied by the
                 Daily Rate multiplied by the Outstanding Invoice
                 Amount
```

The formula uses these definitions:

- ✔ *Daily Rate* is the percentage you set divided by 365 days.
- ✔ *Outstanding Invoice Amount* is the balance remaining unpaid on the invoice.
- ✔ *Number of Days Past Due* is the number of days between the date that you calculate finance charges and one of the following:
    - The invoice date if aging is set to Invoice Date in the Customer Defaults dialog box
    - The due date if aging is set to Due Date in the Customer Defaults dialog box
    - The date of the last finance charge calculation

To clarify these definitions, consider an example: Suppose that today is July 15, and you want to calculate charges for an invoice dated 5/1 (due 5/31) in the amount of $200.00. Your company charges an 18 percent finance charge for invoices 30 days overdue. You age your customer invoices by due date.

First, the invoice is overdue by 44 days (from May 31st to July 15th):

```
(.18/365) x 44 x 200.00 = 4.34
```

The .18/365 is the annual percentage rate divided by 365 days. Multiply that by the 44 days the invoice is past due, and then multiply that times the $200.00 invoice amount. Therefore, a finance charge applied on 7/15 would be $4.34.

Applying finance charges

Okay, now that you understand how the finance charge process works, you can actually apply the charges.

When you decide to apply a finance charge, Peachtree creates but does not print an invoice for the amount due. The charges do appear on customer statements, so you need to apply finance charges before you print customer statements:

1. **Choose Tasks⇨Finance Charge to display the Calculate Finance Charges dialog box.**

2. **Optionally, select a range of customers for whom you want to calculate finance charges.**

   If you leave the customer range blank, Peachtree assumes you want to calculate charges on all eligible customers (by way of the Charge Finance Charges check box).

3. **Enter the date you want Peachtree Accounting to use to calculate finance charges and then click OK.**

   The Apply Finance Charges dialog box seen in Figure 8-9 appears.

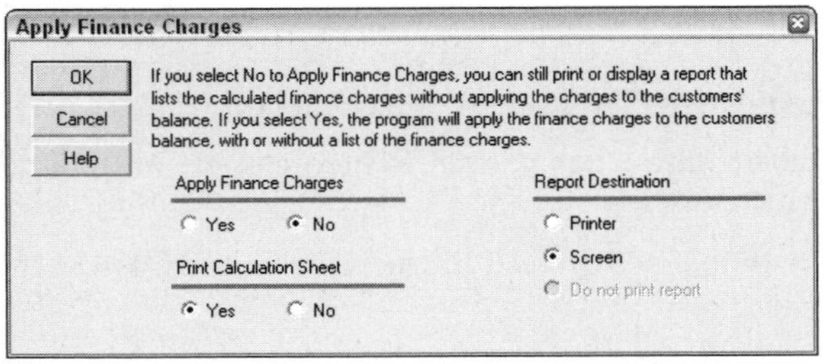

Figure 8-9:
You can preview finance charges before Peachtree applies them to the customer account.

4. **If you'd like to review the finance charges before Peachtree applies them, click No to Apply Finance Charges. Or if you'd prefer to just go ahead and apply the charges, click Yes to the Apply Finance Charges section dialog box.**

5. **Choose a Report Destination (Screen or Printer) and then click OK.**

   The Finance Charge Report Selection dialog box appears. You don't *have* to print the report, but we recommend that you do.

6. **Click OK to print the report in detail.**

7. **If you elected to review the charges before Peachtree applied them, repeat Steps 1 through 6, but choose Yes in Step 4.**

   Peachtree applies the finance charges to the customer.

The finance charge entries are generated with a reference number that begins with the letters *FC* (for finance charge). Therefore, never enter a customer invoice with a reference number that begins with FC. Otherwise, Peachtree uses that transaction when recalculating finance charges.

Producing Statements

Before you print statements the first time, you may want to determine statement default preferences. Refer to Chapter 4 on how to set statement default options.

To print statements, follow these steps:

1. **Choose Reports➪Accounts Receivable.**

2. **Click the Customer Statements folder.**

   Peachtree considers statements a *form*. See Chapter 13 for information on customizing forms.

3. **Double-click the statement form you want to use.**

4. **Select any of the following options from the Statement dialog box:**

   • **Statement Type:** On balance forward statements, only the balances left over from previous statements appear. On open items, the detail for all open items appears.

   • **Print Detail for:** Choose to print or not print the line item detail information for invoices, credit memos, and receipts.

   • **Date:** Select the date range of the transactions you want to print on the statements.

The Filter Range options also allow you to select specific customer IDs or types. You can also choose the Form Delivery option, which lets you choose how you want to deliver forms to the defined range of customers: as paper copies only, as e-mail attachments only, or as both paper copies and e-mail attachments. If you choose either E-mail or Both, the E-mail tab becomes available, letting you set up more form delivery options. See Chapter 13 for details on printing and e-mailing forms.

5. **Click OK.**

When the statements finish printing, Peachtree asks you whether the statements printed correctly and if it's OK to update the Customer file. If you click Yes, Peachtree stores the statement date in the customer record to use it as the balance forward date the next time you print statements. If you click No or Cancel after printing statements, Peachtree does not update the Customer file and maintains no record of having printed a statement. That means Peachtree will continue to list invoices as open items on any statement you print. If you are using Balance Forwarding statements, it is therefore important that you answer Yes when statements print successfully.

Reporting on Money Your Customers Owe

Although Peachtree can't guarantee that you make a profit every month, it does give you some ways to show you (or your investors) your various financial reports. We're sure you like to track the money you're taking in so that you can plan your budget or keep your banker happy. So, in Table 8-1, we provide a description of the reports that pertain to collecting your money.

See Chapter 14 to find out how to print reports.

Table 8-1	Reports Related to Collecting Your Money
Report Name	**What It Does**
Aged Receivables	Lists each customer with their outstanding invoices or credits in aging categories
Cash Receipts Journal	Lists the date, amount, description, and general ledger account number of all receipt transactions created during a specified period

Visit this book's Web site for more information on Peachtree.

Chapter 9

Paid Employees Are Happy Employees

. . . .

In This Chapter
▶ Setting up employee defaults
▶ Writing and printing payroll checks
▶ Paying commissions or bonuses

. . . .

They call it *work* for a reason, some people say. And we can't think of too many people who are willing to work without being paid. If you aren't using an outside payroll service, you may want to consider using Peachtree's payroll features.

Peachtree's payroll features mimic the functions you perform when you prepare payroll checks by hand. But after you've set up basic background information for each employee (yes, you still need to know the employee's gross wages and number of exemptions), we think that preparing payroll in Peachtree is much easier and faster than preparing payroll checks manually. Why? Because you don't need to look up payroll taxes in the Circular E flyer, you don't need to remember which employees have various deductions, and you don't need to subtract the taxes and deductions to determine the net payroll check. Furthermore, you don't need to keep track of the payroll tax liability amounts you, as the employer, must pay. And, if you allow Peachtree to print the checks, you don't need to write them. In this chapter, we show you how to set up your employees and produce paychecks.

Even if you prepare payroll in Peachtree, you're going to have questions about handling various situations. The Circular E booklet that you get from the government every December is your bible for payroll questions. If you don't understand the Circular E, contact your accountant. If you don't understand your accountant, hire a new one.

If you use an outside payroll service, you may want to consider using Peachtree's payroll features to keep your general ledger up to date. That way, you can accurately report your company's financial picture. If your outside payroll service provides you with journal entries, you can ignore Peachtree's payroll features and simply enter the journal entries (see Chapter 17). However, if your outside payroll service doesn't provide you with journal entries, you may want to use Peachtree's payroll features to mimic the payroll process and match your records with theirs.

Understanding Payroll Basics

Before you start setting up employees and paying them, you really need to consider some basic information: whom you pay and when you should start using payroll in Peachtree.

Peachtree uses *payroll tax tables* to calculate the amounts you deduct for taxes (Federal Income Tax, Social Security, Medicare, and so on). Best Software, the company that produces Peachtree, does *not* ship tax tables that calculate federal taxes with the software. To accurately calculate payroll, you must either subscribe to Peachtree's Payroll Tax Table Update service or create your own tax tables. To order tax table updates, call 1-800-336-1420 Monday through Friday, 8:30 a.m. to 5:30 p.m. eastern standard time.

Employees and sales representatives

In this chapter, we're talking about paying people who work for you. You can rule out vendors for this discussion. Vendors don't work for you — they just provide you with goods or services. You pay vendors from the Payments, Write Checks, or Select for Payment window, as detailed in Chapter 6.

Both employees and sales representatives work for you. As you see in this chapter, you pay employees from the Select for Payroll window or the Payroll Entry window. Although employees are always employees, sales reps might be employees or independent contractors. The windows in Peachtree that you use to pay sales reps depend on their employment status: employee or independent contractor.

If you are uncertain about an individual's status, check with your accountant.

Employees work for you, so, in this chapter, we're talking about them. And sales representatives who are also employees work for you, so we're talking about them. We aren't talking about sales representatives whom you treat as independent contractors; you pay them as 1099 vendors from the Payments window or the Select for Payments window. See Chapter 5 for information on designating a vendor as a 1099 vendor. See Chapter 6 for information on paying vendors.

Most sales representatives, whether they're employees or independent contractors, earn commissions. If you want to track commissions to make paying sales reps easier, you need to specifically identify sales reps (both employees and independent contractors) in Peachtree. Interestingly, Peachtree has you set up a sales representative in the same window where you set up employees, even though the sales representative might be an independent contractor and not an employee.

So, being the logical individual that you are, you ask, "If a sales rep isn't an employee, why should I set up a sales rep in the same window where I set up employees?" Peachtree has you set up sales reps in the Maintain Employees/Sales Reps window for two related reasons:

- ✔ If you set up sales representatives in the Maintain Employees/Sales Reps window, you can include the sales rep on invoices.

- ✔ If you include a sales rep on an invoice, you can produce the Sales Rep report, which shows commissioned and noncommissioned sales amounts per sales rep.

Including a sales rep on an invoice *does not* automatically generate a commission amount for the sales rep. The inventory items sold on the invoice must be subject to commission. In the "Writing and Printing Payroll Checks" section, we tell you how to pay sales representatives who are also employees. In the "Determining commission amounts" section, you see a sample of the Sales Rep report. See Chapter 7 for more information about including sales representatives on invoices. See Chapter 11 for information on making an inventory item subject to commission.

When should you start to use payroll?

You can start using payroll at any time during a calendar year, but you may find it easiest to start using payroll on January 1. Why? Because, if you start using payroll on January 1, you won't have to enter any beginning balance information — information to account for paychecks you've already produced this year that need to be included on payroll tax forms and W-2s at the end of the year.

If you can't start using payroll on January 1, try to start on the first day of any payroll quarter: January 1, April 1, July 1, or October 1. Payroll tax laws require that you file payroll tax returns quarterly, and you need to include information only for the current quarter. So, if you start using payroll at the beginning of a quarter, you can enter beginning balance information as lump sums for each quarter of the current year in which you've produced payroll checks.

As a final resort, if you can't start using payroll on the first day of any payroll quarter, start using payroll on the first day of a month. You need to enter beginning balance information for the other months in the current payroll quarter, but you can enter quarterly amounts for other payroll quarters of the current year in which you've produced payroll checks.

Working with Employee Information

In Chapter 4, we show you how the Payroll Wizard walks you through setting up default payroll information for your company. After the default information is in place, you need to set up your employees, establishing individualized information for each of them. For example, different employees claim different withholding exemptions. And some employees may participate in a company retirement plan, but others may not. Or some may receive a health insurance benefit. To set up employees, choose Maintain⇨Employees/Sales Reps. Peachtree displays the General tab of the Maintain Employees/Sales Reps window (see Figure 9-1).

Figure 9-1:
Just as you might expect, you supply general employee information on the General tab of the Maintain Employees/ Sales Reps window.

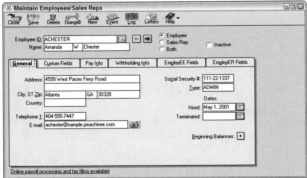

At the top of the window — not associated with any of the tabs in the window — you assign an ID and type in a name. You also can check the Inactive box when an employee leaves the company to avoid accidentally generating a paycheck.

If you need to change an employee's ID, click the Change ID button.

Note that you can set up each person as an employee, a sales rep, or both. Typically, you deduct payroll taxes for employees, and you don't deduct payroll taxes for sales representatives. If you select Sales Rep, three of the six tabs in the window become gray, and the individual doesn't appear in the Payroll windows when you are paying employees. Choose Both if the individual is both a sales representative and an employee.

We discuss each of the six tabs of the Maintain Employees/Sales Reps window individually.

General employee information

You use the General tab (refer to Figure 9-1) of the Maintain Employees/Sales Reps window to give Peachtree general information about each employee — things like the employee's name, address, and social security number (you need those when you produce W-2s at the end of the year). You also can supply the employee's telephone number, date of hire, and e-mail address.

Peachtree provides the Type field to give you a way to group employees. If your company pays worker's compensation insurance, you might want to store the worker's compensation categories in the Type field to make it easier to produce a report that helps you pay your worker's compensation liability.

In the lower-right corner of the tab, you see the Beginning Balances button. Click this button if you're starting payroll on any day other than January 1 and you've already produced paychecks in the current year. Peachtree displays the Employee Beginning Balances window (see Figure 9-2).

Use the boxes in this window to enter payroll amounts you've already paid this year before you started using Peachtree. Each column represents a pay period that you specify: a week, a biweekly or semimonthly pay period, a month, a quarter, or even multiple quarters. For example, suppose that you want to start entering payroll as of July 1, which is the beginning of the third payroll quarter. In the Beginning Balances window, you can enter one column of numbers that represents the sum of all the payroll amounts you've paid for the first six months (two quarters) of the year for each payroll field.

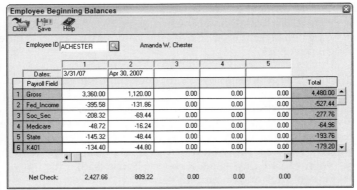

Figure 9-2:
Record
amounts for
paychecks
you've
written this
year before
you started
using
Peachtree.

Although you can enter amounts for each pay period, we don't recommend that approach, simply because it's cumbersome and time-consuming.

At the top of each column you intend to use, right-click to display a calendar and select the ending date of the timeframe represented by the amounts. Then, in the boxes below the date, type the appropriate amounts for each payroll field, entering deductions as negative amounts and earnings as positive amounts. Based on the information in Figure 9-2, we're starting payroll on May 1. In the first column, we include the quarterly amount for the first quarter of the year. In the second column, we include the monthly amount for April, the first month of the second quarter.

Click the Save button when you finish, and Peachtree redisplays the Maintain Employees/Sales Reps window.

Custom fields

If you choose Maintain⇨Default Information⇨Employees, you can view the screen where you establish the custom fields that appear in the Maintain Employees/Sales Reps window. When you click the Custom Fields tab, you can type the appropriate information for the employee in each custom field box. Custom field information is optional.

Payroll information

On the Pay Info tab of the Maintain Employees/Sales Reps window (see Figure 9-3), you tell Peachtree the method and frequency you use to pay the employee. We cover both of these in this section, starting with frequencies.

Figure 9-3:
Tell
Peachtree
how often to
pay your
employees.

Setting payroll frequency

Peachtree allows you to pay your employees using any of five frequencies:

- ✔ Weekly
- ✔ Biweekly
- ✔ Semimonthly
- ✔ Monthly
- ✔ Annually

You don't need to pay all your employees using the same frequency; that is, you can pay some employees weekly, some biweekly, and some monthly. The choice is yours. Most companies tend to pay all employees at the same time, but Peachtree doesn't make you operate that way.

Determining pay method

Pay methods tell Peachtree how to calculate wages — and you set up the pay methods your company uses in Chapter 4. When you open the Pay Method list box (click the drop-down arrow to the right of the box), you see that you can choose Salary, Hourly – Hours per Pay Period, or Hourly – Time Ticket Hours:

- ✔ Choose Salary to pay your employees a flat rate, regardless of the number of hours they work in a pay period.

- ✔ Choose Hourly – Hours per Pay Period to pay your employees based on hours they work in a pay period.

- ✔ Choose Hourly – Time Ticket Hours to pay your employees for hours they work in a pay period as recorded on Time Tickets they submit.

You use time tickets when you intend to bill your customers for the time your employees or your vendors work on projects for them. You can, but don't have to, pay employees based on the time tickets they submit. To find out more about this pay method, see Chapter 10.

When you choose Hourly – Hours per Pay Period, Peachtree displays the standard number of hours associated with the frequency you select:

- ✔ Frequency: Standard hours
- ✔ Weekly: 40
- ✔ Biweekly: 80
- ✔ Semimonthly: 88
- ✔ Monthly: 176
- ✔ Annually: 2112

You can change the value that appears in the Hours per Pay Period box. For example, you can set the number of hours to zero to ensure that you don't accidentally pay an employee for time not worked.

You indicate the amount, per pay period, that you want to pay the employee. In Figure 9-3, we're paying the employee time-and-a-half for overtime and double-time for special occasions (maybe Sundays). For salaried employees, you typically don't see an Overtime field.

If you plan to use time tickets to bill your customers for the time an employee works on projects — even if you don't pay the employee based on time tickets — supply an amount in the Hourly Billing Rate box.

Peachtree Premium users can track an employee's raise history. Click the Raise History button, and Peachtree displays a dialog box where you can record the following:

- ✔ The raise date
- ✔ The pay rate to which the raise applies (Regular, Overtime, or Special in our sample company)
- ✔ The base amount associated with that pay rate, the Raise Amount, or the Raise Percentage (you enter one and Peachtree calculates the other)
- ✔ Any notes you may want to make about the raise; for example, you might want to note that the raise was based on the employee's annual performance review or was an out-of-cycle raise due to the on-going stellar performance of the employee

The window also shows the calculated new amount for that pay rate, but Peachtree doesn't change the amount that appears on the Pay Info tab. You must make that change manually.

Withholding information

On the Withholding Info tab, you provide — you guessed it — tax withholding information, such as the employee's marital status and the number of exemptions he or she claims for federal, state, and local withholding. You also can supply additional federal, state, and local withholding amounts as appropriate along with the 401k deduction amount if your company has a 401k plan. Don't forget to check the Retirement Plan box if your employee participates in a 401k or other retirement plan. Check the Statutory Employee box if IRS guidelines qualify the employee as an employee based on the law. Briefly, four categories of independent contractors qualify by law as employees. If you don't know or aren't sure whether you have independent contractors whom you must, by law, treat as employees, ask your accountant.

Peachtree reserves Special1 and Special2 for you to use in payroll tax formulas where a value in the calculation is unique for each employee.

Employee fields

You really need to understand only one aspect of the EmployEE Fields tab of the Maintain Employees/Sales Reps window (see Figure 9-4). You use that tab to indicate anything about the employee that *doesn't* follow the payroll defaults you set up for the company back in Chapter 4.

Figure 9-4:
Indicate any nonstandard information about employee fields for the selected employee.

For example, you may change the G/L account to send wages to a different account than the default account. Or if an employee doesn't participate in the company's dental plan (such as Amanda in Figure 9-4), you'd remove the check mark from the STD column (STD represents *standard,* as in the company default). If there had been a check in the Calc column, you would remove it as well.

You remove the check mark from the STD column so that Peachtree allows you to remove the check mark from the Calc column. What's the Calc column? Well, when you place a check mark in the Calc column, Peachtree expects to use a payroll tax table to calculate the amount for the field. You remove the check mark from the Calc column under two conditions:

✔ When you're not going to use a calculation to figure the amount for the employee; instead, you want to supply a fixed amount in the Amount column

✔ When you don't want to calculate the field for the employee

If the employee's calculation is different from the standard (default) calculation, and you remove the check mark from the STD column but don't remove the check mark from the Calc column, you can select a different calculation for the employee. Simply click in the Tax Name column to use the lookup list.

If you don't intend to calculate the field for the employee, you must remove the check marks from both the STD column and the Calc column. Otherwise, Peachtree still calculates an amount based on the formula in the payroll tax table.

Employer fields

The EmployEE Fields tab and the EmployER Fields tab in the Maintain Employees/Sales Reps window closely resemble the same tabs in the Employee Defaults dialog box. That makes sense because Peachtree gets the information it displays in the Maintain Employees/Sales Reps window from the information you enter in the Employee Defaults dialog box.

The EmployER Fields tab, like the EmployEE tab, is used to indicate anything about the employee that *doesn't* follow the defaults you set up for the company.

Writing and Printing Payroll Checks

Now you come to the part that your employees like most — the part where you produce paychecks. Peachtree enables you to pay employees en masse or one at a time; we discuss both methods. Typically, you pay groups of employees at the same time, so we think you can make more use of the group method.

We recommend that you let Peachtree print paychecks for you. You can save *lots* of time and reduce the possibility of introducing errors because you won't be typing in information.

Using the Direct Deposit service

For an additional fee, Peachtree supports use of a direct deposit solution in all versions of Peachtree except Peachtree First Accounting. Using direct deposit, you still create paychecks in Peachtree the same way that we describe in preceding sections in this chapter, identifying employees who participate in direct deposit as you create the paychecks. You don't actually print the paychecks to give to employees; instead, through the Direct Deposit service, money is electronically transferred from your bank account to each employee's bank account on payday. If you want to print a stub for your employees, you can do so as you create the paychecks. Using the Direct Deposit solution, employees can select one or more bank accounts into which money can be deposited; the employees can identify fixed amounts or percentages to deposit to each account. Directly deposited paychecks appear in Account Reconciliation in lump sums that should match your bank statements. Checks processed through the Direct Deposit service become read-only in Peachtree, and you cannot edit them.

In this section, we show you how to produce and print paychecks and how to pay commissions and bonuses — two other common payroll needs.

Paying a group of employees

Paying a group of employees is similar to paying a group of vendors. In this section, we walk you through how to select employees to pay and how to print paychecks.

If you write your checks by hand or use an outside payroll service, plan to print the paychecks that Peachtree produces on plain paper, because Peachtree posts the information to the general ledger when you print the checks.

Follow these steps:

1. **Choose Tasks⇨Select for Payroll Entry.**

   Peachtree displays the Select Employees – Filter Selection dialog box you see in Figure 9-5. Use this dialog box to select the majority of employees you want to pay.

   Try to make the selection include everyone you want to pay, even if the selection includes more people than you intend to pay. After you make choices in this dialog box, you have another opportunity to exclude employees.

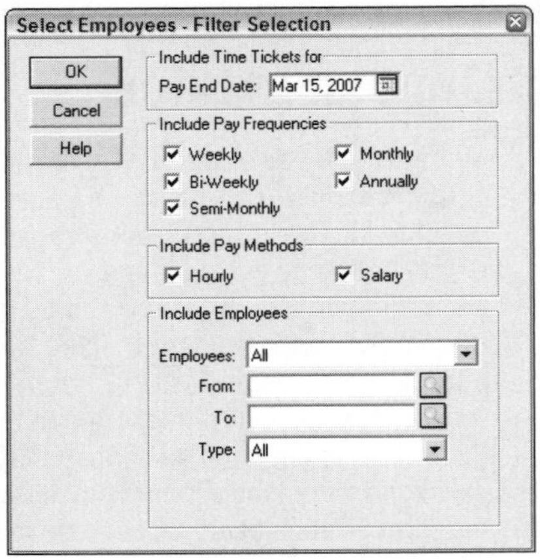

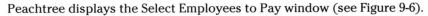

Figure 9-5:
Identify the
employees
you want
to pay.

2. **In the Pay End Date box, select the date that represents the last day of the pay period.**

3. **In the Include Pay Frequencies section, check all of the boxes that represent the pay frequencies you want to include.**

   For example, include employees you pay weekly. As you can see from the dialog box, you can include all pay frequencies. If you don't have any monthly or annual employees, you can leave the boxes checked without affecting anything.

4. **In the Include Pay Methods section, choose to pay hourly employees, salaried employees, or both.**

5. **Use the Include Employees section to limit the range of employees you pay.**

   If you want to pay all employees who meet the other criteria you establish in this dialog box, simply choose All Employees. Otherwise, in the From box, select the first employee you want to include. Then, in the To box, select the last employee you want to include.

   We suggest that you include all employees because you have another opportunity in the next window to exclude an employee.

   If you have enabled direct deposit, the Employees drop-down list contains two additional choices besides All and Range; you see Direct Deposit Only and Manual Check Only.

6. **Click OK.**

   Peachtree displays the Select Employees to Pay window (see Figure 9-6).

7. **If you don't like the selection you see, click the Select toolbar button to redisplay the Select Employees – Filter Selection dialog box (refer to Figure 9-5).**

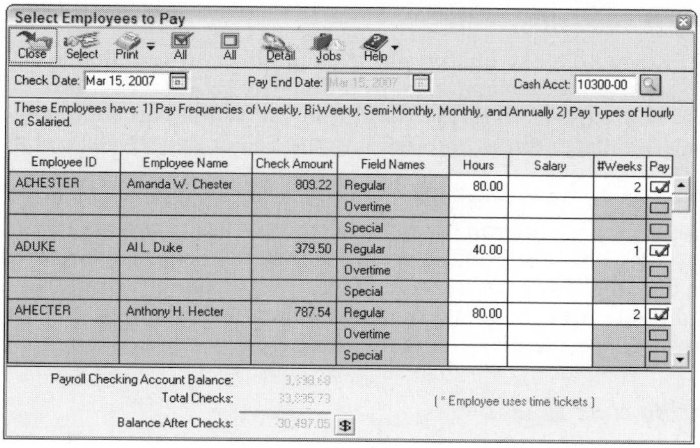

Figure 9-6:
Confirm that
the payroll
checks
you're about
to print are
the ones
you want to
produce.

The Select Employees to Pay dialog box has some options you should keep in mind:

- ✓ You can change the cash account from which the checks will be written if necessary.

- ✓ An asterisk next to an employee's name signifies that you've set up the employee's pay method as Hourly – Time Ticket Hours, and that employee's paycheck is based on the number of time ticket hours in the current pay period. Find out more about time tickets in Chapter 10.

- ✓ If you've enabled direct deposit, you see an extra column in the Select Employee to Pay window to the right of the Pay column; the additional column is titled DD. A red check mark in this column identifies employees who are set up to use direct deposit. You can remove the check mark, but you cannot add a check mark to anyone who is not set up to use direct deposit.

- ✓ You can change the number of hours worked for hourly employees or the salary amount for salaried employees; Peachtree recalculates the taxes and net check amount.

- ✓ You can change the number of weeks in the pay period. Typically, you see 1, 2, 12, or 52; these numbers indicate the frequency with which you pay each employee (weekly, biweekly or semimonthly, monthly, or annually). Changing the number of weeks in the pay period affects the pay period beginning date on the paycheck stub. Peachtree calculates the beginning date by subtracting the number of weeks from the Pay Period Ending Date.

  You can print the Pay Period Beginning Date on a paycheck stub. You need to customize the payroll check form to add the field. See Chapter 13 for information on customizing forms.

- ✓ You can avoid paying an employee by removing the check mark from the Pay column.

Viewing the details

You can view and make changes to the details of any employee's check. Highlight the employee and click Detail on the toolbar. Peachtree displays the Select Employees to Pay – Detail window. When you finish viewing or changing details, click OK to redisplay the Select Employees to Pay window.

Don't change Social Security or Medicare amounts. If you do, you'll find discrepancies on your payroll tax reports, and the 941 quarterly payroll tax return won't be accurate. You can, however, change the Federal Income Tax and state income tax amounts with no side effects. Make changes to the hours/salary first and the taxes second; if you make the changes in the opposite order, Peachtree will recalculate the taxes and ignore your tax changes.

Allocating time to jobs

If you use jobs and want to allocate an employee's time to various jobs, follow the steps in the "Paying a group of employees" section to display the Select Employees to Pay window. Then follow these steps:

1. **In the Select Employees to Pay window, click the employee.**

2. **Click the Jobs button to display the Labor Distribution to Jobs window (see Figure 9-7).**

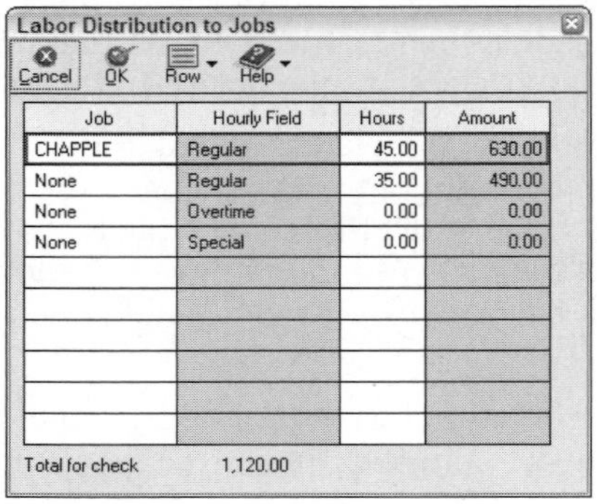

Job	Hourly Field	Hours	Amount
CHAPPLE	Regular	45.00	630.00
None	Regular	35.00	490.00
None	Overtime	0.00	0.00
None	Special	0.00	0.00
Total for check	1,120.00		

Figure 9-7:
Allocate employee hours to Jobs.

3. **Click in the Job column on the line displaying the type of pay you want to allocate — Regular, Overtime, or Special.**

   Peachtree inserts a blank line.

4. **Click the blank box in the Job column to display a lookup list button.**

5. **Use the Lookup list indicator to select a job.**

6. **In the Hours or Amount column, assign hours or dollars to that job.**

   Peachtree assigns the hours or dollars to the selected job and adjusts the unassigned hours or dollars accordingly.

7. **Repeat Steps 3 through 6 as needed to continue distributing hours or dollars.**

8. **Click OK when you're finished to redisplay the Select Employees to Pay window.**

Listing the checks that you plan to print

Wouldn't it be nice to know how many checks Peachtree is planning to print? (You may have noticed that you don't see that number in the window any-place.) Well, if you click drop-down arrow on the Print button and then click Report, Peachtree prints a report that shows you the details of checks you're printing. At the end of the report, you also find the number of checks you're printing. To preview checks on-screen, click the drop-down arrow on the Print button and then choose Preview. See Chapter 13 for details on printing forms (checks are called forms in Peachtree).

Printing checks

If you click the Print button in the Select Employees to Pay window, Peachtree displays the Print Forms: Payroll Checks window. From this window, you can confirm (or change) the first check number, select a check form, identify the number of copies to print of each check, and select a printer.

If you click the Practice button, you can print practice checks to see Xs and 9s on the form where words and numbers will appear. Click Print, and Peachtree prints the checks and displays a dialog box asking you to confirm that the checks printed properly. Click Yes to post the checks; click No if you need to reprint the checks for any reason—like a printer jam.

Paying employees individually

Do you need to pay only one or two employees? Use the Payroll Entry window and follow these steps:

1. **Choose Tasks⇨Payroll Entry to display the Payroll Entry window (see Figure 9-8).**

2. **Use the Lookup list indicator next to the Employee ID field to select an employee to pay.**

   Peachtree fills in the employee's regular payroll information. On the left side of the window, you see Pay Level information. On the right side of the window, you see payroll fields, such as the employee's taxes and deductions, as well as other payroll liabilities you incur such as Federal Unemployment Tax.

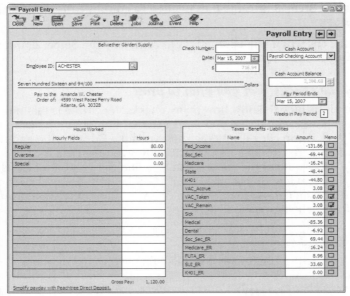

Figure 9-8:
Use this
window to
pay an
individual
employee.

3. **If necessary, change the information.**

   Set the Pay Period Ends date and the Cash Account.

   If an hourly employee doesn't work all of the hours in the pay period, adjust the number of hours on the left side of the window.

   Don't change Social Security or Medicare amounts. If you do, you'll find discrepancies on your payroll tax reports, and the 941 quarterly payroll tax return won't be accurate. You can, however, change the Federal Income Tax and state income tax amounts with no side effects. Make changes to the hours/salary first and the taxes second; if you make the changes in the opposite order, Peachtree will recalculate the taxes and ignore your tax changes.

4. **To assign the employee's hours to a job, click the Jobs button at the top of the screen.**

   For details, see "Allocating time to jobs," earlier in this chapter.

5. **Click the Print button to print the check.**

   Peachtree displays the Print Forms: Payroll Checks window.

   You can preview checks before printing them by clicking the drop-down arrow on the Print button and choosing Preview.

Don't assign a check number before clicking the Print button. If you do, Peachtree prints "Duplicate" on the check because Peachtree assigns the check number to the check when you print it.

6. **Confirm (or change) the first check number, select a check form, identify the number of copies to print of each check, and select a printer.**

   For details on selecting and printing a form, see Chapter 13. If you click the Practice button, you can print practice checks to see Xs and 9s on the form where words and numbers will appear.

7. **Click Print.**

   Peachtree prints and posts the checks, updating the employee's record and the general ledger.

If you don't print checks — say because you are entering after-the-fact payroll information provided by a payroll service — you can simply save the check. If you save the check instead of printing it, assign it a check number.

Paying commissions, bonuses, or other additions

Many companies pay employees bonuses at the end of the year. And employees who act as sales representatives usually earn commissions. It may seem strange to you that we're talking about two different situations in the same breath, but Peachtree handles both situations the same way. In fact, you can use the technique we show you here to handle any form of additional lump-sum income that you must pay through payroll, such as jury duty or maternity leave. We refer to these lump-sum income amounts as *payroll additions*.

Setting up a payroll item

You can use a pay level to record a bonus or commission, but we recommend that you use the technique we describe here for three reasons:

- ✔ You can control whether to include the payroll addition in gross pay when calculating payroll taxes or other payroll fields, such as retirement contributions. (Peachtree automatically includes pay levels in gross pay when calculating payroll fields.)

- ✔ The payroll addition appears as a separate item on payroll reports, making the payroll addition easier to track.

- ✔ Setting up a payroll addition item is less work than setting up a pay level.

Follow these steps to set up a payroll addition item for commissions:

1. **Choose Maintain⇨Default Information⇨Employees to display the Employee Defaults dialog box.**

2. **Click the EmployEE Fields tab and scroll down to find a blank line.**

3. **In the Field Name column, type the name of the payroll addition.**

   The name you use will appear on the paycheck stub.

4. **Assign the line to a general ledger account — usually your wage expense account.**

Because commissions (and bonuses, jury duty pay, maternity leave pay, and so on) vary from employee to employee, you don't check the Calc column and create a payroll tax table to calculate the amount. You also don't need to supply an amount in the Amount column. You need to tell Peachtree only whether to include additional pay when Peachtree calculates gross wages for each tax. For example, you may want Peachtree to _include_ commission pay in gross wages when calculating FIT, Social Security, and Medicare. At the same time, you may want Peachtree to _exclude_ commission pay in gross wages when calculating a pension plan deduction.

Suppose that you want Peachtree to include additional pay in gross wages when calculating Federal Income Tax. Follow these steps:

1. **Choose Maintain⇨Default Information⇨Employees.**

2. **On the EmployEE Fields tab of the Employee Defaults dialog box, scroll up to find the Federal Income Tax entry (it's probably called Fed_Income).**

3. **In the Adjust column for Fed_Income, click the button to display the Calculate Adjusted Gross dialog box (see Figure 9-9).**

4. **If necessary, scroll down in the EmployEE Field Names area on the left side of the dialog box until you see Commission.**

5. **Place a check mark in the Use column to have Peachtree add commission pay to gross wages before calculating federal income tax.**

   If you're not sure whether you want Peachtree to include a payroll addition when calculating adjusted gross wages, ask your accountant.

6. **Click OK to redisplay the Employee Defaults dialog box.**

   You need to repeat these steps for each payroll field for which Peachtree's calculation of adjusted gross wages should include commission pay — at a minimum, Social Security and Medicare.

   If you adjust the gross wage calculation for Social Security and Medicare, be sure that you click the Adjust button for these payroll fields on _both_ the EmployEE Fields tab and the EmployER Fields tab.

7. **Click OK to close the Employee Defaults dialog box.**

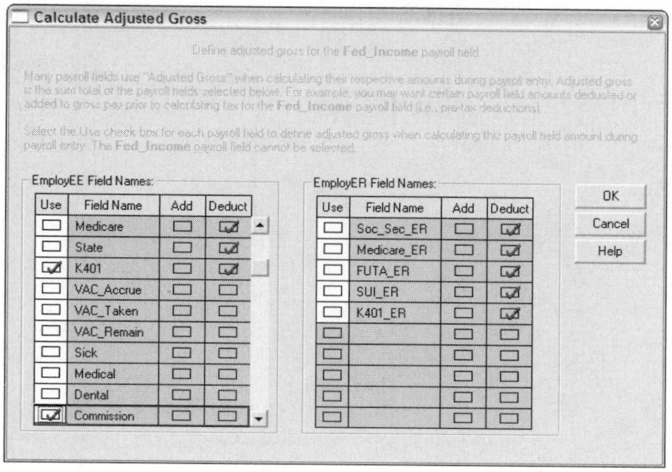

Figure 9-9:
Identify the
amounts
Peachtree
should add
together to
calculate
adjusted
gross
income
before cal-
culating the
selected tax.

To actually pay an employee a commission, simply fill in the amount in the field on the employee's paycheck. Peachtree adjusts appropriate taxes, based on settings you established in the various Calculate Adjusted Gross dialog boxes.

Don't change the Social Security or Medicare amounts on paychecks. If you do, you may find discrepancies on your payroll tax reports and the 941 quarterly payroll tax return won't be accurate. You can, however, change the Federal Income Tax and state income tax amounts on paychecks with no side effects.

The W-2 form and payroll additions

If you want, you can show commissions in Box 14 on the W-2. The assignment is optional; that is, Peachtree includes the commission wages in Boxes 1 (gross wages), 3 (Social Security wages), and 5 (Medicare wages) automatically. Showing the wages in Box 14 simply identifies the component of Gross Wages (Box 1) that were commissions.

To include commissions in Box 14, follow these steps:

1. **Choose Maintain⇨Default Information⇨Employees to display the General tab of the Employee Defaults dialog box.**

2. **Click the W-2s button to display the Assign Payroll Fields for W-2's dialog box (see Figure 9-10).**

3. **In the text box next to number 14, type the name of the payroll field.**

4. **From the list box, select the appropriate field to print in Box 14.**

   In the example, we used Commission.

5. **Click OK twice to save the changes.**

W-2s button

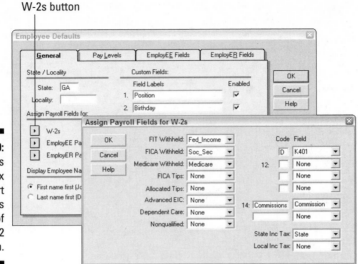

Figure 9-10:
Use this
dialog box
to report
commissions
in Box 14 of
the W-2
form.

Determining commission amounts

With respect to commissions, one burning question pops immediately to mind: How do you know how much commission to pay an employee?

When you produce an invoice that contains items that are subject to commission *and* you assign a sales rep to the invoice, Peachtree's Sales Rep report shows you the commissioned sales for each sales rep. Choose Reports⇨ Accounts Receivable. From the Report List on the right, select Sales Rep Reports. You can print this report (see Figure 9-11) for any date range. See Chapter 7 for more information on invoicing and Chapter 14 for more information on printing reports.

In Figure 9-11, Derrick Gross made three sales that contained commissioned inventory items and one sale that contained no commissioned inventory items. As his employer, you'd multiply the commissioned amount by Derrick's commission rate and pay him the resulting number.

Customer returns usually affect commissions due. We have a few recommendations concerning paying commissions:

> ✔ Print the Sales Rep report only once each month and pay commissions only once each month for the *preceding* month — to make sure that you've processed all invoices for the month.

✔ Add the Amnt Recvd field to the report, as we did in Figure 9-11, and summarize the report by customer so that you see the invoices that have been paid and pay commissions only on paid invoices. See Chapter 14 for information on how to add a field to a report.

✔ Understand that the Total Sales column on the report does *not* include sales tax, but the Amnt Recvd columns *does* include sales tax. When you calculate the commission amount, be sure to calculate it on the Total Sales column.

✔ Hold back a specified amount from each rep's commission and pay that amount when the sales rep decides to leave your company. This practice protects you if you pay a commission for a sale that you later determine you won't collect. Be sure to include this policy in your employee information packet, because you can be sure your employees are tracking the commissions due to them.

✔ Reversing a commission for a merchandise return is *not* a problem. Simply enter a credit memo and assign the sales rep to the credit memo. Reversing a commission for a return where you don't get any merchandise back is a little trickier. We suggest that you set up a nonstock inventory item that you assign to your Sales Returns and Allowances account, making sure to set the item up as subject to commission. When you issue the credit memo, use the nonstock, subject-to-commission inventory item.

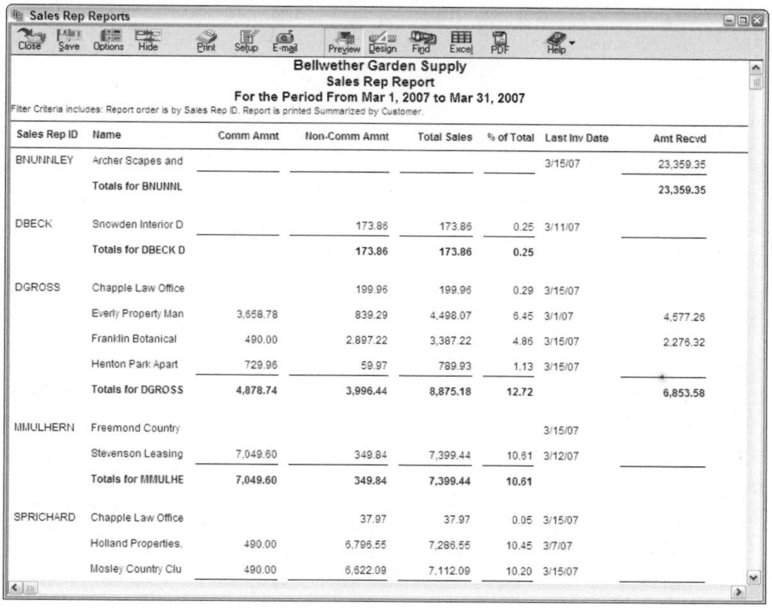

Figure 9-11: Use the Sales Rep report to help you identify commission amounts to pay.

Sales Rep Reports

Bellwether Garden Supply
Sales Rep Report
For the Period From Mar 1, 2007 to Mar 31, 2007
Filter Criteria includes: Report order is by Sales Rep ID. Report is printed Summarized by Customer.

Sales Rep ID	Name	Comm Amnt	Non-Comm Amnt	Total Sales	% of Total	Last Inv Date	Amt Recvd
BNUNNLEY	Archer Scapes and					3/15/07	23,359.35
	Totals for BNUNNL						23,359.35
DBECK	Snowden Interior D		173.86	173.86	0.25	3/11/07	
	Totals for DBECK D		173.86	173.86	0.25		
DGROSS	Chapple Law Office		199.96	199.96	0.29	3/15/07	
	Everly Property Man	3,658.78	839.29	4,498.07	6.45	3/1/07	4,577.26
	Franklin Botanical	490.00	2,897.22	3,387.22	4.86	3/15/07	2,276.32
	Henton Park Apart	729.96	59.97	789.93	1.13	3/15/07	
	Totals for DGROSS	4,878.74	3,996.44	8,875.18	12.72		6,853.58
MMULHERN	Freemond Country					3/15/07	
	Stevenson Leasing	7,049.60	349.84	7,399.44	10.61	3/12/07	
	Totals for MMULHE	7,049.60	349.84	7,399.44	10.61		
SPRICHARD	Chapple Law Office		37.97	37.97	0.05	3/15/07	
	Holland Properties.	490.00	6,796.55	7,286.55	10.45	3/7/07	
	Mosley Country Clu	490.00	6,622.09	7,112.09	10.20	3/15/07	

Dates for credit memos should be in the period when you enter the credit memo — which is *not* necessarily the period in which you sell the item. That way, you are always able to pay commissions for a specified period, and you pay a net amount.

Writing the Payroll Tax Liability Check

You have to pay the payroll tax liability, and the IRS frowns greatly if you don't pay it in a timely fashion. The IRS classifies each employer as either a semiweekly or monthly depositor, and your classification determines when your payroll tax deposit is due after a payday. You make your federal tax deposit at any bank, and you complete Form 8109 as your deposit ticket. On Form 8109, you specify the amount of the deposit, the type of tax (such as 941), and the period for which the tax applies (first quarter, second quarter, third quarter, or fourth quarter).

For simplicity's sake, we strongly urge you to write your federal payroll tax liability check and make your payroll tax deposit *at the same time* that you generate paychecks. That way, you can't get into trouble regardless of whether you are a semiweekly or monthly depositor.

You write your payroll tax liability check from the Payments window. The only tricky part is determining how much you owe.

Use the Payroll Tax Liability report to easily determine the amount of your payroll tax liability. Choose Reports⇨Payroll, and from the Report List on the right, choose Tax Liability Report. If you print the default version of the report, you see each tax name listed and each employee under that tax name, along with the amount withheld and the liability amount for one month. We like the summary version of this report for determining the amount of the tax liability check. For monthly depositors, the summary version is easier to read than the 941 Worksheet. Semiweekly depositors don't need to mess with the 941 B form anymore; simply use the Tax Liability Report for the specified timeframe.

Although Peachtree prints all taxes on the report by default, you also can print the Tax Liability report for only one kind of tax: federal, state, or local. If you're viewing the report on-screen, click the Options button, and Peachtree displays the Options dialog box for the report. Use the Tax list box to choose to print either only federal, state, or local taxes. If you leave the Tax list box set to print all taxes and place a check mark in the Print Report in Summary Format box, you can produce a report that looks like the one shown in Figure 9-12.

Tax Liability Report — _ □ ×

Close | Save | Options | Hide | Print | Setup | E-mail | Preview | Design | Find

Bellwether Garden Supply
Tax Liability Report
For the Period From Mar 1, 2007 to Mar 31, 2007
Filter Criteria includes: Report order is by Employee ID. Report is printed in Summary Format.

Tax Description	Gross	Taxable Gross	Tax Liability
FUTA	45,181.52	45,181.52	361.46
940 Total			361.46
FIT	44,526.57	44,526.57	4,547.11
FICA EE	45,181.52	45,181.52	2,801.27
FICA ER	45,181.52	45,181.52	2,801.27
Medicare EE	45,181.52	45,181.52	655.14
Medicare ER	45,181.52	45,181.52	655.14
941 Total			11,459.93
GA State Taxes			
GASUI ER	45,181.52	45,181.52	1,355.43
GASIT	44,526.57	44,526.57	1,925.45
GA State Total			3,280.88
Report Total			15,102.27

Figure 9-12:
A summa-
rized version
of the Tax
Liability
Report.

Use the totals in the Tax Liability column for each tax to determine the amount of money you owe for each of your payroll tax liabilities. Then open the Payments window and write a check to your local bank. Set the G/L Account on the Apply to Expenses tab at the bottom of the window to your payroll tax liability account(s) and the Cash Account to the account from which you're writing the check — you might use a payroll checking account (if you have a separate account) or an operating checking account.

Paying your payroll tax liability doesn't affect the numbers that appear on the Tax Liability report. The report shows what you *should* pay and doesn't consider what you may have already paid, which is *another* good reason to pay your tax liability at the same time you generate paychecks.

Exploring Payroll Reports

Besides the Payroll Tax Liability report we describe in "Writing the Payroll Tax Liability Check," Peachtree offers several reports that you can use for a variety of tracking needs. Table 9-1 shows you a description of the reports that pertain to payroll. See Chapter 14 to learn how to print reports.

Table 9-1	Other Reports Related to Payroll
Report Name	**What It Does**
Check Register	Lists each paycheck with the check number, payee, and the amount.
Current Earnings Report	Shows, for the current period, much of the same information on the Payroll Register: breakdowns (by payroll field) of each paycheck. The Current Earnings report, however, subtotals each employee.
Employee Compensation Report	A Peachtree Premium Only report. This report lists, for each employee, the raise date, the pay level on which the raise was based, the pay level amount before the raise, the raise amount and percentage, new pay level amount, and any raise notes you supplied.
Employee List	For each employee, lists the ID, name, contact name, address, Social Security number, and pay type.
Exception Report	Shows the difference between the tax amount Peachtree calculates and the tax amount withheld for each specified payroll tax.
Payroll Journal	Shows the accounts Peachtree updated for each paycheck in the period.
Payroll Register	Lists every paycheck in the specified time period; provides the same information as the Current Earnings report but without subtotaling each employee.
Payroll Tax Report	Shows, for the selected tax, each employee, Social Security number, the number of weeks worked, the gross, the taxable gross, the excess gross, and the tax amount. You can print this report for every payroll tax for which you've set up a calculation and marked the Appears on Payroll Tax Report Menus check box.
Quarterly Earnings Report	Shows the same information as the Current Earnings Report but for the current quarter.
Yearly Earnings Report	Shows the same information as the Current and Quarterly Earnings Reports but for the year.

Visit this book's Web site for more information on Peachtree.

Chapter 10

Billing for Your Time

In This Chapter

▶ Setting up time and expense items

▶ Entering Time and Expense Tickets

▶ Paying employees for hours worked

▶ Using tickets to create customer invoices

*Y*ou've probably heard the saying, "Time is money." Some companies, particularly those employing service-oriented professionals such as accountants, consultants, lawyers, and architects, bill their customers for the time spent to complete projects. These companies often have employees track time and expenses, such as travel, for each of their projects. Then the employer bills the customer for the employee time and expenses. In some cases, the companies also pay employees based on time worked.

In this chapter, you find out how Peachtree Premium and Peachtree Complete support these billing functions — complete with a clock that lets you time your activities.

See Chapter 12 to find out how you can use jobs in Peachtree to create reimbursable expenses — expenses you incur that may have nothing to do with time spent by anyone but that you want to include on an invoice. Using time and expense tickets provides an alternative — and possibly better — method for creating reimbursable expenses if you don't need jobs for any other reason. (Chapter 12 lists information concerning the restrictions imposed if you use Peachtree jobs.) If you find that your time and billing needs are more extensive than the features provided by Peachtree, you might consider Timeslips, which links with Peachtree.

Time and billing functions are not available in Peachtree First Accounting or Peachtree Accounting.

Creating Time and Expense Items

If you plan to use the time and expense features in Peachtree, you need at least two (but probably more) inventory items (yeah, we know that it's weird to use inventory items for time and expense features, but it's true). You use inventory items with an item class of Activity item to enter time-related activities, and you use inventory items with an item class of Charge item to enter expense activities.

To create inventory items to use on time activities, follow these steps:

1. **Choose Maintain⇨Inventory Items to display the Maintain Inventory Items window (see Figure 10-1).**

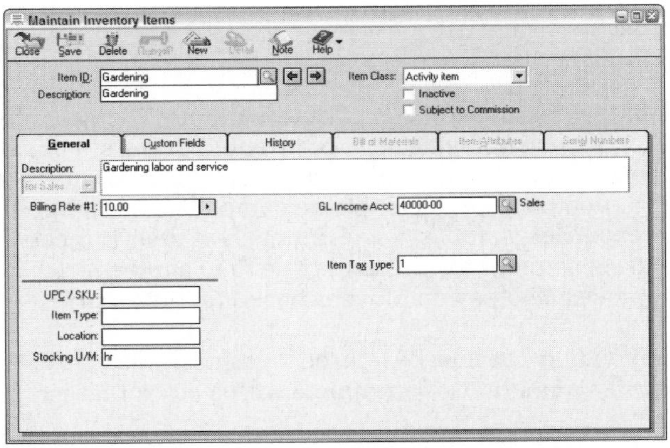

Figure 10-1: Set up at least one Activity item and one Charge item if you intend to record both time and expenses.

2. **In the Item ID text box, type an label that identifies the item.**

3. **In the Item Class list box, choose Activity item for a time activity or Charge item for an expense activity.**

4. **In the text box below the Item ID box, supply a description.**

   This description appears on reports but *not* on invoices to your customers.

5. **In the Description text box on the General tab, fill in the description that you want to appear on customer invoices for time spent on this activity.**

The description in the longer description box appears on the customer's bill unless you choose to display the description from the time ticket. For details on the time ticket's description block, see the "Entering Time Tickets" section.

6. **Enter up to ten billing rates for the activity by clicking the button beside the Billing Rate box.**

   You may assign more than one billing rate to an employee or a vendor so that you can bill the same employee or vendor at different rates for, say, different customers or different situations.

7. **Use the lookup list button to select a GL Income Account for the activity.**

8. **Use the lookup list button to select an Item Tax Type for the activity.**

   UPC/SKU, Stocking U/M, Item Type, and Location are all optional fields.

9. **Click Save.**

Entering Time Tickets

Peachtree's Time Tickets feature eliminates the need for timecards and old-fashioned push-in, punch-out tracking of employee hours. You can use Peachtree's Time Tickets to

- ✔ Record time spent by employees or vendors to bill to a customer or job

- ✔ Track the cost of employee time spent on jobs

- ✔ Provide employees with a method to track time so that you can pay them based on time worked

Chapter 9 provides information about one of Peachtree's pay methods, Hourly – Time Ticket Hours, which you can use to pay your employees based on the hours entered on time tickets. If you pay an employee based on time worked, you also need a way to account for employee time that you don't intend to charge to a customer or job — such as overhead time spent doing marketing or bookkeeping. Although you won't be billing the time to a customer, you need to include overhead hours on the employee's paycheck.

Peachtree allows you to enter overhead Time Tickets and marks any overhead time you record as unbillable. And, as you might expect, you aren't able to include that time on a bill.

If you don't pay your employees based on time tickets, you don't need to assign time to overhead activities.

Follow these steps to enter a time ticket:

1. **Choose Tasks⇨Time/Expense⇨Time Tickets to display the Time Tickets window (see Figure 10-2).**

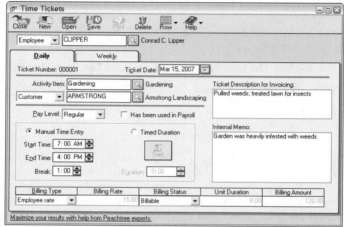

Figure 10-2:
Use this window to enter time tickets.

2. **In the upper-left list box, select either Employee or Vendor and then select an employee or vendor.**

3. **In the Ticket Date box, enter the date you performed the work.**

4. **In the Activity Item list, use the lookup list button to make your selection.**

5. **In the list box below the Activity Item box, choose Customer, Job, or Administrative. If you choose Customer or Job, select the appropriate customer or job using the lookup list button.**

   If you choose Customer or Job, you can include the time ticket on a bill; if you choose Administrative, Peachtree considers the time ticket unbillable.

6. **In the Ticket Description for Invoicing box, you can enter up to 160 characters of text to use instead of the activity name on the customer's invoice.**

7. **In the Internal Memo box, you can provide up to 2000 characters of descriptive information.**

You can't include the Internal Memo description on a customer's invoice, but Peachtree prints it on reports. Use it to provide details about the work performed.

To start a new paragraph while typing in the Internal Memo box, press Ctrl+J.

8. **If you are entering a Time Ticket for an employee, choose a Pay Level.**

Don't mess with the Has Been Used In Payroll check box; instead, let Peachtree fill it in. If the box is checked, you've paid the employee for the Time Ticket; unchecked means that you haven't included the Time Ticket on a paycheck yet.

9. **Choose Manual Time Entry or Timed Duration and then do the following:**

   • For Manual Entry, supply a start and stop time as well as a break time, if appropriate.

   • For Timed Duration, click Start, and Peachtree runs a timer (the Start button then becomes the Stop button).

Regardless of your choice, Peachtree calculates the duration of the time ticket.

You can't save a time ticket or close the Time Ticket window while the timer is running.

10. **Choose a Billing Type, as follows:**

   • **Employee Rate:** Uses the Hourly billing rate you entered on the Pay Info tab when you set up the employee in the Maintain Employees/ Sales Reps window

   • **Activity Rate:** Uses the rate you entered when you set up the activity in the Maintain Inventory Items window

   • **Override Rate:** Ignores both the employee and activity rates and allows you to enter any rate you want

   • **Flat Fee:** Ignores the duration (and value) of the time ticket and allows you to establish an amount for the ticket

All billing types are available for employees, but only some are available for vendors.

11. **Choose a Billing Rate.**

The available rates depend on the choice you make for Billing Type in Step 10. For example, you can establish only one employee rate, so if you choose Employee as the Billing Type, you can't change the billing rate. However, you can establish up to five rates for an activity, so you can choose a billing rate if you select Activity as the Billing Type. For Override Rate, you must type a Billing Rate.

12. **Choose a Billing Status: Billable, Non-Billable, Hold, or No Charge.**

    Billable and Non-Billable are self-explanatory. If you select Hold, you can't bill the ticket to a customer until you change the ticket's status. If you select No Charge, Peachtree changes the ticket's value to $0, so you can show your customer on the invoice that you performed work but didn't charge for it.

13. **If you choose Flat Fee as the Billing Type, enter a Billing Amount.**

    For all other Billing Types, Peachtree calculates the Billing Amount.

14. **Click Save.**

Whew! This process seems like a lot of steps to enter a ticket, but it goes quickly. The daily Time Ticket window appears in Figure 10-2, but Peachtree also provides a weekly view. You can enter time tickets in the weekly view, and you can print the weekly timesheet by clicking the Print button in the window.

The columns in the weekly view aren't terribly wide, and most contain lookup list box selectors. As you enter information for a particular column, the list boxes extend to cover up columns to the right of the current column. The visual effect may make you think that columns have disappeared — but they haven't.

Entering Expense Tickets

Okay, good news here. Almost everything you just read in the preceding section about time tickets applies also to expense tickets. For example, you can enter expense tickets for both employees and vendors. And you can assign an expense ticket to a customer or job so that you can recover the expense. Or you can assign an expense ticket to overhead, making it unbillable. If you assign an expense ticket to an employee, you also can place a check mark in the Reimbursable to Employee box; Peachtree prints reimbursable expense tickets in the Reimbursable Employee Expense report, making it easy for you to pay employees for their expenses.

Choose Tasks➪Time/Expense➪Expense Tickets to display the Expense Tickets window. In the Ticket Description for Invoicing box, you can type up to 160 characters, which can print on the customer's invoice. In the Internal Memo box, you can type up to 2000 characters.

Unit Price is tied to the Charge Item you select — you may see up to ten available unit prices. And you have the same four Billing Status options for expense tickets that you have for time tickets: Billable, Non-Billable, No Charge, and Hold.

Paying Employees

Suppose that you pay employees from time tickets. You can use either of the payroll windows we describe in Chapter 9. Figure 10-3 shows the Payroll Entry window (choose Tasks⇨Payroll Entry). When you set the Pay Period End date, Peachtree automatically calculates the paycheck using time tickets from that pay period that are assigned to Customer or Administrative (in that unnamed list box we mentioned in Step 5 in the "Entering Time Tickets" section). If your employee assigned the time tickets to Job instead of Customer or Administrative, you need to click the Jobs button when you're paying the employee to see and select those time tickets.

Repaying employees for reimbursable expenses

Peachtree doesn't try to repay your employees automatically for expense tickets. You must print the Reimbursable Employee Expense report (shown in the following figure) for the specified pay period to identify expenses for reimbursement.

Then you can repay the employee in one of two ways:

✔ Use the Payments window (choose Tasks⇨ Payments) to write a separate expense reimbursement check to the employee. If you want to track the reimbursable expense checks to the employee, set the employee up as a vendor.

✔ Include the reimbursement in the employee's paycheck by setting up a payroll field as an addition. See Chapter 9 for details on setting up additions. You need to assign the reimbursement to a general ledger account but probably *not* to your wage expense account. And, because reimbursements aren't usually subject to payroll taxes, you need to click the Adjust button for each payroll tax and make sure that you're not including the reimbursement item. When you pay the employee, type a positive amount for the reimbursement to add it to the paycheck.

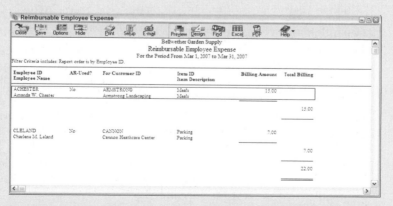

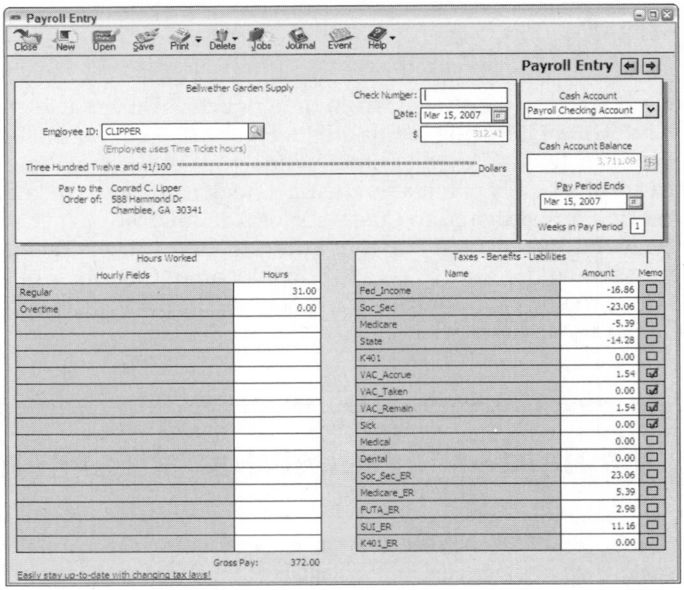

Figure 10-3:
Paying an
employee
for time
worked.

Using Tickets to Bill Customers

If your employees or vendors assign time or expense tickets to customers or
jobs, you can bill the customers for those costs. Follow these steps to bill
customers using tickets:

To be sure you don't forget to bill your customers for time or expense tickets,
print the Aged Tickets report before you create invoices.

1. **Choose Tasks⇨Sales/Invoicing to display the Sales/Invoicing window.**

2. **Complete most of your invoice as usual.**

   Select a customer using the lookup list indicator next to the Customer ID
   box and assign shipping information, terms, and line item information if
   this invoice includes more than reimbursable Time and Expense Tickets.
   For details on entering invoices, see Chapter 7.

3. **In the lower-left corner of the window, click the Apply Tickets/Expenses
   button to display the Apply Tickets/Reimbursable Expenses window
   (see Figure 10-4).**

   You can view available time tickets on the Time Tickets tab and expense
   tickets on the Expense Tickets tab. To find out more about the Reimbursable Expenses tab, see Chapter 12.

4. **To include a ticket on the invoice, click the Use check box next to the
   ticket on the appropriate tab.**

WriteUp buttons

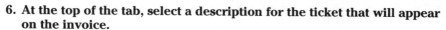

Apply Tickets/Reimbursable Expenses

Cancel OK WriteUp WriteUp Use NoBill Use NoBill Detail Help

| Customer ID: | ARMSTRONG | Customer Name: | Armstrong Landscaping |

Time Tickets | Expense Tickets | Reimbursable Expenses

○ Use Ticket Description for Invoicing   Sort List By: Date
○ Use Item Description for Invoicing   Consolidate By: No Consolidation

Ticket Date	Activity Item	Hours	Billing Rate	Ticket Amount	Invoice Amount	Use	No Bill
Mar 15, 2007	Gardening	12.00	15.00	180.00	180.00	☐	☐
CLIPPER	Conrad C. Lipper						
Mar 12, 2007	Gardening	8.00	15.00	120.00	120.00	☐	☐
CLIPPER	Conrad C. Lipper						

Total Time Tickets Selected:	0.00	0.00
Total Time Tickets Not Selected:	300.00	
Total Time Tickets Available:	300.00	

Figure 10-4:
Use the tabs in this window to select time tickets and expense tickets to include on a customer's invoice.

5. In the Invoice Amount column, verify or change the figure.

To build some profit into a ticket or a reimbursable expense, you change the amount in the Invoice Amount column. To mark up costs or reduce a group of tickets or reimbursable expenses, click the WriteUp button to display the Select Tickets to Write Up/Down dialog box. You can adjust tickets up or down by a dollar amount or a percentage. To mark up, supply a positive number; to mark down, supply a negative number.

If you change your mind and decide that you *don't* want to mark tickets up or down, click the Remove WriteUp button (the one with the "not" symbol in its image) in the Apply Tickets/Reimbursable Expenses window.

6. At the top of the tab, select a description for the ticket that will appear on the invoice.

The first option, Use Ticket Description for Invoicing, tells Peachtree to use the description supplied on the time ticket. The second option, Use Item Description for Invoicing, tells Peachtree to use the description supplied when you set up the item in inventory.

If you leave the Consolidate By list box setting at No Consolidation, Peachtree creates separate lines on the invoice for each ticket you choose to bill. You can use other entries in the list to consolidate each type of ticket you use and reduce the number of lines on the invoice.

7. Click OK.

The reimbursable expenses appear on the customer's invoice.

8. Supply G/L accounts, select a job if appropriate, print, and post the invoice as usual.

See Chapter 7 for details on completing an invoice.

When you print tickets as separate lines on the invoice, Peachtree prints the description you supplied on the expense when you created it. You see either ticket descriptions or item descriptions on the customer's invoice depending on the selection you make in the Apply Tickets/Reimbursable Expenses window. When you consolidate expenses on the invoice, Peachtree does not supply a description. Instead, Peachtree prints the name of the G/L account you choose as the description on the invoice and the total of all the tickets. If you want, you can type a description on the line for the consolidated tickets in the Sales/Invoicing window, and Peachtree uses that description instead of the G/L account name.

Keep the following notes in mind when you work with tickets:

✔ You can delete tickets from the Apply Tickets/Reimbursable Expenses window if you decide not to invoice the client for them. Place a check mark in the No Bill box to the right of the expense. Deleting the ticket does *not* delete the transaction that created the ticket; instead, deleting in the Apply Tickets/Reimbursable Expenses window disconnects the ticket and the customer.

You can't undo a deletion you make in the Apply Tickets/Reimbursable Expenses window. As soon as you delete a ticket, the connection between the ticket and the customer is *permanently* broken unless you erase the ticket and reenter it completely.

✔ Be aware that using a ticket makes it disappear from the Apply Tickets/Reimbursable Expenses window. If you subsequently delete the line from the invoice, the reimbursable expense *does not* reappear in the window. If you mistakenly use the ticket and post the invoice, delete the invoice and reenter it to make the ticket available again.

✔ You can edit a ticket you intend to bill to a customer. You can find the transaction by opening the Time Tickets window or the Expense Tickets window and clicking the Edit button.

Tracking Ticket Traffic

(Say that section title three times fast!)

The Reimbursable Employee Expense report is one example of the reports Peachtree offers to help you keep track of time tickets. Table 10-1, provides you with a description of the various other reports that pertain to time and expenses. See Chapter 14 for more details on printing reports.

Table 10-1	Other Reports Related to Time and Billing
Report Name	*What It Does*
Aged Tickets	Shows unbilled tickets and how old they are based on the aging brackets you set up in Customer defaults
Employee Time	Lists, by employee, tickets and billing status
Expense Ticket Register	Lists, by ticket number, detailed information about expense tickets
Tickets Recorded By	Lists the tickets entered for each employee or vendor
Tickets Used in Invoicing	Lists tickets that were included on customer invoices
Tickets by Item ID	Shows tickets organized by item ID so that you can see which activities are being used the most
Time Ticket Register	Lists, by ticket number, detailed information about time tickets
Ticket Listing by Customer	Lists each ticket assigned to the customer in the specified time period
Payroll Time Sheet	Shows you the tickets entered by employee for the specified time period

Visit this book's Web site for more information on Peachtree.

Chapter 11

Counting Your Stuff

*T*his chapter is about stuff. Many businesses sell stuff you can touch, while others sell stuff you *can't* touch. Some stuff is made up of pieces of other stuff. Peachtree lets you sell all these kinds of stuff. Enough stuff.

Of course, we're talking about inventory. And not just the goods you place on your shelves but other kinds of nonphysical items such as services, labor, activities, and items you charge to your customer's bill.

We'll just warn you up front. The material in this chapter is rather dry, and you probably won't consider it too funny. However, inventory management is typically a crucial part of keeping your books. Peachtree makes handling inventory a lot easier than trying to track it all by hand.

Creating Inventory Items

When you create inventory items, you set up the goods and services you sell. You set a price (actually, you can set up to ten prices) at which you want to sell your product and the account you want Peachtree to adjust when you sell this item or service. But before you can set up selling prices, you need to supply basic information about the item.

To create your virtual inventory, follow these steps:

1. **Choose Maintain⇨Inventory Items.**

   Peachtree displays the Maintain Inventory Items window, with multiple tabs for each item. The header information consists of the item ID, description, and class.

2. **In the Item ID field, type an item ID.**

   Keep in mind that the Item ID appears in lookup lists for sales transactions and so on. Peachtree allows item IDs with up to 20 alphanumeric characters.

   IDs are case sensitive and can't contain the asterisk (*), question mark (?), or plus symbol (+).

3. **Enter a description containing up to 30 characters.**

   This description appears in the item lookup lists. In the following section, you'll see how to type descriptions that you can use for sales or purchase transactions. For example, in the lookup description, you might refer to a specific birdbath as "Con PBB w/birds," but when you sell this item, you'll want to be a little more descriptive, such as "Concrete bird bath with 2 bluebirds on pedestal base."

   If you discontinue an inventory item, you can mark it inactive; redisplay the item in the Maintain Inventory window and check the Inactive box.

4. **Choose an Item Class to identify the type of inventory item.**

   Selecting the right classes for your inventory items helps ensure that Peachtree meets your business needs. Peachtree Premium supports 11 item classes, Peachtree Complete supports 9 item classes, and the other versions support 7 item classes. Chapter 4 provides more information on the different Peachtree inventory classes, but these are the basics:

   - **Stock:** Inventory items you want to track for quantities, average costs, vendors, low stock points, and so on.

   - **Non-stock:** Items such as service contracts that you sell but do not put into your inventory.

   - **Master Stock:** Items that consist of information shared by a number of substock items.

   - **Serialized Stock:** Items that have serial numbers that you plan to track. Serialized stock items appear only in Peachtree Premium edition.

   - **Assembly:** Items that consist of components that must be built or dismantled.

- **Serialized Assembly:** Items that consist of serialized components that you plan to build or unbuild. Serialized Assembly items appear only in Peachtree Premium edition.

- **Service:** Services provided by your employees that you bill to your customers.

- **Labor:** Charges you bill to a customer for subcontracted labor on that customer's projects.

- **Activity:** Records of how time is spent when performing services. Activity items appear only in Peachtree Premium and Peachtree Complete editions. Chapter 10 gives you more information on setting up Activity and Charge items.

- **Charge:** On-the-job expenses of an employee or vendor. Charge items appear only in Peachtree Premium and Peachtree Complete editions. Chapter 10 gives you more information on setting up Activity and Charge items.

- **Description Only:** Timesaver when you track nothing but the description.

If you save an item as a stock item, an assembly item, an activity item, or a charge item, you can't change its item class. Although you probably wouldn't want to, Peachtree does allow you to interchange the item class between nonstock, description, labor, and service items.

5. **Check the Subject to Commission box if you want to track the sales of the item and have it reported on the Accounts Receivable Sales Rep report.**

General options

You enter basic item information such as descriptions, account numbers, sales prices, and pricing methods on the General tab.

Why does Peachtree list different description lines? Well, the first description, the one you entered in the header information (Figure 11-1), appears when you open the inventory item lookup list.

Peachtree also provides the For Sales description and the For Purchases description. The description (up to 160 characters) you enter for sales appears on quotes, sales orders, sales invoicing, and receipts. The for purchases description appears on purchase orders, purchases/receive inventory, and payments. You can modify either the for sales or the for purchases description when you create a transaction.

Item Class drop-down list

Sales Purchase description box

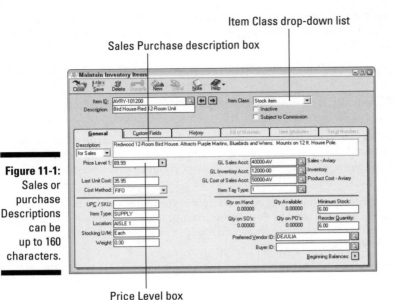

Figure 11-1:
Sales or
purchase
Descriptions
can be
up to 160
characters.

Price Level box

Follow these steps to enter general inventory information:

1. **Click the arrow under description to select the description you want to enter.**

2. **Enter a description as you want it to appear on transactions.**

   Entering information in the For Sales and For Purchases boxes is optional. If you do not specify a sales description, Peachtree uses the lookup description when you enter a quote, a sales order, an invoice, or a receipt. If you don't specify a purchase description, Peachtree uses the for sales description when generating purchase orders, purchases, or payments. If a sales description doesn't exist, Peachtree uses the lookup description.

3. **Type the price you want to charge.**

   Peachtree refers to the amounts that appear on your quotes, sales orders, and invoices as *sales prices*. The sales pricing levels correspond with those you assign your customers in the Maintain Customers/Prospects window (see Chapter 7).

   If you charge only one price for this item, no matter which customer, enter only Price Level 1. To enter additional sales prices, click the arrow. The Multiple Pricing Levels dialog box as shown in Figure 11-2 appears.

   Be consistent when entering item sales price levels (for example, from lowest to highest or highest to lowest).

Items prices can be a static number you assign, or you can create a calculation using the current price or the last cost as the foundation of the formula. By default, Peachtree uses the pricing calculation you entered when creating inventory defaults. (See Chapter 4.) You can, however, click the Edit button to display the Calculate Price Level box and create a different calculation. You can increase or decrease the price by a percentage or an amount. When you're finished, click OK twice to close both the Calculate Price Level dialog box and the Multiple Price Levels window.

4. **In the Last Unit Cost box, enter the last price you paid for this item (optional).**

   After you enter transactions against the inventory item, the Last Unit Cost box becomes unavailable. Peachtree automatically updates the Last Unit Cost as you enter purchases, payments, adjustments, or beginning balances, calculating the amount based on the costing method you select in Step 8.

5. **If necessary, select a different Cost Method.**

   The Cost Method is a *very important* field. You can't change a costing method after an inventory item is saved.

Edit button

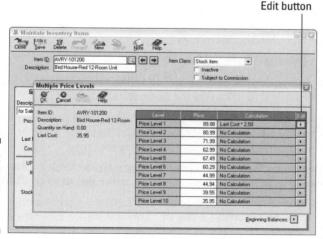

Figure 11-2:
Set up to ten sales prices for each item.

Costing methods apply only to serialized items and serialized assemblies, stock items, master stock items, and assemblies. In addition to tracking serialized items and serialized assemblies by their specific unit cost, Peachtree supports three other costing methods: average cost, LIFO (last in, first out), and FIFO (first in, first out). The sidebar "How do costing methods work?" gives you more information on what these methods mean. Typically, you set all inventory items to use the same costing method, so you probably determined a default method when you set up default inventory items information in Chapter 4. If you're not sure, check with your accountant for advice about different costing methods.

6. **If necessary, change the GL accounts for the item.**

You can review setting up the default GL accounts in Chapter 4.

7. **Choose an item Tax Type.**

The tax type you select applies when you enter the inventory item on quotes, sales orders, invoices, or receipts. If you assign an exempt tax type to an item, the item will never be taxed. If you assign a taxable tax type to an item, you can still exempt the item from tax at the customer or invoice level.

8. **Enter an optional UPC or SKU number for your barcoded items.**

9. **Enter an item type (optional).**

You'll appreciate this when you're generating reports. Grouping items is much easier when they're marked, for example, "supplies" or "raw materials." Item types are case sensitive.

10. **Enter a storage location for the unit (optional).**

Someday you may need to know where the unit is located, such as Bin 17 or Shelf B3 or in Mom's garage. The storage location is helpful also when doing a physical inventory.

11. **Enter a unit of measure (optional).**

You may sell your products on an individual basis (each), in pairs, per dozen, per pound or kilogram, or per ounce.

Peachtree Premium for Distribution and Peachtree Premium for Manufacturing are the only editions that include the ability to purchase and sell your products in different units of measure.

12. **In the Minimum Stock box, enter the quantity at which you want Peachtree to remind you it's time to reorder the item (optional).**

When the quantity on hand reaches the minimum stock quantity, Peachtree prints the item on the Inventory Reorder Worksheet.

Although entering a minimum stock point is optional, you need to enter a minimum stock point if you want Peachtree Premium to automatically create a purchase order when the stock gets low.

13. **Enter a reorder quantity (optional).**

Reorder quantity is the quantity you generally purchase when you order the inventory item. Entering a reorder quantity point is also optional, but again you need to enter a reorder quantity if you want Peachtree Premium to automatically create a purchase order when the stock gets low.

14. **Tell Peachtree where you prefer to buy this item by selecting the vendor ID in the Preferred Vendor field lookup box (optional).**

    Selecting a Preferred Vendor doesn't mean that's the *only* vendor from which you can purchase the item. It just means that this vendor is your *favorite* vendor. You must supply a Preferred Vendor if you want Peachtree Premium to automatically create purchase orders for reorder or for drop ship transactions and non-drop ship transactions.

15. **Select the employee who is the usual buyer for this item.**

    The information can appear on the Buyer Report and can be used to select items for automatic purchase orders.

16. **If you're not creating an assembly item, a master stock item, or a serialized item and are ready to move on, click Save to save the inventory item.**

    Later in this chapter, we show you how setup serialized items. Additionally, we see how to set up a bill of materials for an assembly item and master stock items with their substock items.

If you entered the item ID incorrectly, click the Change ID button and enter a new inventory item ID

Whew! That's a *lot* of stuff to enter for one item! Fortunately, the rest of the Maintain Inventory Items window is easy and doesn't involve too many tough decisions.

Custom fields

If you're using other Peachtree modules, such as A/R, A/P, P/R, or Job Cost, you've seen custom fields before. Use custom fields to store miscellaneous pieces of information about the inventory item that just don't seem to fit anywhere else in the Maintain Inventory Items window. Examples of such items are a substitute item number, the product average shelf life, or information about an alternate vendor for the product. One of our clients uses a custom field to store the chemical makeup of each item.

History

The History tab displays a summary of inventory transactions for stock, assembly, and serialized items for past periods. Peachtree shows units sold and received as well as sales and costs by accounting period. Peachtree does not retain history for nonstock, service, and the remaining class items.

How do costing methods work?

If you're not sure which option to choose in the Cost Method box, you may want to know how Peachtree handles these options. Peachtree supports three main costing methods: Average, FIFO (first-in, first-out), and LIFO (last-in, first-out). (Those terms kinda remind us of Jack and the Beanstalk — Fee Fie Foe Fum. . . .) Peachtree also supports Specific Unit as a costing method, but that method, available only in Peachtree Premium, applies only to those items with a serialized inventory class.

If you use the Average costing method, Peachtree adds the total amount paid for the items and divides that by the total units on hand. The average is recalculated each time you purchase more of the item. Remember that Peachtree calculates costs on a daily basis. As an example, say you have on hand five widgets for which you paid $6 each and three more widgets for which you paid $7 each. That's a total of $51 for the eight widgets or an average of $6.375 each.

If you use the FIFO costing method, Peachtree calculates costs at the *earliest* purchase price, inventory increase adjustment, build, sales return, or assembly unbuild (for the component item) for a particular item. FIFO produces the lowest possible net income in periods of falling costs and the cost of the most recently purchased item most closely approximates the replacement of the item.

If you use the LIFO costing method, Peachtree calculates costs at the most recent *(last)* purchase price, inventory increase adjustment, build, sales return, or assembly unbuild (for the component item) for a particular item. LIFO produces the lowest possible net income in periods of rising costs and the cost of the most recently purchased item most closely approximates the replacement of the item.

Serial numbers

The Serial Number tab is one location where you can view the in-stock serial numbers of the current item as well as determine whether you provide a warranty with the item. The Serial Number tab becomes available only if you class the inventory item as a Serialized Stock item or a Serialized Assembly item.

Peachtree Premium is the only edition that support serialized inventory items.

Peachtree assigns to each serial number a status that you can't change except by entering transactions such as buying or selling. Table 11-1 shows the different statuses and what they mean.

Table 11-1	Serialized Inventory Item Status Codes
Status	*What It Is*
Available	Serial numbers with this status are available for selection on transactions.
Sold	Serial numbers with this status are no longer available because the serial number for the item has been removed from inventory by a transaction such as a sale.
Adjusted	Serial numbers with this status have been taken out of inventory using an inventory adjustment.
Returned	Serial numbers with this status have been returned to the vendor using a credit memo.
In Progress	Serial numbers with this status have been added to work tickets that have not yet been closed. This status is available only in the Peachtree Premium for Manufacturing and Peachtree Premium for Distribution editions.
New	Serial numbers with this status have been added to the system by a transaction but the transaction hasn't been saved.
Error	Serial numbers with this status have been imported into Peachtree with an on-hand quantity. However the transaction that added the serial number to the system (the originating transaction) is missing.

Peachtree Premium for Distribution and Peachtree Premium for Manufacturing editions also include Work Tickets to help track the build progress of an assembled item. Work Tickets contain information about what's needed to build an assembly and whether all the items are available. Work Tickets follow a build through its process, and you can check off the build steps as they're completed.

Serial number statuses are displayed on the Serial Numbers tab in the Maintain Inventory Items window, on the Serial Number Entry window, and on the Serial Number Selection window. Serial number statuses are reported on the Serial Number History report.

Also on the Serial Numbers tab, you can indicate whether the current item has a warranty and determine the length of the warranty period (see Figure 11-3). Peachtree allows up to 90 days, months, or years for a warranty period.

You can customize your invoice to display the warranty information and warranty expiration date. See Chapter 13 for information on customizing forms such as invoices.

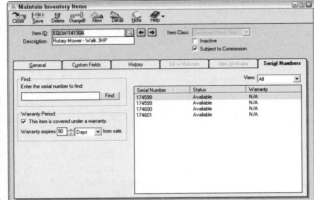

Figure 11-3:
Enter the
serialized
inventory
warranty
period.

Whoa Nellie! Working with Master Stock Items

If you have lots of items and each of those items comes in a different flavor such as color, size, or condition, you can end up with an out-of-control inventory list. To help you harness your inventory list, Peachtree calls another of its inventory classes Master Stock. You use Master Stock items when you might have several variations of similar items, such as T-shirts in various colors and sizes, or both new and used lawn mowers (as demonstrated in Figure 11-4).

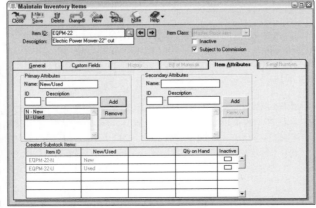

Figure 11-4:
Peachtree
automat-
ically
creates
Substock
inventory
items.

Master Stock items are available only in Peachtree Premium and Peachtree Complete editions.

When you create a Master Stock item and designate its various attributes, Peachtree creates Substock items for each category you determine. In our example, instead of creating new and used versions of each lawn mower, we can set up one Master Stock item, assign it to either the new or used version of the Sales and Cost of Sales accounts, and then use the Item Attributes tab to create new and used versions of the item. The Item Attributes tab becomes available only if you are working with a Master Stock item. Use the following steps to create a Master Stock item:

1. **In the Name box under Primary Attributes, type a name that describes the distinction you're making for the item.**

   In the example, we typed New/Used.

2. **In the ID box, type an ID that will identify the Substock item.**

   Peachtree will append this ID to the ID of the Master Stock Item.

3. **In the Description box, type a description for the Substock item.**

   We typed N and New for the first Substock item and U and Used for the second Substock item.

4. **Click the Add button.**

   The ID and Description will appear in the box immediately below the ID and Description boxes, and the *full* item ID will appear in the bottom of the box in the Created Substock Items list.

5. **Repeat Steps 2–4 for each Substock item.**

   Peachtree creates separate entries for each substock item; you'll see these entries if you click the lookup list indicator next to the Item ID field. This method makes creating items with similar characteristics quick and easy.

6. **Click the Save button to save both the Master Stock Items and each of the substock items you created.**

You can't sell Master Stock items; instead you sell one of the Substock items. Because you don't sell Master Stock items, Peachtree doesn't track the Last Unit Cost, the UPC/SKU, or any quantity information shown on the General tab of the Maintain Inventory Items window.

During reporting, you can summarize report information for Substock items by filtering most inventory reports to show only Master Stock Items. For example, if you print the Inventory Profitability Report and filter it for Master Stock items, you see the Master Stock item and numbers that are the totals for all associated Substock items. On reports, you can't filter for particular substock items.

In the Beginning (Balance, That Is) . . .

Chances are, you've been in business for some time and have a current stock of inventory goods. If so and you are setting up your Peachtree company for the first time, you need to enter beginning balances for the items you have on hand.

To enter inventory item beginning balances, follow these steps:

1. **Choose Maintain⇨Inventory Items.**

   The Maintain Inventory Items window appears.

2. **From the General tab, click the Beginning Balances button (in the lower-right corner of the window).**

   The Inventory Beginning Balances dialog box appears, as shown in Figure 11-5.

Figure 11-5: Only stock items and assemblies appear in the Inventory Beginning Balance dialog box.

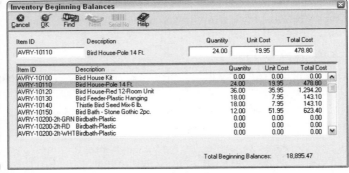

3. **In the list box, click the inventory item.**

   The item appears at the top.

4. **Enter a Quantity and the Unit Cost, which is the price you paid for the unit.**

   If you bought the items at a lot (bulk) price and don't know the cost of each one, skip the unit cost and enter the total cost you paid for the goods. Peachtree divides the total cost by the quantity and displays the result in the Unit Cost box.

5. **Repeat Steps 3 and 4 for each inventory item in which you have stock.**

6. **Click OK to update the inventory balance.**

Puttin' Them Together, Takin' Them Apart

Some stuff is made up of pieces of other stuff. Peachtree calls the pieces *components* and the complete items *assemblies*. Maybe your company sells bird feeders as a standalone product or as part of a package deal that includes a post, a hook, and birdseed. The package deal is an assembly. Or, maybe you sell a "doobob." (Elaine, that one's for you!) This doobob is made up of several thingamajigs and a couple of whatchamacallits. You don't actually sell thingamajigs or whatchamacallits (components) to your customers, but you still need to keep track of their quantities so you know how many doobobs (assemblies) you can make. In either situation, you create the assembled items by building them out of a list of component parts, both in your physical inventory and in your virtual store.

Peachtree Premium for Distribution and Peachtree Premium for Manufacturing editions also include work tickets to help track the build progress of an assembled item. Work tickets contain information about what's needed to build an assembly and whether you have all the items available. You can use work tickets to follow a build through its process, and you can check off the build steps as they are completed.

Creating a bill of materials

The bill of materials is a list of the individual parts that make up assemblies. Before you can create an assembly item, you need to make sure that each component part is set up in Peachtree.

After you use an assembly on a transaction, you can't add or remove component items from the bill of materials unless you are using Peachtree Premium for Manufacturing edition or Peachtree Premium for Distribution edition. If you're using any of the other editions, you need to create a new assembly item to change component parts.

Create a bill of materials by following these steps:

1. **Choose Maintain⇨Inventory Items to display the Maintain Inventory Items window.**

2. **Create the inventory item ID, description, and other information.**

   Make sure that you choose Assembly as the Item Class.

3. **Click the Bill of Materials tab to display a screen like the one in Figure 11-6.**

   Because assemblies are made up of other components, you need to use the Bill of Materials tab to list the component items. Assemblies must have at least one component (Item ID) listed in the bill of materials.

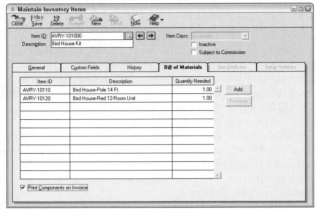

Figure 11-6:
Assemblies
must have
at least one
item listed in
the bill of
materials.

4. **Select or enter the first item to be included in the assembly.**

   Peachtree automatically fills in the description, but you can change the description.

5. **Enter a Quantity Needed to build one assembly.**

6. **Repeat Steps 4 and 5 for each component item.**

   If you run out of lines on the bill of materials list and have additional components, click the Add button. Peachtree inserts a blank line above the current item.

7. **If you want Peachtree to print the list of the individual components on the invoice, check the Print Components on Invoice box.**

8. **Click Save to save the assembly item.**

Building assemblies

When you build an assembly item, Peachtree takes the individual components and reduces their quantity on hand. Peachtree does not allow negative component quantities when building assemblies. Therefore, you need enough component parts in stock to build the requested number of assemblies.

When building an assembly, Peachtree generates a *debit* entry for the *assembly's* inventory GL account and *credits* the *component's* inventory GL account for the cost of the assembly items.

Follow these steps to build assemblies:

1. **Choose Tasks⇨Assemblies.**

2. **In the Item ID lookup box, select the assembly item ID.**

   Peachtree displays each assembly component along with the current quantity on hand.

3. **In the Reference box, enter an optional reference number or any piece of information to identify this transaction, perhaps your initials.**

   Peachtree doesn't require reference numbers, but making sure that every transaction you enter into Peachtree has some type of a reference number is a good idea.

4. **Choose the transaction date, which is typically the date the changes in your inventory occurred.**

5. **Select an Action to Build or Unbuild the assembly.**

   You might want to "unbuild" an assembly, for example, if you need to sell the individual components.

6. **Enter the build or unbuild Quantity.**

   Whether you're building or unbuilding, enter a positive number. As you enter the quantity you want to build, the assembly New Qty on Hand amount changes, as well as the component quantity required. If you're unbuilding assemblies, Peachtree shows the component item quantity returned to stock.

7. **Enter a Reason to build the assemblies.**

   You don't *have* to enter a reason. No doubt, you know exactly right now why you're building them, but will you remember six months from now?

   Optionally, select an employee name from the Supervisor list. The Supervisor is the person overseeing the assembly build or unbuild.

8. **Click Save to record the transaction.**

Making Inventory Adjustments

Let's face it; inventory counts get out of whack sometimes. Items get damaged, lost, or stolen. Sometimes, for reasons unknown, you might find several products that you didn't know you had, stashed away in a corner. So periodically, you'll need to adjust your inventory.

Whether you take a physical inventory count of all your goods, or just need to adjust the quantity on hand of a single product, you use Peachtree's Inventory Adjustment feature.

Follow these steps to make adjustments to your inventory:

1. **Choose Tasks⇨Inventory Adjustments to display the Inventory Adjustments window you see in Figure 11-7.**

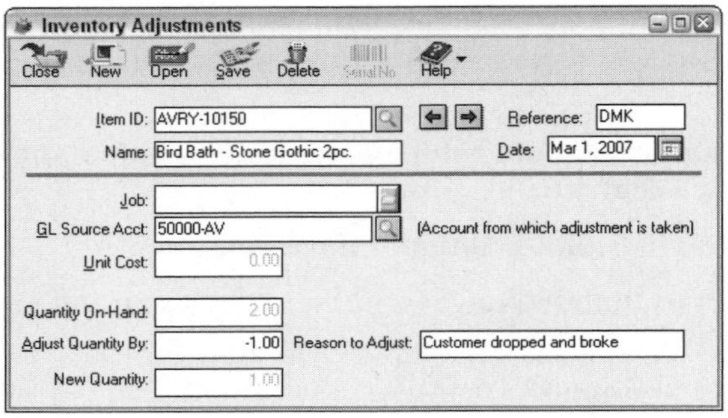

Figure 11-7:
To reduce quantity on hand, enter a negative quantity.

(Inventory Adjustments window screenshot)

Item ID: AVRY-10150   Reference: DMK
Name: Bird Bath - Stone Gothic 2pc.   Date: Mar 1, 2007
Job:
GL Source Acct: 50000-AV   (Account from which adjustment is taken)
Unit Cost: 0.00
Quantity On-Hand: 2.00
Adjust Quantity By: -1.00   Reason to Adjust: Customer dropped and broke
New Quantity: 1.00

2. **Enter a Reference number or any piece of information to identify this transaction, perhaps your initials.**

Peachtree doesn't require reference numbers, but making sure that every transaction you enter into Peachtree has some type of a reference number is a good idea.

3. **Select a Date for the inventory adjustment.**

4. **If you use Peachtree's job costing, select the job (and optionally, the phase or cost code) to which you want to charge the adjustment.**

Chapter 12 tells you all about job costing.

5. **Choose the GL Source Account you want to charge for the adjustment cost.**

If you decrease the item quantity, Peachtree debits the GL Source Account and credits the Inventory Account you listed in the Maintain Inventory Items window for the item. If you increase the item quantity, Peachtree credits the GL Source Account and debits the item's Inventory Account.

6. **Enter a Unit Cost.**

The Unit Cost defaults to the last purchase price you entered in the system. If you use the Inventory Adjustment transaction to *increase* your inventory count, you can change the unit cost. If you're *reducing* the quantity on hand, however, the unit cost field becomes disabled. Peachtree determines the cost of the adjustment based on the item's costing method at the time of the adjustment.

The unit cost is very important! Not putting in a cost can throw off your entire inventory valuation.

7. **In the Adjust Quantity By box, type a quantity to adjust.**

   You enter the quantity as a negative number if you need to decrease your quantity on hand. Peachtree displays the new quantity on hand.

8. **Optionally, in the Reason to Adjust box, describe why you're creating the transaction (for example, damaged or annual inventory).**

   You may know quite well why you're creating this adjustment, but will you remember later?

9. **Click Save to save the transaction.**

Adjusting Prices

One day you suddenly realize you haven't raised the prices on your products for a long time. Your costs have gone up and you know you have to pass some of that increase on to your customers. We know this isn't a step you take lightly. After all, you still want to be competitive, but you *are* in the business to make money, *not lose it.* So you make the decision to increase your prices.

Originally, you entered the sales prices when you created the inventory item in the Maintain Inventory Items window. You *could* go back to the Maintain Inventory Items window and pull each item up individually, change the sales prices, and then save the inventory item again.

Oh no, you say! I have too many inventory items to change the prices individually. Isn't there a faster way? Yes. Peachtree provides an easy way to update prices on all your inventory items, a range of items, or a single item. For example, you can mark up sales prices for all your stock items by 10 percent. You can even adjust the prices for only the products you purchase from a specific vendor. Peachtree allows you to adjust the item sales prices up or down.

Make a backup before you change item prices.

To adjust sales prices, follow these steps:

1. **Choose Maintain➪Item Prices to display the Maintain Item Prices – Filter Selection dialog box you see in Figure 11-8.**

2. **Enter any desired filter information.**

   The Filter Selection box gives you lots of different ways to select the products that need a price increase. If you don't choose any settings from the filter box, Peachtree assumes you want to change the price of *all* your products. However, you can select just stock items, or stock items you purchase from vendor JONES-01, or only the products that cost more than $10 but less than $50, or . . . you get the idea. You can select any of these combinations from the Filter Selection box. In Figure 11-9, we changed the price on only our plastic birdbaths.

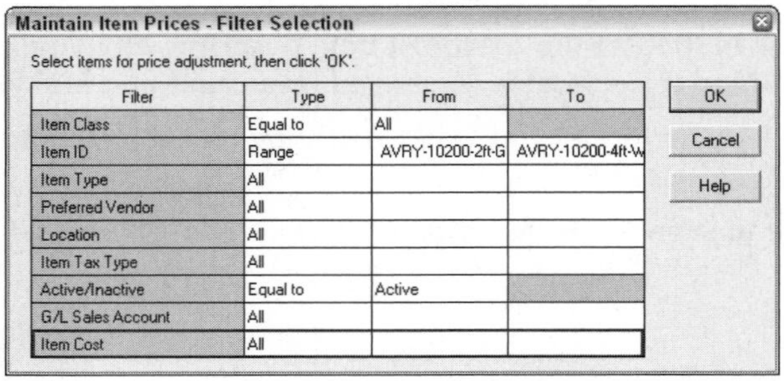

Figure 11-8:
Adjust
inventory
sales prices
for all or
some of
your items.

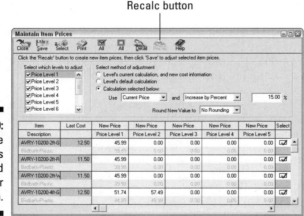

3. **Click OK to display the Maintain Item Prices window, shown in Figure 11-9.**

Figure 11-9:
Peachtree
displays
items based
on your filter
selection.

4. **Because Peachtree assumes that you want to change all ten pricing levels, you have to remove the check mark next to each price level that you do not want to change.**

   Now you have to make some decisions regarding your method of adjustment. Do you want to adjust your price levels manually or through calculations?

5. **Select an adjustment method:**

   - **Level's current calculation and new cost information:** Selected price levels and items that use cost or level one in calculating the price are recalculated based on the current cost or the updated level-one price.

   - **Level's default calculation:** Each price level and item selected are recalculated using the calculation in Inventory Item Defaults. This method overrides any customized calculations you may have set up for individual items in Maintain Inventory Items.

   - **Calculation selected below:** If you're using a calculation for changing your prices, select the Calculation selected below method and then click the Use arrow and choose an adjustment method: Current Price or Last Cost. Some companies mark up their products by a flat percentage, say 25 percent over cost. In that case, they'd select the Last Cost option. If you want to increase the current sales price, say a $1.00 item that you now want to sell it for $1.15, you'd choose the Current Price option.

6. **If you selected the Calculation selected below method, follow Steps 7 and 8. If not, jump ahead to Step 9.**

7. **Choose a markup method and enter an amount or percentage to mark up the item.**

   Peachtree allows you to change prices on the selected items by an amount or a percentage. If you choose Amount, enter the amount as a positive or negative dollar amount. If you choose Percent, enter the amount as a positive or negative percentage (for example, enter 6 for a 6-percent markup).

   Enter a negative number if you want to mark down the current price.

   When you modify and save the calculation method in the Item Prices box, Peachtree retains that calculation as the default for the item in Maintain Inventory Items.

8. **Select a method for rounding the new prices:**

   - **Next Dollar:** Peachtree rounds the item prices up to the nearest dollar amount. For example, if you increased the price of a product you previously sold for $11.60 by 15 percent, the calculated price is $13.34, but Peachtree rounds the new price up to $14.00.

   - **Specific Cent:** Use this if you want to round all prices up to a specified cent level. For example, at a 95-cent price level your products would sell for 5.95, 7.95, 11.95, and so on. If you choose Specific Cent, specify the cents (95 in our example) in the Amount box.

   - **Do Not Round:** Select this if you don't want the prices rounded.

9. **Click the Recalc toolbar button to see the new item prices, or you can manually change individual prices.**

> *TIP*
>
> Click the Detail button to display additional information about an item or click the Print button to print a report of your proposed price adjustments.

10. **Click Save to record the new prices.**

11. **Click Close to close the Maintain Item Prices dialog box.**

When Does Peachtree Assign a Cost to Items?

We'll be honest here. This section is Boring with a capital *B*. You certainly don't have to read this information, but our experience shows that many clients want to know how Peachtree's inventory system works — not just the mechanics of entering items or transactions, but what's happening behind the scenes. We don't give you any steps or tasks to accomplish — just some plain old facts about inventory.

This whole inventory state of affairs can be confusing. You've probably already noticed that Peachtree's inventory module is perfect for a buy/sell situation, where you purchase a product and then resell it, but it doesn't work very well for tracking raw materials used in production, especially if scrap is involved. Add that factor to all the different item transactions that can affect the cost, and sometimes the entire picture becomes blurred.

Peachtree calculates the value of inventory items on a daily basis. To ensure that increases to inventory are posted before decreases to inventory, Peachtree posts transactions in the following order:

1. Purchases

2. Payments

3. Increase adjustments

4. Assembly builds (for an assembly item)

5. Sales returns

6. Receipts return

7. Assembly unbuilds (for a component item)

8. Purchase returns

9. Payment returns

10. Assembly unbuilds (for an assembly item)

11. Sales

12. Receipts

13. Decrease adjustments

14. Assembly builds (for a component item)

Peachtree creates three types of system-generated adjustments: the purchase return adjustment, the assembly unbuild adjustment, and the system cost adjustment. You can't erase these types of adjustments. They appear in the Inventory Adjustment Journal and on the Item Costing Report. The reference for a system cost adjustment is SysCost, the reference for a purchase return adjustment is the reference number of the purchase transaction (usually the invoice number), and the reference for the assembly unbuild adjustment is the reference number of the assembly unbuild transaction.

Figure 11-10 shows an inventory adjustment journal with a system-generated cost (SysCost) adjustment.

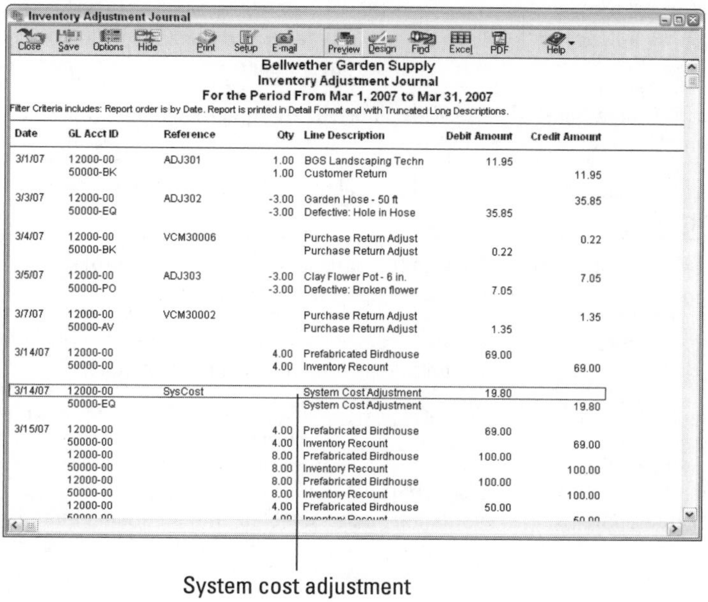

Figure 11-10: See system-generated adjustments in the Inventory Adjustment Journal.

System cost adjustment

Reporting on Your Inventory

Here comes the spiel you may have seen in many other chapters. . . . While it would be nice to print a sample of every report Peachtree offers, (especially in this chapter because Peachtree has a number of valuable inventory reports), there simply isn't space in this book to do so. So, in Table 11-2, we provide you with a description of the reports that pertain to maintaining your inventory. (Chapter 14 describes how to print and customize reports.) Many inventory reports include only stock and assembly item information.

Table 11-2	Reports Related to Inventory
Report Name	**What It Does**
Assemblies Adjustment Journal	Shows built and unbuilt assembly transactions in journal format.
Assembly List	Lists each assembly with the components that make up the assembly.
Buyer Report	Lists each item along with the buyer. You can sort this report by buyer ID, item ID, or item description, or preferred vendor ID.
Component Use List	Lists component items and the assemblies on which they are used. Sort by component item or assembly item ID.
Cost of Goods Sold Journal	Shows, in journal format, the cost of goods sold.
Inventory Adjustment Journal	Lists, in journal format, inventory adjustments.
Inventory Profitability Report	Lists each item with units sold, cost, gross profit, adjustments, and percent of total.
Inventory Reorder Worksheet	Displays reorder amounts for inventory items when they fall below the specified minimum stock amount.
Inventory Stock Status Report	Lists items, quantity on hand, and reorder quantity.
Inventory Unit Activity Report	Lists items' beginning quantity; units sold, purchased, adjusted, and assembled; and an ending quantity on hand.

Report Name	What It Does
Inventory Valuation Report	Shows the quantity on hand, value, average cost, and percent of inventory value for all in-stock items.
Item Costing Report	Lists each inventory item with costing information for quantities received and sold.
Item List	Lists each item, item description, class, type, and quantity on hand.
Item Master List	Lists items with detail information as entered in Maintain Inventory Items.
Item Price List	Lists each item with quantity on hand and each available sales price.
Physical Inventory List	A worksheet you can use to check the actual quantity of items on hand versus what the system reports on hand.
Serial Number History Report	Lists serialized items along with their status. Sort this report by item ID or description or by serial number.

One report you should definitely know is the Inventory Valuation report, which shows the quantity on hand, value, average cost, and percent of inventory value for all in-stock items. To arrive at the percent of inventory value number, Peachtree takes the value of the item divided by the total value of items that have a positive item value. The example in Table 11-3 shows you how the percent-to-total value works.

Table 11-3	Sample Inventory Valuation		
Transaction #	Quantity	Total Item Value	% of Inventory
1	4	10.00	33.33
2	1	−5.00	
3	2	20.00	66.67
	Total	25.00	

In Table 11-3, Peachtree calculates the percent of inventory on the percent of the positive item values (items 1 and 3), which equal $10.00 + $20.00, or $30.00.

Visit this book's Web site for more information on Peachtree.

Chapter 12

Tracking Project Costs

In This Chapter

▶ Creating estimates and jobs

▶ Creating phase codes and cost codes

▶ Using jobs for invoicing

Some businesses lend themselves well to organizing work by projects, and for the purposes of this discussion, *project* is synonymous with *job*. In particular, these companies perform the same general type of work for each customer — that is, all their projects are similar. Companies who use *job costing* (assigning costs to jobs) in their business want to track expenses and revenues for each job so that they can determine the net profit from the job. These companies often bid for the services they sell by providing an estimate. Then, if they get the work, they want to compare the estimated costs to the actual costs so that they can improve their estimating skills for future jobs and increase revenues.

In this chapter, we describe the job costing features available in Peachtree Premium and Peachtree Complete. In Peachtree Accounting, you can create jobs but not phases or cost codes, which are fields that enable you to capture more details about jobs. Peachtree First Accounting doesn't support job costing.

Understanding Job Costing

What kinds of companies use job costing? Well, job costing is widely used in the construction industry, but it also can be used by a variety of other businesses, such as convention planners, party planners, landscapers, cleaning services, and printers (the people who produce things like letterhead).

Do you need to use job costing? If the jobs you perform tend to stretch out over time, you're more likely to use job costing. However, if you complete a job in a short period of time — a week or less — you probably don't need to use Peachtree's job costing, because the time you'd spend entering job information would exceed the value you'd receive from that information.

Creating custom fields for jobs

In Chapter 4, we set up defaults for other areas of Peachtree; for jobs, you can establish only custom fields because this feature has no other preferences to set. Choose Maintain⇨Default Information⇨Jobs to display the Job Defaults dialog box. Place a check mark next to any of the five field labels to enable the custom field. Then type a label description for each custom field. Click OK when you're finished.

Reviewing job examples

Before you dive in and start creating things, we think you'd benefit by examining a few examples. We think that you might better understand the order in which we choose to create things after you read these examples.

Jobs are a method of organizing accounting information. Throughout this chapter, we explain the various facets of jobs by using one example: a company that builds swimming pools. Consider each swimming pool the company builds to be a separate job.

Phases

You can use *phases* to further break down the costs of a project. Phases are optional; use them only if you want to organize your project in some way and look at costs and revenues at a more detailed level. In the case of our swimming pool builder, we might use five phases:

- ✔ Design
- ✔ Permits
- ✔ Site preparation
- ✔ Installation
- ✔ Finishing/landscaping

Peachtree allows you to assign each phase to a cost type: Labor, Materials, Subcontract Labor, Equipment Rental, and Other.

Cost codes

If you need a further breakdown of any of these cost types for a particular phase — for example, you may need to track the costs of specific materials such as concrete and tile — you can create *cost codes*. If you choose to create cost codes for a phase, you won't assign a cost type to the phase. Instead, you can assign a cost type to each cost code: Labor, Materials, Subcontract Labor, Equipment Rental, and Other.

Cost codes, like phases, are optional. You may find that you need cost codes for only one cost type, perhaps Labor. You can set up specific cost codes for Material, such as tile, lumber, and concrete, and then assign those cost codes as needed to phases. For phases that don't need a cost code, you can simply use the phase — and its cost type.

If you use cost codes, we recommend that you try to use the same ones for every project. That way, you can set up one set of cost codes and assign them, as needed, to any phase of any project. You may also be able to use the same phases (or a subset of phases) for each project.

Consider one more example. Suppose that you manage an apartment complex, and you want to monitor the costs associated with each building on the property. You could set up each building as a job. Then, as you make purchases for a particular building, you can assign the purchases to that building. Your job reports show you the costs of each building in the complex. Note that we haven't suggested using phases or cost codes because they're optional.

Suppose, however, that you want to track costs for the complex at a more detailed level — by apartment. In that case, you could set up the apartments in each building as phases and assign expenses to particular apartments.

"So what's your point? Why are you telling me all this now?" you ask. Well, when setting up a job in Peachtree, you must decide whether the job uses phases. Similarly, when setting up a phase you must decide whether the phase uses cost codes. You need to understand what each entity is so that you know what to create and the order in which to create things.

Coding Costs

To create a cost code, follow these steps:

1. **Choose Maintain⇨Job Costs⇨Cost Codes to display the Maintain Cost Codes window (see Figure 12-1).**

2. **In the Cost Code ID box, type an ID (up to 20 alphanumeric characters).**

3. **In the Description box, type a description for the cost code.**

4. **Select a cost type for the cost code to categorize it in a general way.**

   You can select Labor, Materials, Equipment Rental, Subcontractors, or Other.

5. **Click the Save button.**

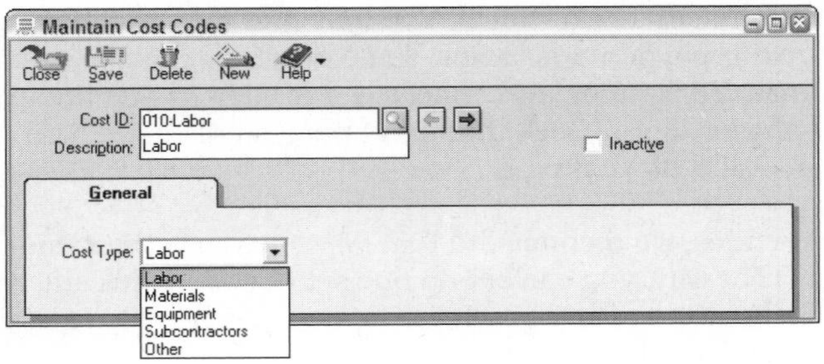

Figure 12-1:
Create a
cost code.

Repeat these steps to set up other cost codes you need for your jobs.

If you no longer need a cost code, you can mark it inactive. To do so, redisplay the cost code in the Maintain Cost Codes window and add a check mark to the Inactive box.

Establishing Phases

To create a phase, follow these steps:

1. **Choose Maintain⇨Job Costs⇨Phases to display the Maintain Phases window (see Figure 12-2).**

2. **In the Phase ID box, type an ID (up to 20 alphanumeric characters).**

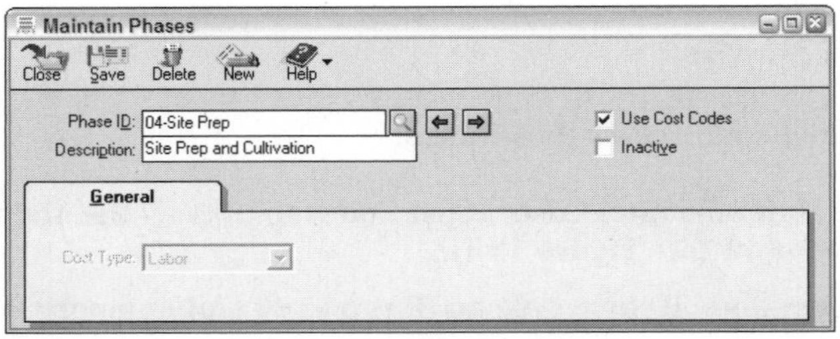

Figure 12-2:
Create a
phase that
uses cost
codes.

3. **In the Description box, type a description for the phase.**

4. **Decide whether to use cost codes:**

   • If you plan to use cost codes for the phase, place a check mark in the Use Cost Codes box. Peachtree disables the ability to select a cost type.

- If you don't plan to use cost codes, choose a cost type for the phase to categorize it in a general way. You can select Labor, Materials, Equipment Rental, Subcontractors, or Other.

5. Click the Save button.

Repeat these steps to set up other phases you need for your jobs.

If you no longer need a phase, you can mark it inactive. To do so, redisplay the phase in the Maintain Phases window and add a check mark to the Inactive box.

Creating Jobs and Estimates

To set up a job, follow these steps:

1. Choose Maintain⇨Job Costs⇨Jobs to display the Maintain Jobs window (see Figure 12-3).

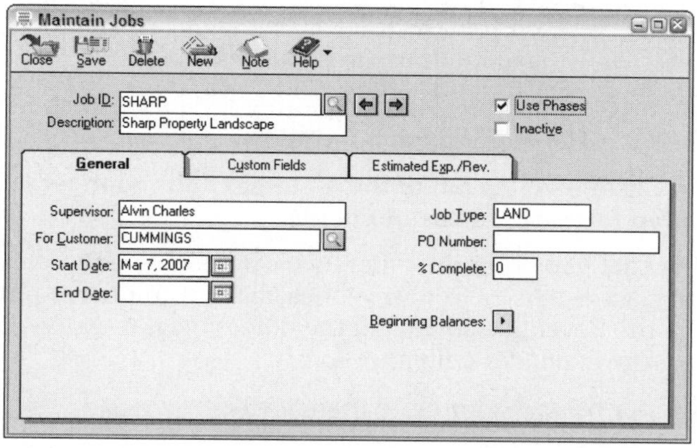

Figure 12-3:
Set up a job in this window.

2. Type the job ID.

You can use up to 20 alphanumeric characters, excluding the asterisk (*), the question mark (?), and the plus sign (+). IDs are case sensitive, so POOL-1, for example, is different from pool-1.

3. In the Description box, provide a description for the job.

4. If the job uses phases, place a check mark in the Use Phases check box.

5. On the General tab, fill in any pertinent information, all of which is optional.

Peachtree doesn't limit the number of jobs you can assign to customers, but you don't *need* to assign jobs to customers. If you don't need jobs for any reason other than charging customers for expenses, you can use time and expense slips. See Chapter 10 for details.

6. If you work on the job before you enter it in Peachtree and you have historical revenues and expenses for the job, do the following:

You may want to read the next two steps before entering beginning balances. If you choose to use phases and cost codes with your job, you can follow these steps to enter beginning balances by phase and cost code.

   a. Click the Beginning Balances button to display the Job Beginning Balances window.

   b. Use the Job Entries tab to enter beginning balances. From the Job Balances tab, you can view the beginning balance of all jobs in the system.

   c. Enter a date for the balance you intend to enter and a beginning balance in either the Expenses column or the Revenues column.

   Make sure that you enter the difference between revenues and expenses. If you subtract expenses from revenues, and the number is positive, enter it in the Revenues column; if the difference is negative, enter the amount in the Expenses column.

   d. When you finish entering beginning balances, click Save to redisplay the Maintain Jobs window.

7. Click the Custom Fields tab of the Maintain Jobs window to supply information for enabled custom fields.

Make sure that you enter the difference between revenues and expenses. If you subtract expenses from revenues and the number is positive, enter it in the Revenues column; if the difference is negative, enter the amount in the Expenses column.

You can enter balances for more than one date.

8. When you finish entering beginning balances, click Save to redisplay the Maintain Jobs window.

9. Click the Custom Fields tab of the Maintain Jobs window to supply information for enabled custom fields.

10. Click the Estimated Exp./Rev. tab and use the Lookup list indicators (the magnifying glass) to enter estimated expenses and revenues.

These estimates are optional. In Figure 12-4, you see the Estimated Exp./Rev. tab for a job that uses phases. If you don't use phases with your job, you see only two boxes: one for total estimated expenses and one for total estimated revenues.

11. Click Save to store the job's information.

Job reports and masking

Some of the job reports enable you to filter jobs using a job mask, which can be useful if you have several different characteristics about each job that you want to track. For one type of information you want to track, you can use the Job Type field. For the rest, you can use a coding scheme for the Job ID. Suppose, for example, that you work in three cities — Tampa, St. Petersburg, and Clearwater — doing design, planting, and maintenance. You also want to differentiate jobs for residential and commercial customers. You can use the Job Type field to store the information about design, planting, and maintenance. Then you can create a coding scheme for the job ID that will enable you to use masking to print reports that display

information on a subset of jobs. In the example, you might want to create a ten-character Job ID that is composed of one character (T, S, or C) representing the city, one character (C or R) representing commercial or residential, four characters representing the customer's name, and four characters representing a job number. On most job reports, you can filter by Job Type and then mask for Tampa jobs by typing T********* in the Job Mask field. You could mask for commercial jobs in Clearwater by typing CC******** or residential jobs in St. Petersburg by typing SR********. To use the mask, you supply asterisks for the characters that can change; the total number of characters you type is equal to the length of the job ID.

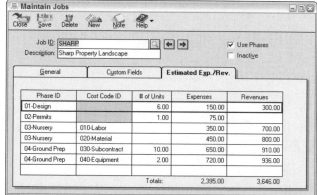

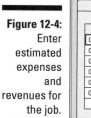

Figure 12-4: Enter estimated expenses and revenues for the job.

Phase ID	Cost Code ID	# of Units	Expenses	Revenues
01-Design		6.00	150.00	300.00
02-Permits		1.00	75.00	
03-Nursery	010-Labor		350.00	700.00
03-Nursery	020-Material		450.00	800.00
04-Ground Prep	030-Subcontract	10.00	650.00	910.00
04-Ground Prep	040-Equipment	2.00	720.00	936.00
		Totals:	2,395.00	3,646.00

When you complete a job, you can mark it inactive. To do so, redisplay the job in the Maintain Jobs window and add a check mark to the Inactive box.

Assigning Jobs to Transactions

Okay, you've set up jobs (and maybe phases and cost codes, too). Now you can use them when you create purchases and invoices.

Purchasing

Suppose that you're buying something to use on a job and you want to assign the expense to the job. To do so, you use the Purchase Orders window, the Purchases/Receive Inventory window, or the Payments window. The method is the same, regardless of the window you choose. In the following steps, we show you the process in the Purchases/Receive Inventory window:

1. **Choose Tasks➪Purchases/Receive Inventory to display the Purchases/ Receive Inventory window (see Figure 12-5).**

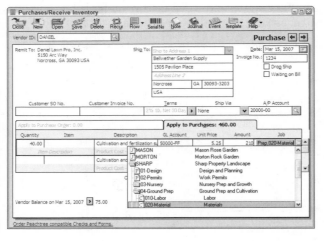

Figure 12-5:
Assign a job to a purchase of anything but stock inventory items.

2. **Fill in the purchase information at the top of the window as you would for any purchase.**

3. **In the bottom portion of the window, enter the information for the item that you're purchasing.**

You can't purchase a stock inventory item to use on a job. If you already own a stock item that you want to use on a job, you can enter an inventory adjustment (see Chapter 11), or you can place the item on the customer's invoice. If you invoice the customer, you don't need to make the inventory adjustment.

4. **In the Job column, use the lookup list indicator (this time it looks like a file folder) to assign the line to a job.**

   If the job uses phases or cost codes, you see a folder in the list representing the job. You need to double-click the folder to open it and select the appropriate phase or cost code.

   As you can see in Figure 12-4, when you open the Job list, the box partially overlays the Amount box. (For details on filling in a purchase, see Chapter 5.)

5. **Continue entering lines as needed; you can include lines that you assign to jobs and lines that you don't assign to jobs on the same purchase.**

6. **Click the Save button to save the purchase.**

Invoicing customers

By default, Peachtree sets up purchases you assign to jobs as reimbursable expenses that you can include on an invoice to a customer. You also can choose not to include these reimbursable expenses on customer bills.

Follow these steps to work with reimbursable expenses generated by assigning jobs to purchases or payments:

1. **Choose Tasks⇨Sales/Invoicing to display the Sales/Invoicing window.**

2. **Fill in the invoice information at the top of the window as you would for any invoice.**

   For details on filling in an invoice, see Chapter 7.

3. **In the bottom portion of the window, enter one line of information for each of the items that you're selling.**

4. **In the Job column, use the list box selector (it looks like a file folder) to assign the lines to a job, as appropriate.**

5. **To include a reimbursable expense on an invoice, click the Apply Tickets/Expenses button in the lower-left corner of the window to display the Apply Tickets/Reimbursable Expenses window (see Figure 12-6).**

   You won't know if reimbursable expenses exist for a customer until you click the Apply Tickets/Expenses button.

6. **Click the Reimbursable Expenses tab to see expenses you entered and assigned to a job in the Purchases/Inventory window and the Payments window.**

   (If you ignored our advice and assigned an expense to a job in the Write Checks window, that expense will also appear on the Reimbursable Expenses tab.)

WriteUp button

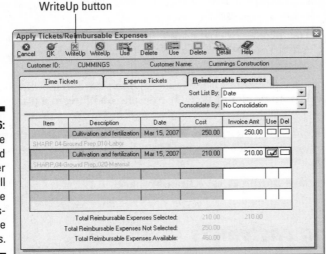

7. **To include a reimbursable expense on the invoice, click the Use check box next to that reimbursable expense.**

8. **To build some profit into a reimbursable expense, change the amount in the Invoice Amt column.**

   To mark up or down a group of reimbursable expenses, click the WriteUp toolbar button to display the Select Reimbursables to Write Up/Down dialog box, where you can identify reimbursable expenses to mark up by either a dollar amount or a percentage.

If you change your mind after marking up reimbursable expenses, you can click the Remove WriteUp button that appears immediately to the right of the WriteUp button. (We know it's confusing, because they both seem to be called WriteUp, but you can point your mouse at each button to display a ToolTip that describes each button's function. The Remove WriteUp button's image is the universal "No" sign.)

When you use reimbursable expenses, keep these points in mind:

✔ You can delete reimbursable expenses from the Apply Tickets/ Reimbursable Expenses window if you decide not to bill the client for them. Place a check mark in the Del box to the right of the expense. Deleting the reimbursable expense does *not* delete the transaction that created the reimbursable expense. Instead, deleting in the Apply Tickets/Reimbursable Expenses window breaks the tie between the reimbursable expense and the customer.

You can't undo deleting here. After you delete a reimbursable expense, the connection between the reimbursable expense and the customer is *permanently* broken unless you erase the purchase or payment that created the reimbursable expense and reenter it.

↙ Be aware that deleting or using a reimbursable expense makes it disappear from the Apply Tickets/Reimbursable Expenses window. If you use a reimbursable expense and subsequently delete the line from the invoice, the reimbursable expense *does not* reappear in the window. If you mistakenly use a reimbursable expense and post the invoice, delete the invoice and reenter it.

↙ You can edit a reimbursable expense you intend to bill to a customer by editing the purchase or payment that assigns the expense to a job. To find the transaction, open the window where you first created it — for example, the Purchases/Receive Inventory window — and click the Edit button.

Adding Overhead to a Job

To run your business, you incur certain expenses that accountants call *overhead* — expenses such as telephone, postage, and electricity. You can think of overhead expenses as expenses you incur even if you don't sell anything. (Of course, you wouldn't incur overhead for long if you didn't sell anything, because you'd go out of business, but you get our drift.)

If your company uses job costing, you probably want to divide your overhead and assign it to jobs. There's no standard method to do this in Peachtree, but you *can* do it. The method we're going to describe assumes that you know the amount of overhead to add to each job. It could be a percentage of the expenses you incur or an hourly rate. If you don't know, you need to ask your accountant to figure out the overhead burden rate for you.

After you have the rate from your accountant, you need to know your expenses by job so that you can apply the overhead burden rate to each job.

We suggest that you customize the Job Ledger report (choose Reports↪Jobs and select the Job Ledger report). On the Fields tab, include the following fields: Job ID, Job Description, Phase ID, Cost Code ID, Transaction Date, Transaction Description, Actual Expenses, and Hours with Totals. When you print the report, you have all the information you need to apply the burden rate to your expenses and then assign the overhead to various jobs. You might want to export the report to Excel and calculate the burden amount there (you know, burden rate times expense amount). For more information on customizing reports, see Chapter 14.

Okay. Now that you've calculated the overhead amount, enter the amount into Peachtree using a journal entry.

For this task, you need a suspense account. We use a suspense account to handle amounts that are temporary in nature. You can set up a suspense account as any kind of account: asset, liability, income, or expense. But we suggest that you make it an account you're likely to notice if it appears on reports because, ultimately, your suspense account shouldn't have a balance. For help in creating an account, see Chapter 3.

To assign overhead to a job, you make a journal entry. Don't worry — it's easy. (For more details on entering journal entries, see Chapter 17.) Follow these steps:

1. **Choose Tasks⇨General Journal Entry to display the General Journal Entry window (see Figure 12-7).**

2. **Supply a Date and a Reference number for the journal entry, and ignore the Reverse Transaction check box.**

3. **Supply two lines for every overhead amount you want to assign, choosing the Suspense account on both lines.**

4. **Assign the job to the Debit line, not the Credit line.**

5. **Click Save to save the entry.**

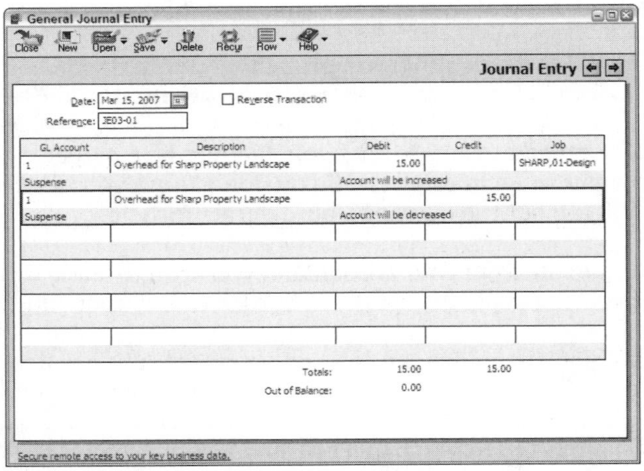

Figure 12-7:
Create the journal entry to assign overhead to jobs.

This journal entry debits and credits the same account, which makes the entry have no effect on your books. However, assigning the job to the debit side of the transaction allocates the overhead expense to the job.

Reporting on the Job

Table 12-1 shows a list of the other reports that relate to job costing. You can exclude balance forward information on the Job Ledger, the Job Profitability Report, and the Job Register. See Chapter 14 to find out how to print reports.

Table 12-1	Other Reports Related to Job Costing
Report Name	*What It Does*
Cost Code List	Lists all defined cost codes, along with their description and cost type.
Estimated Job Expenses	Shows estimated expenses, actual expenses, the difference by job, and if appropriate, the difference by phase and by cost code. Along with other filters, you can filter this report by cost code ID and by using a job mask.
Estimated Job Revenue	Shows estimated expenses, actual revenues, the difference by job, and if appropriate, the difference by phase and by cost code. Along with other filters, you can filter this report by cost code ID and by using a job mask.
Job Costs by Type	Shows estimated and actual expenses by cost type for jobs that have phases.
Job Estimates	For each job (and, if appropriate, phase and cost code), lists estimated units and expenses. Along with other filters, you can filter this report by cost code ID and by using a job mask.
Job Ledger	Shows all transactions that you've assigned to each job. Along with other filters, you can filter this report by cost code ID, using a job mask, and by vendor ID.
Job List	Lists each job's ID, description, the starting and ending dates for the job, the customer to whom you assign the job, and the percentage complete.
Job Master File List	Lists all the details you entered in the Maintain Jobs window for each job.
Job Profitability Report	Shows the actual expenses and revenues for each job — and phase and cost code, if appropriate. Along with other filters, you can filter this report by cost code ID, using a job mask, and by vendor ID.

(continued)

Table 12-1 *(continued)*

Report Name	What It Does
Job Register	Shows an overview of job transaction dollars as of a certain date. Along with other filters, you can filter this report by cost code ID, using a job mask, and by vendor ID.
Phase List	Lists all defined phases, along with their description, cost type, and whether the phase uses cost codes.
Unbilled Job Expense	Helps you identify existing reimbursable expenses that you can bill to a customer. Along with other filters, you can filter this report by cost code ID, using a job mask, and by vendor ID.

Visit this book's Web site for more information on Peachtree.

Part III
The Fancy Stuff

The 5th Wave   By Rich Tennant

"The new technology has really helped me get organized. I keep my project reports under the PC, budgets under my laptop, and memos under my pager."

In this part . . .

In this part, we cover many of the tasks you *don't* do every day. First, we show you how to customize Peachtree to make it work your way. Then we show you how to customize forms and produce and modify reports — after all, you put information *into* Peachtree, so you should be able to get it out and see the effects of your business habits. Then we cover reconciling the bank statement and the stuff you do monthly, quarterly, or annually. We also provide some real–life situations encountered by people just like you and ways you might handle similar situations.

Last, we show you how to easily keep your accounting information safe — a *very* important chapter. Why? Because you spend so much time putting stuff into Peachtree that it would be criminal to lose it just because your hard drive crashes or your office is robbed.

Chapter 13

Working with Forms

- -

In This Chapter

▶ Previewing and printing forms

▶ E-Mailing your forms

▶ Customizing your forms

- -

*I*t's important to understand the differences among the types of information you produce with Peachtree. Peachtree provides three types of documents: forms, reports, and financial statements. In this chapter, we discuss forms, which Peachtree defines as documents you exchange with your customers, vendors, or employees. You print these documents on preprinted forms or on blank paper.

Reports are typically specific to a module such as Accounts Payable or Payroll and provide feedback about one or more customers, vendors, employees, or inventory items. Financial statements tell you the overall value of your company and whether the company as a whole made or lost money. You can find out about reports in Chapter 14 and financial statements in Chapter 15.

You print forms on preprinted forms or on blank paper. You can purchase preprinted forms from your local printer, or you can use the offers you receive in your Peachtree software box. Chapter 21 lists Web contact information on a couple of sources for forms: Deluxe Forms and Peachtree Forms.

If you contact Deluxe Forms at 1-800-328-0304 and reference this book and discount code R03578, you'll receive 20 percent off your first order.

Printing Forms

You use essentially the same steps for printing all forms whether you're printing a quote, a purchase order, a check, or a customer invoice. Peachtree can print your forms one at a time or together in a batch. Peachtree also includes forms for printing customer, vendor, and employee labels as well as collection letters, 1099s, and various payroll forms such as W2s and 941 reports.

A variety of forms are available, and you can customize any form.

Previewing forms in the document window

Because Peachtree has several forms, you may want to see what your quote, purchase order, check, or invoice would look like in each form. You can use the Preview feature to examine the transaction:

1. **Display the transaction you want to preview on the screen.**

   If necessary, click the Open button and select a previously posted transaction.

2. **Click the drop-down arrow on the Print button and choose Preview.**

   The Preview Forms dialog box appears, listing the available forms (see Figure 13-1). The forms listed vary depending on the transaction type.

3. **If you want to change the form, do the following:**

   a. **Click the Change Form button.**

      Peachtree assumes that you want to use the same form you used the last time you printed, but the Change Form button lets you select a different form. The Preview Forms dialog box appears.

   b. **Select the form you want to print and then click OK.**

   c. **Click Preview.**

Print drop-down arrow   Change Form button

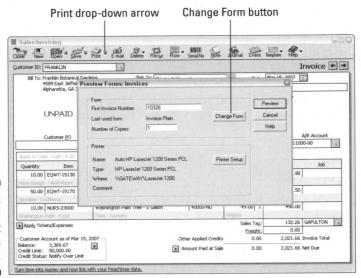

Figure 13-1: Choose the form that best suits your needs.

4. **Click anywhere on the form to enlarge the view; click a second time to enlarge the view even more (see Figure 13-2).**

   No need to strain your eyes. Whenever the mouse pointer turns into a magnifying glass, you can click to zoom in or out on the form — this feature works also in reports. See Chapter 14 for more information on reports.

   You can click the Close button if you need to make changes to the transaction. Peachtree redisplays the transaction window.

5. **To print the transaction on the selected form, click Print.**

   Peachtree prints the form, saves the transaction, and returns you to a blank transaction window.

Printing from the document window

In the preceding section, you discover how to preview and then print a document from the preview window. If you don't want to preview the document, you can print directly from the data entry window.

Print button   Magnify glass

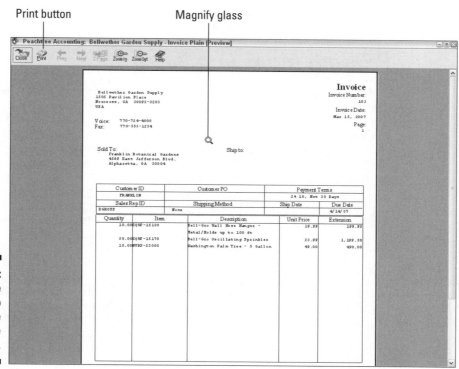

Figure 13-2:
Click the document to enlarge or reduce the view.

To print a form, follow these steps:

1. **With a document displayed in the window, click the Print button (or press Ctrl+P).**

   You'll see the Print Forms dialog box, like the one shown previously in Figure 13-1.

2. **Verify the transaction number, printer, number of copies, and form name.**

   If you did not manually enter a transaction number in the data entry screen, Peachtree automatically uses the next number.

   Peachtree maintains a different series of numbers for each form type. For example, checks have a different numbering system from purchase orders or customer invoices.

   To test the form alignment, click the Practice button to print practice forms. You'll see Xs and 9s on the form where words and numbers will appear.

3. **Click Print.**

   Peachtree automatically saves a transaction after printing. Saving a transaction posts the transaction and, if applicable, updates the general ledger as well.

Printing forms in a batch

Sometimes, when you're entering data such as invoices, you don't want to stop and go through the steps to print each invoice separately. In this case, you may like Peachtree's batch printing feature. If you want to print several invoices at the same time, create each invoice without assigning an invoice number and then click Save. Then, whenever you're ready to print your transaction, Peachtree can print all unnumbered invoices at the same time. You can batch print any form *except* receipts and deposit tickets.

The following steps show you how you can batch print forms such as statements, quotes, sales orders, purchase orders, and both A/P and P/R checks:

1. **Click Reports and select an area.**

2. **Select the type of form.**

   You can find forms in four report areas: Accounts Receivable, Accounts Payable, Payroll, and Mail Merge. (We cover mail merge in Chapter 14.)

Peachtree displays reports with an icon that looks like a piece of paper with lines on it and displays forms in small folders. Forms are at the bottom of the list.

3. **Click the forms folder to open it and display a list of forms.**

4. **Double-click the form you want to print.**

Peachtree displays an options dialog box specific to the form you selected. (See Figure 13-3.) The dialog box appearance varies according to the chosen form.

You can select a forms printing method also from the Print dialog box and select to send only e-mailed forms, only paper forms, or both. Peachtree looks at the default method for sending forms assigned to each vendor (Chapter 5) or customer (Chapter 7). The next section shows you how Peachtree handles e-mailing forms.

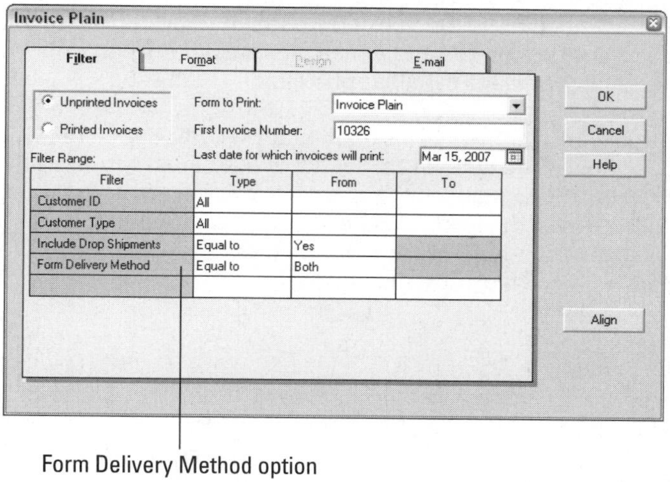

Figure 13-3: Select printing options from this dialog box.

Form Delivery Method option

5. **Verify the beginning transaction number, printer, number of copies, and form name, and then click OK.**

After printing the forms, Peachtree displays a dialog box asking whether the forms printed properly.

6. **Answer the dialog box by clicking Yes or No.**

If you click Yes, Peachtree assigns the numbers to the forms. If you click No, the forms remain unnumbered, and you need to reprint them.

E-Mailing Forms

Some customers or vendors prefer that you e-mail their forms rather than making the trek to the mailbox (or even *worse*, the post office). You can e-mail forms in a batch, or many transaction windows allow you to send e-mail copies in replace of or in addition to paper forms. Peachtree provides a place to store an e-mail address in the Maintain Customer or the Maintain Vendor screen. You have the option of e-mailing the form to the stored address or to one you type in.

Most forms are eligible for e-mailing. You can e-mail invoices, statements, collection letters, sales orders, and purchase orders. You can't e-mail deposit tickets, receipts, customer or vendor labels, any payroll forms, and for obvious reasons, vendor or payroll checks.

To generate e-mail in Peachtree, you must have a MAPI-compliant, default e-mail application installed on your computer. If your default e-mail system is AOL, you will not be able to send e-mail alerts from Peachtree because AOL is not a fully MAPI-compliant e-mail application.

During batch printing, if you are e-mailing forms, Peachtree provides several additional options. The E-mail tab, available with most forms, addresses how you want Peachtree to manage the printing. You decide if you want to e-mail only the form, e-mail the form plus generate a paper copy for your records, and a few other options. To see the options, click the E-mail tab of the form option window. (See Figure 13-4.)

Figure 13-4:
You can assign a different numbering sequence to e-mailed forms.

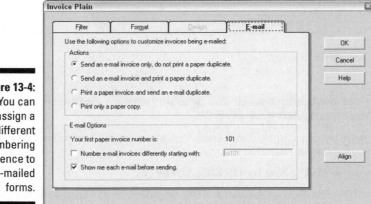

If you're not batch printing the forms you want to e-mail, you need to display the transaction:

1. **In the transaction window, for example, the Sales/Invoicing window, choose File⇨E-mail or click the E-mail button.**

   The E-Mail Forms window appears so that you can confirm the transaction number and the form name.

2. **Click Send.**

   Peachtree launches your e-mail program and automatically inserts the recipient information as stored in your customer or vendor file. If your Peachtree options specified to send a copy to a sales or buyers representative, their e-mail information appears in the Cc: line (see Figure 13-5).

3. **If you want to change the recipients, type a different e-mail address or click the address book icon and select a recipient from the address book.**

4. **Click Send.**

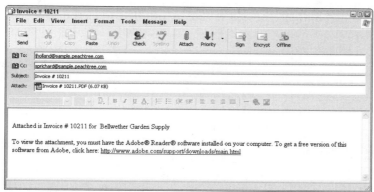

Figure 13-5:
The e-mail body contains a link to obtain a free PDF reader.

When e-mailing a form, Peachtree sends the form as a PDF (Portable Document Format) attachment. To view or print the form, the recipient must have the Adobe Reader software, which is a free download from the Internet at www.adobe.com/products/acrobat/readstep2.html.

Customizing Forms

You can customize any form to better meet your needs. You can move, add, or delete fields, change fonts, and even add graphical images.

Exploring the Form Designer

The Form Design window enables you to create customized forms or edit existing forms to match the needs of your business. To use the Form Designer, follow these steps:

1. **Choose Reports⇨Accounts Receivable** or the report area for the form you want to modify.

2. **In the report list, locate and click the folder containing the form you want to modify.**

   Because Peachtree lists forms after reports, you may need to scroll down the Report List a bit (see Figure 13-6).

3. **Click *once* on the form you want to modify and then click the Design button.**

   The selected report appears in Form Design view (see Figure 13-7).

If you accidentally double-click the desired form, Peachtree assumes you want to print it, not modify its design. It displays a dialog box containing filter and format options you can set before printing. Click the Cancel button, and be sure to click *only once* on the form you want to modify. Then you can click the Design button.

Maximize the design window for optimal viewing.

Design button

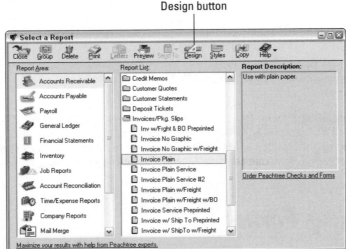

Figure 13-6:
Peachtree
displays a
list of
available
forms.

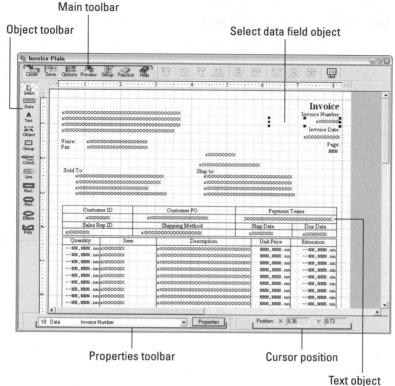

Figure 13-7:
A customer invoice in Design view.

The design window has two main parts: the toolbars and the design area, which displays Peachtree data fields, text fields, and other objects such as rectangles or pictures. Five toolbars appear on the design window. Each toolbar has a specific function:

- ✔ **Alignment toolbar:** Use this toolbar to line up two or more objects.
- ✔ **Main toolbar:** Use this toolbar to accomplish many common steps, including saving the form and closing the design window.
- ✔ **Object toolbar:** Use this toolbar to add new objects to the window.

  Use the Selection tool, the first tool on the Object toolbar, to select objects that you want to move, modify, or delete.

- ✔ **Properties toolbar:** Use this toolbar to determine an object's content, size, order, position, and appearance.
- ✔ **Cursor position toolbar:** Use this toolbar to determine the location of selected objects.

Everything on a form is a type of object. You can find data field objects, text field objects, text objects, shaped objects, and even grouped objects. Take a look at the first of two main object types you find on a form. A *data field object* is the most common object you see on a form. Peachtree obtains information, either from the Maintain window or from the Tasks window, and places it in data fields. Peachtree indicates data field objects with XXX's for words and NNN's for numbers.

The second most common form object is a *text object*. This is text that shows specific words, such as "Sold to" or "Thank you for your business." You can easily identify text objects because you just read them on the screen.

To modify any type of object, you first need to select the object. "Okay," you say, "but how do I know which object to modify?" Well, you click any object to select it. The object has eight small black box "handles" around it, and the Properties toolbar indicates the name of the selected object.

Moving objects

You won't throw your back out moving form design objects. You can move an object by selecting it and dragging it to a new location. If you select the wrong object, click anywhere in a blank area of the window to deselect the object.

You can move an object also by selecting it and using your arrow keys to move it to a new position. This technique works well when you want to move the object only a little bit.

Deleting objects

Deleting objects is easy, too. If you want to get rid of something on a form, click the object to select it and then press the Delete key. Poof . . . it's gone! For example, if you don't want the word *Duplicate* to print on a check to which you have assigned a check number, delete the Duplicate Check Message field in the check form you use.

If you delete the wrong object, immediately choose Edit➪Undo to reverse the last step you took.

Adding data field objects

If you want to add data field objects to a form, you need to tell Peachtree where you want to place the field and which field you want to add. To do so:

1. **Click the Data button on the Object toolbar.**

   As you move your mouse over the form design area, the mouse pointer turns into a thin, black cross.

2. **Click the mouse at the approximate location where you want to place the new data object, hold down the mouse button, and drag the mouse to the right and slightly downward to draw the approximate size of the object you want to add.**

   The outline of the new object appears while your mouse is pressed. (See Figure 13-8.)

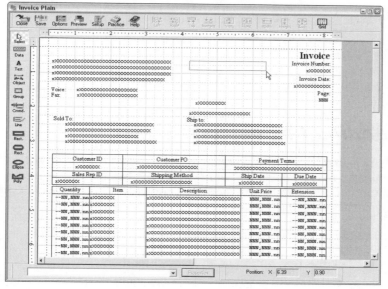

Figure 13-8: Draw an imaginary box to hold the data.

3. **Release the mouse button.**

   The Data Object Properties dialog box appears, as shown in Figure 13-9.

4. **Click the Data Field Name drop-down list, and then click the field you want to add.**

   You see only fields applicable to the current form. A little later in this chapter, we show you how to modify any field.

5. **Click OK to close the Data Object Properties dialog box and add the object to your form.**

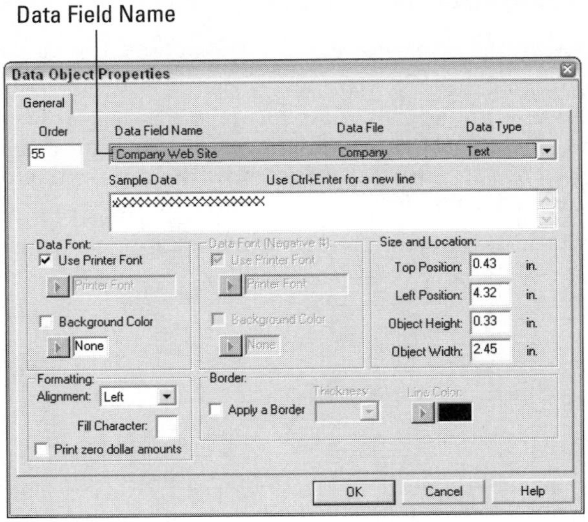

Data Field Name

Figure 13-9:
Select a
data field
to add to
your form.

Adding text objects

Data field objects contain variable information that will . . . well, vary, or change from one document to the next. Text field objects are static. The information won't change; the same words appear on each and every document that uses this form.

You add a text object pretty much the same way you add data fields.

1. **Click the Text button on the Object toolbar.**

   As you move your mouse over the design area, the mouse pointer turns into a thin, black cross.

2. **Click the mouse at the approximate location where you want to place the new text object, hold down the mouse button, and drag the mouse to the right and slightly downward to draw the approximate size of the text object you want to add.**

3. **Release the mouse button.**

   The Text Object Properties dialog box appears, as shown in Figure 13-10.

4. **Enter the text you want to appear on the form.**

   If you need a second line, press Ctrl+Enter to move the insertion point to the next line.

5. **Click OK to add the next text object to your form.**

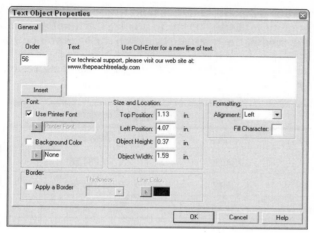

Figure 13-10:
Enter text
information
here.

Resizing an object

If an object is too long, too short, too narrow, or too wide, resize it with your mouse.

Select the object you want to resize; then position the mouse over one of the object "handles." As you do so, the mouse pointer turns into a double-headed black arrow. Then you drag the handle in the direction you want to resize the object. As you drag the handle, you'll see the box boundaries resize. When you reach the desired size, release the mouse button.

Formatting field properties

With all those XXX's and NNN's on the screen, how do you know what a data field looks like? Well, you examine the field properties. The properties tell you what each field represents as well as its size and appearance. You can modify properties for both data fields and text objects.

To view or modify object properties, you must first click the object you want to modify. With the object selected, click the Properties button on the Properties toolbar. Peachtree then displays the Object Properties dialog box.

Using the Object Properties dialog box, you can choose a specific font, size, and color for each object, or you can change how you want numbers to print when designing forms. We talk about numbers first.

Peachtree designates numbers that appear before the decimal point with a capital N and numbers that appear after the decimal point with a lowercase n. Suppose that you wanted standard decimal points and commas. Using

NNN,NNN.nn as your template, one thousand would print as 1,000.00 and ten thousand would print as 10,000.00. To change the number format for the selected field, modify the template to match the appearance you want.

In Table 13-1, we show the values 1234.56 and −1234.56 using various formats.

Table 13-1	Number Samples	
Format	*Positive*	*Negative*
NNN,NNN.nn	1,234.56	−1,234.56
NNN,NNN.nn−	1,234.56	1,234.56−
(NNN,NNN.nn)	1,234.56	(1,234.56)

To change the font for the selected object, follow these steps:

1. **If a check mark appears in the Use Printer Font box in the Object Properties dialog box, remove it by clicking the box,**

2. **Click the font selection arrow located below the Use Printer Font box**

   The Font dialog box appears, allowing you to select a font type, style, size, and color, as well as special effects.

3. **Click OK after making your font selections.**

4. **When you finish using the Data Object Properties dialog box, click OK to close it.**

To make all objects the same font, press Ctrl+A to select all objects; then right-click on top of a highlighted field and choose Font. In the Font dialog box, select the font you want for the entire form, and click OK.

Aligning objects

When you select multiple objects in the Forms Design window, Peachtree can align those objects in relation to each other. You can align their top, bottom, left, or right edges together, or you can choose to align the centers vertically or horizontally. To align multiple objects:

1. **Click the Selection tool and then select the objects you want to align.**

   To select multiple objects, use Windows selection techniques and hold the Shift or Ctrl keys and click each object you want to modify as a group.

To select contiguous objects, hold down the Shift key and click the first and last objects in the group you want to modify. To select noncontiguous objects, hold down the Ctrl key and click each object.

2. Click a tool on the Alignment toolbar.

The objects align based on your choice.

When you've selected multiple objects to align them, how does Peachtree determine which of the selected objects' edges to use when aligning fields? If you pay close attention, you'll notice that all the selected objects have gray handles, except the object you selected last, which has black handles. Peachtree aligns the objects to the one with the black handles — we call it the "foundation" object. Rule to remember: Select the foundation object last.

Grouping fields

When you have a series of rows of data, such as lines on an invoice, customer statement, or purchase order, instead of creating each field individually, use the Group command to list data fields displayed in columns and rows.

To create a group object, follow these steps:

1. Click the Group button on the Object toolbar.

2. Click the mouse at the approximate location where you want to place the new group object, hold down the mouse button, and drag the mouse to the right and slightly downward to specify the approximate size of the group object you want to add. Release the mouse button.

The Group Object Properties dialog box appears, as shown in Figure 13-11.

The Group Object Properties dialog box has several columns to help you define the fields you want to include in the group table. The list of available fields in the Group Object Properties dialog box varies depending on the type of form:

- **Show Field:** Check this box to include the data field in the group table.

- **Column Number:** This option specifies the order in which the data fields appear in the group table. You can't change order directly here; use the Move Field up- and down-arrow buttons to change the column number.

- **Field Name:** Identify the fields included in the group table.

- **Number Format:** While this column is untitled in the Group Object Properties box, it appears to the right of the Field Name column. In numeric data fields, a number button (#) appears here. Clicking the # button displays the Number Formatting window. (See "Formatting field properties" earlier in this chapter.)

Move Field button

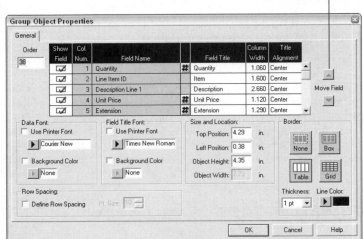

Click the Number Format button and add two or three spaces at the end of the number signs. This adds some space between the numbers and the group box borders.

- **Field Title:** Peachtree calls the heading that prints for the column a *field title*. You can change this option for any of the data fields or leave it blank.

- **Column Width:** You can enter a column width to three decimal places.

- **Title Alignment:** This aligns the title within the column.

You can set other options for your grouped object, including row spacing, the font for the data or headings, and whether to define a border to print around the grouped object.

By checking the Row Spacing box, you can define the spacing between rows of data fields in the Group object. The value you enter determines additional space between data rows. You can enter any amount from –10 to 100. For example, if you use a 10-point font for data and you want the data rows double-spaced, enter a 10 in the Row Spacing box.

3. **Make your group object selections and then click OK.**

Peachtree places the grouped object on your page.

Saving forms

After you've modified a form, you'll want to save it. In fact, we recommend that you save the form *as* you're modifying it. Then resave it again every few steps or so. To save a form:

1. **Click the Save button to display the Save As dialog box.**
2. **Enter a name for the form.**

   You can't use the same name as one of Peachtree's standard forms. You must give your form a unique name.
3. **Optionally, in the Description box, type a description of the form.**
4. **Click Save to save the form for future use.**

Peachtree identifies custom forms by a red flag on the form icon.

Delete any customized form by highlighting the form name in the Select a Report window (refer to Figure 13-6) and clicking the Delete button.

We would have loved to include a discussion of Shapes, Commands, Field Order, and Graphical objects. Unfortunately, these topics are beyond the scope of this book, but you can find information about them in your *Peachtree Users Guide*.

Visit this book's Web site for more information on Peachtree.

Chapter 14

Making Reports Work for You

*P*eachtree includes almost 100 standard reports, ranging from a list of your chart of accounts to a check register to a job profitability report. In each chapter in Part II, you find a list of the standard reports Peachtree supplies appropriate to the subject of the chapter. In this chapter, we show you how to print those reports to your screen, your printer, a PDF file, e-mail or an Excel workbook. We also show you how to modify and save reports. We even show you how to merge information with Microsoft Word.

Previewing Standard Reports

Save a tree! You may find that you want to take only a brief look at your information. Peachtree allows you to print any report to the screen before or instead of printing it on paper.

To preview reports on your screen, follow these steps:

1. **Choose Reports and then select the module you need, such as Accounts Payable.**

   The Select a Report window (see Figure 14-1) appears with an alphabetical listing of available reports.

2. **Click the report to view.**

Customized report

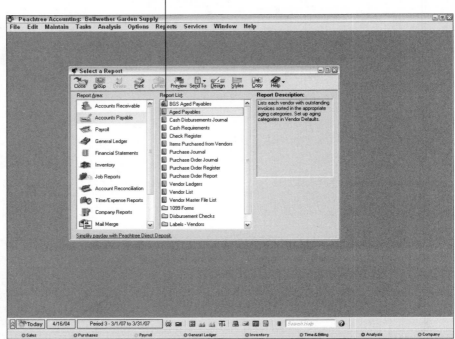

Figure 14-1:
Select
reports to
preview.

3. Click the Preview button.

Peachtree displays a dialog box that allows you to limit the information that appears on the report. In most cases, the dialog box contains three tabs: Filter, Fields, and Fonts.

4. Click OK.

Peachtree displays the selected report on the screen. You can use the scroll bars to view more of the report.

 While previewing the report on-screen, click the Setup button to display the Page Setup dialog box, where you can change the paper size, source, orientation, and printer selection.

In most screen reports, you can "drill down" to view the details of the transaction. As you move the mouse pointer over the transaction, the pointer changes to a magnifying glass that contains a Z (for zoom). Double-click, and Peachtree displays the transaction in the window where you entered it. You can make changes to the transaction and save it; in most cases, Peachtree automatically updates the report to reflect the changes. If the report isn't automatically updated, click the report's Options button and then click OK to refresh the report.

Printing Reports

After you've previewed your report on the screen, you may decide that you want a paper copy or need to send the report to someone.

Peachtree provides several ways to transmit a report. You can print it to paper, send it by e-mail, or print it to a PDF file. You access these different methods through the report toolbar, which is shown in Figure 14-2.

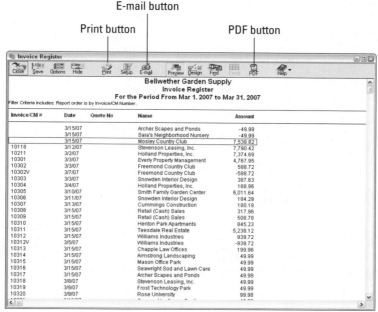

Figure 14-2:
Use the toolbar buttons to print your report.

To print the report on paper, click the Print button. You see a dialog box where you can select which printer you want to use, as well as which pages to print and how many copies to print.

To print the report to a PDF file, click the PDF button. The Save As dialog box appears. You can specify the PDF file name and location.

PDF stands for Portable Document Format. To view or print the report in PDF, you must have the Adobe Reader software, which is a free download from the Internet at www.adobe.com/products/acrobat/readstep2.html.

To e-mail the report, click the E-mail button. A window from your default e-mail program appears with the report as a PDF attachment (see Figure 14-3). Peachtree fills in the e-mail subject and the message body with information pertaining to the creation date and report title. Enter the recipient's e-mail address and then click Send.

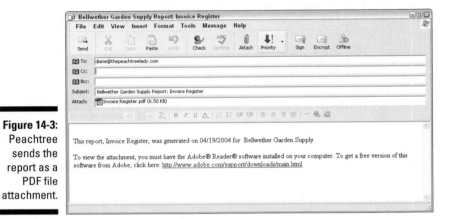

Figure 14-3:
Peachtree sends the report as a PDF file attachment.

Finding the Facts

Some reports can be quite lengthy, and locating a specific number can look like a total blur. While previewing a report, you can click the Find button to search for specific text or numbers. When you click the Find button, Peachtree displays the Find on Report dialog box, as shown in Figure 14-4.

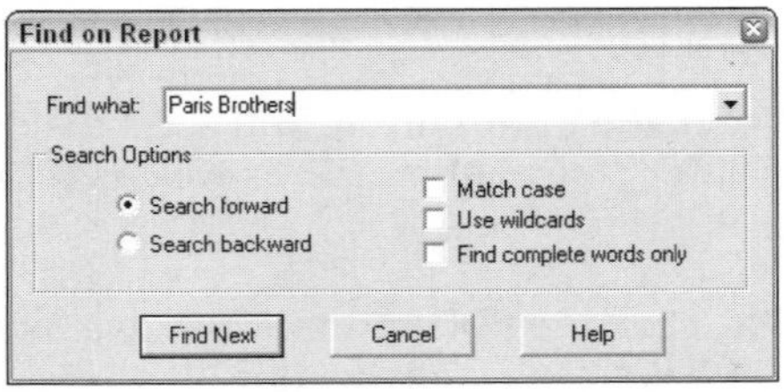

Figure 14-4:
Use this window to search for data within a previewed report.

You can make several search option selections:

- ✔ **Find what:** Use this box to enter the information you want to search.

- ✔ **Search direction:** Use this option to determine whether to search up or down the report, depending on the location of the line with the thin blue border around it.

- ✔ **Match case:** Use this checkbox if you want your search to be case-sensitive. Peachtree will search only for text that matches the case of whatever you enter in the Find what text box. For example, if you enter *SMITH* in all capital letters and select Match case, Peachtree will search for any occurrence of *SMITH* but will not search for *smith* or *Smith*.

- ✔ **Use wildcards:** Peachtree recognizes the ? and the * as wildcards, meaning you can use them in the search to indicate unknown characters. The question mark (?) represents a single character and the asterisk (*) can represent any number of characters. Using the sample Aged Receivables report, if you check the Use wildcards box and type *a?m* in the Find what box, Peachtree could find *armstrong, alma, palm,* or any other similar combination. If you type *a*m*, Peachtree would find all the words just listed, along with *Natasha Cannon, M.D.* and *Dash Business Systems,* for example.

- ✔ **Find complete words only:** Use this box to tell Peachtree you want to be specific and locate exactly what you type. For example, if you check this box and type *build* in the Find what text box, Peachtree locates only the word *build*, not *builders* or *building*. You can use this option along with the Match case option.

If you use the Find box to search for text or numbers, even on a different report or financial statement, Peachtree stores the last 20 values used during the current Peachtree session. You can choose one of your previously entered values by selecting it from the drop-down list.

Enter the text or numbers you want to locate, check any desired options, and then click Find Next. Peachtree locates and highlights the first occurrence of the item. Click Find Next again to locate the next occurrence. Peachtree displays a message box when no more occurrences are found. Click OK and then click Cancel.

Customizing Reports

Sometimes, the standard reports don't contain enough information to meet your needs. Or perhaps they contain more information than you're looking for. Maybe you want to see the information only for a particular customer or vendor and over a different time frame than that specified in the report. You can modify the date range, field information, font, and page layout of any report.

Using filters

Filtering is the process of restricting the report data to a different set of specifications than Peachtree shows in standard reports. Suppose that you take a standard report, for example, the Customer Ledgers, and view it a little differently.

In Figure 14-5, you see the Filter tab of the Customer Ledgers report. By default, the standard Customer Ledgers report shows all activity for all customers for the current month. But what if you want to see the transactions (both sales and receipts) for the entire year for customer Cummings Construction? By using filtering, you can have Peachtree display that information.

Figure 14-5:
You can choose sorting options, the time frame, and other limits for a selected report.

To use a filter, follow these steps:

1. **Choose the report name you want to filter.**

   In the example, we chose the Customer Ledgers report under Accounts Receivable.

2. **Click Preview.**

   A dialog box appears in which you can set a variety of options for the report you want to display. The first thing we want to change is the time frame. By default, this report displays the current month, but we want to see the transactions for the entire year.

   If you double-click the report, the report displays on-screen with the default options. Click the Options button to see the dialog box.

3. **Click the drop-down arrow next to the Date box and change the date to represent the period you want.**

   In our example, we want This Year. You can enter a more specific date range by entering the beginning and ending dates in the From and To boxes.

4. **Click in the From box on the Customer ID filter line and type (or look up and select) the first Customer ID you want to view.**

   In this example, we use CUMMINGS. Notice that when you select a specific ID, the Type column changes from All to Range.

   If you want to see a list of IDs from a certain point down through the list, enter only the From ID and leave the To ID blank. For example, if you want to see every customer from SMITH through WILLIAMS, who is the last customer on the list, enter SMITH in the From box and leave the To box empty.

5. **Click in the To box on the Customer ID filter line and type (or look up and select) the last Customer ID you want to view.**

   If you're looking for one specific customer, enter the same ID in both the From and To boxes.

   Some reports allow you to select multiple IDs that are not contiguous. Click the Type box next to the Customer ID, select Equal to, and then click the From ID box. Hold down the Ctrl key and click the IDs you want to view (see Figure 14-6).

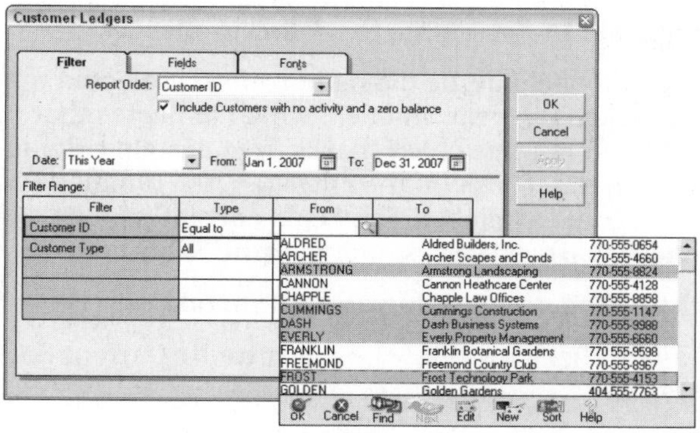

Figure 14-6:
Select
multiple IDs
by holding
down the
Ctrl key to
select or
deselect
an ID.

6. **Click OK to display the report on-screen.**

   Peachtree displays transactions for the specified time frame and the specified customers.

7. **Click Close when you've finished reviewing the report.**

Adding, deleting, and moving report fields

Reports in Peachtree consist of data fields. Those data fields come from the various modules in Peachtree. For example, information on an Aged Receivables report contains information from a variety of Customer and Sales fields, and the payroll register displays information from a variety of Employee and Payroll entry fields. You have the option of including or excluding any available fields to create a customized report.

For example, we want to add the current balance to the Chart of Accounts and remove the Active/Inactive field. To customize a report, follow these steps:

1. **Choose Reports⇨General Ledger.**

2. **Locate and double-click the report you want to modify.**

   In the example, we'll modify the Chart of Accounts report. A standard Chart of Accounts report displays four columns: the account ID, the account description, an active or inactive status of the account, and the account type.

3. **Click Options.**

   The options for the Chart of Accounts report appear.

   If you want to modify a report that's not currently displayed on-screen, highlight the report in the Select a Report window and click the Preview button. The options for the selected report then appear.

4. **Click the Fields tab to determine the fields to display.**

   You can display any field in the dialog box on the selected report. You'll find some fields appear dimmed, which indicates that they can't be changed. As you remove check marks from certain columns on the Fields tab or change settings on the Filter tab, the dimmed (unavailable) columns may become available. The fields currently being displayed have a red check mark in the first column (the Show column).

5. **Select the check box of the field you want to add.**

   For this example, check the Show box next to the Current Balance field (see Figure 14-7).

6. **Clear the Show check box of the field you want to remove.**

   In the example, we cleared the check box of the Active/Inactive field. Removing the check mark removes the field so that it no longer appears on the report. When you remove a field from a report, the columns previously displayed to the right of the removed field move to the left. In this example, when we add the Current Balance column, it became the fifth column, but when we removed the Active column, Current Balance became the fourth column.

We want the Current Balance to appear next to the Account Description. No problem! We just use the Move Up command to change its location.

7. Click the field name you want to move.

Use caution not to click the Show column, or you'll turn off the display of the field. When you select a field, a red border appears around the entire selected line.

8. Click the Move Up or Move Down button to move the field up or down one column at a time. Continue clicking the Move Up or Move Down button until the field appears in the location you want.

Click the check box in the Column Break section to make the selected field appear on a new column on the report. If you want to place more than one field in a column, first make sure that you check the Show check box and then remove the check from the Break check box. Doing so means that Peachtree doesn't place a break (a column) between the fields.

9. Click OK, and the report redisplays with the changes you selected.

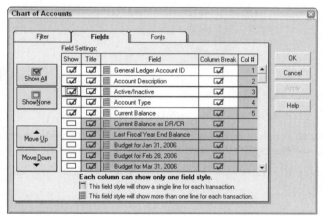

Figure 14-7: Adding the current balance makes the report have five columns.

Changing report's column width

Adding too many columns may cause some to fall off the edge of a page. Well, they don't really fall off, but it does cause the report to print two or more pages in width. You have several choices at this point. You can print the report in landscape mode, print multiple pages in width, remove some report columns, or stack some of the columns as described in the previous section or — and this is probably the best choice — change the column widths.

Use the following steps to change the column width:

1. **Preview the report on-screen and then click the Design button.**

   Short blue column marker lines appear to the right of each column, as shown in Figure 14-8. If you see a long vertical dashed line, your report prints multiple pages wide.

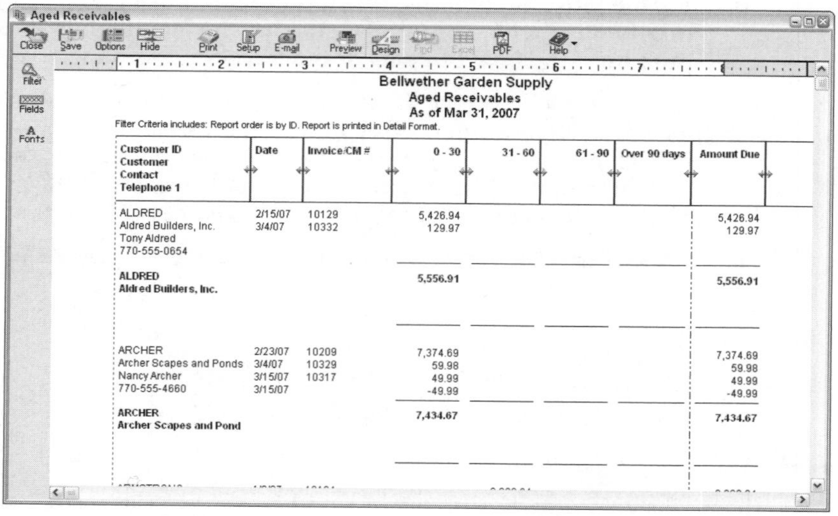

Figure 14-8:
Drag the column markers to change the column width.

2. **Drag the short blue column markers to the left to make a column narrower or to the right to widen a column.**

   You'll know the report fits on one page when the long blue dashed line disappears.

Keeping in style

What's your style — Classic, Elegant, Contemporary, or Professional? By default, Peachtree uses the Professional style, which simply means that all reports print in an Arial font. You can display any or all of your reports in any of the aforementioned styles. Here's a description of Peachtree's furnished styles:

✔ **Classic:** The entire report uses a Times New Roman (black) font.

✔ **Contemporary:** The report heading appears as an Arial (red) font, the data uses a Times New Roman (black) font, and the report totals appear in Times New Roman (red) font.

✔ **Elegant:** The entire report uses a Garamond font. Headings and report totals appear in navy blue, and the body data appears in black.

✔ **Professional:** The entire report appears in an Arial (black) font.

If you have a color printer, the reports print in the same colors that appear on the screen.

Here's an easy way to modify a report style:

1. **Double-click the report you want to modify.**

   The report appears on-screen.

2. **Click the Design button.**

   The report changes to Design mode and three icons appear on the left side of the screen.

3. **Click the Fonts button.**

   The options dialog box shown in Figure 14-9 appears.

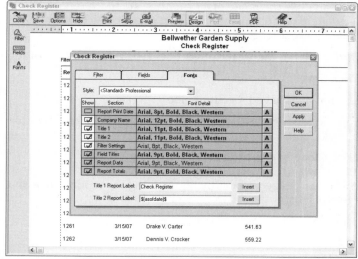

Figure 14-9:
Click the Filter or Fields button to change displayed fields or filter-specific information.

4. **Click the down arrow to the right of the Style box to display a list of available styles.**

5. **Click the style you want for this report and then click OK.**

   The report redisplays on the screen with the new style.

You can also create and save your own styles, choosing the font, color, and sizes you prefer. However, we simply don't have the room in this book to show you how.

Saving a customized report

Sometimes you customize reports for a one-time use, while other reports you use frequently. To save yourself the trouble of recreating the customized report each time you want to display it, save the report with a name that you'll recognize.

To save a customized report, follow these steps:

1. **Display the customized report on the screen.**

2. **Click the Save button.**

   A Save As dialog box appears.

3. **Enter a name for the report.**

   You can't use the name of a Peachtree standard report. You must give it a unique name. For example, you might call a customized Chart of Accounts report "My COA."

4. **Optionally, in the Description box, type a description of the report.**

5. **Click Save.**

   The report is saved for future use.

   You can identify custom reports by the red flag Peachtree places on the report icon.

6. **Click Close to close the report window.**

Delete any customized report by highlighting the report name and clicking the Delete button.

Mail Merge

One common marketing tool is to offer existing customers a discount to encourage them to purchase again. Make your customers feel really special by sending them a personalized letter with this distinctive offer. What? You don't have time to send them a personalized letter? It takes only a few minutes to send such letters using Peachtree's Mail Merge feature.

You can use one of the standard letters included with Peachtree or create your own letter. Combine the letter and the customer contact information that you already have in Peachtree, and in a very short time you can have a personalized letter for every customer in your database. Don't want to send this letter to everyone? That's okay. You can choose which customers should receive the letter.

This type of mailing is called a *mail merge* because you're merging the generic letter and the variable customer information. Peachtree includes a variety of mail merge letters for customer, vendors, or employees. The underlying engine for this mail merge uses Microsoft Word. If you're already familiar with Microsoft Word's Mail Merge feature, you can even customize your own letters to merge with your Peachtree data.

For more details on using Word and Mail Merge, you might want to check out *Word 2003 For Dummies* by Dan Gookin (published by Wiley).

You can create mail merge letters one at a time through the Maintain windows, or you can create them in a batch from the Reports menu. We take a look at both methods in the following sections.

You must have both Microsoft Excel and Microsoft Word installed on your system for the Peachtree mail merge process to work correctly.

Merging one record at a time

Perhaps you're in the process of setting up a new employee and want to send a letter welcoming him or her to your firm. As you enter the new employee information in Peachtree, creating a welcome letter is just a click away. Follow these steps:

1. **Choose Maintain⇨Employees.**

2. **Enter and save the new employee's information.**

   Refer to Chapter 9 for setting up a new employee.

   You can create letters for customers, vendors, or employees from their Maintenance window.

3. **With the employee information still on the screen, click the Letters button.**

   The Mail Merge Template Selector window appears, as shown in Figure 14-10.

4. **Click the letter template you want to use.**

   In the case of the employee letters, there's only one example, but you can also create your own.

Letters button   Word button

Figure 14-10:
Send mail
merge
letters to
customers,
vendors, or
employees.

5. **Click the Word button.**

Microsoft Word opens with the completed letter ready for you to print
or further modify if desired. (See Figure 14-11.)

Optionally, click the E-mail button to e-mail the letter rather than open it
in Microsoft Word.

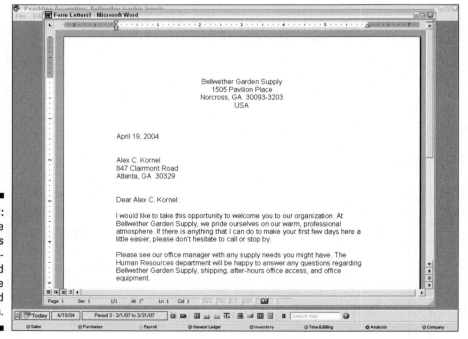

Figure 14-11:
Peachtree
interacts
with Micro-
soft Word
to create
personalized
letters.

Merging multiple records

When merging multiple records, you can select all or a specific group of customers, vendors, or employees. The fields you can filter vary depending on the type of data you are merging.

1. **Choose Reports⇨Mail Merge.**

   A list of available mail merge forms appears.

2. **In the Report List, click the desired folder and then click the letter you want to send.**

3. **Click the Letters button.**

   A filter dialog box opens where you can select the specific IDs, date ranges, and other criteria.

4. **Select the filter criteria you want to use.**

   Refer to the "Using Filters" section earlier in this chapter.

5. **Click the Word button.**

   Microsoft Word opens with all the completed letters ready for you to print or further modify if desired.

Excel with Peachtree

If you have Microsoft Excel, you can send any report, including financial statements, to an Excel workbook.

Why would you want to send a report to Microsoft Excel? Well, perhaps you'd like to sort the report in a different manner than Peachtree offers, total a report that Peachtree can't total, or add a column based on a calculation. How about creating a chart based on the data? We like to use the Excel function to copy customer sales information that can be sorted and ranked in Excel. Those are just a few things you can do by copying a report to Excel.

Follow these steps to copy report data to Excel:

1. **Display the Peachtree report on your screen or highlight the report name in the Select a Report window.**

2. **Click the Excel button to display the Copy Report to Excel dialog box.**

3. **Select the option you want to copy the report to Excel.**

You have two ways you can copy the report. You can choose Create a New Microsoft Excel Workbook, or you can choose Add a New Worksheet to an Existing Microsoft Workbook. The latter option appends the report to an existing Excel file. Click the Browse button to select an existing file.

4. Click OK to copy the report to Excel.

Peachtree copies only values, not formulas, to Excel.

Occasionally Peachtree doesn't recognize that you have Excel on your system. If the Excel button isn't available, but you know you have Excel on your computer, right-click the report name (before you bring the report up on the screen) and choose Excel. Doing so displays the report options dialog box and then the Copy Report to Excel dialog box mentioned in Step 2.

For more details on using Excel, you might want to check out *Excel 2003 For Dummies* by Greg Harvey (published by Wiley).

Stay in a Group Now

If you have a number of reports that you need at the same time, you can create a report group to print them all at once. Report groups print directly to the printer or Microsoft Excel; they can't be previewed on the screen.

In Chapter 17, we suggest reports that you should print at the end of the month. Placing those reports in a report group makes the report printing process much easier.

Follow these steps to create a report group:

1. From anywhere in the Select a Report window, click the Group button.

The Report Groups window appears, as shown in Figure 14-12. All standard and custom reports appear in the Report Index list. To help you find a particular report, you can limit the reports you see in the Report Index list to only the reports for a particular module. Click the Report Index drop-down arrow and select the module.

2. To build a report group, select the first report you want to include in the group in the Report Index list and click the Add button.

Added reports appear on the right side of the window. Peachtree prints the reports in the order they appear on the right side of the window.

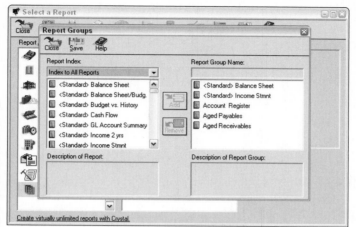

Figure 14-12:
Select the reports you want to include in the report group.

3. **Add any additional reports to the group.**

   You can mix and match report categories. For example, you may want to print an Aged Payables report and an Aged Receivables report.

4. **When you finish adding reports to the group, click the Save button.**

   The Save As dialog box appears.

5. **Enter a name for the group, such as Monthly Reports.**

6. **Optionally, in the Description box, type a description of the reports.**

7. **Click Save to save the report group.**

8. **Click Close to close the Report Groups window.**

When you're ready to print the report group, click Report Groups in the Select a Report window, and then click the name of the report group to print.

Click Print to print the reports to the printer with no further action on your part, or click the Excel button to send the reports to Microsoft Excel. If you send the reports to Excel, Peachtree opens each report in its own workbook.

Visit this book's Web site for more information on Peachtree.

Chapter 15

Reviewing the Financial Picture

*B*efore you advance to the next Peachtree accounting period, you'll probably want to print a series of reports for your records and possibly for your accountant. Reports you may find useful include the general ledger, trial balance, balance sheet, and income statement. Peachtree provides lots of other reports you may want, but these are the most common ones. You'll probably want to include them in a report group. (See Chapter 14 to find out how to create a report group.)

The preceding reports fall into two categories: general ledger reports and financial statements. We begin by taking a look at the general ledger reports.

Reviewing Standard General Ledger Reports

Two of the standard reports you'll use frequently are General Ledger and Trial Balance. Peachtree lists both of these reports in the General Ledger report area of the Select a Report window. (You can find out how to display, filter, and customize reports in Chapter 14.)

The General Ledger report is the mother of all accounting reports. This report lists all transactions you enter into Peachtree *that affect the general ledger.* Figure 15-1 shows a sample General Ledger report. Note the column titled Jrnl. The reference in this column represents the source of the transaction. Table 15-1 lists the different Jrnl codes and their source.

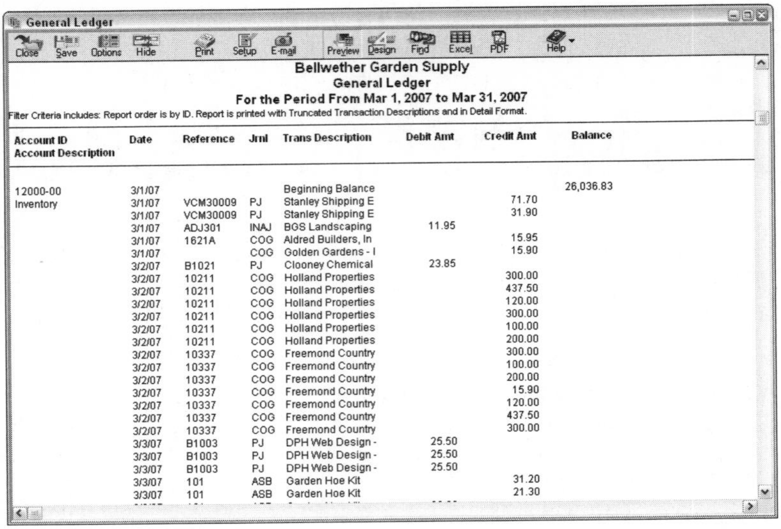

Account ID Account Description	Date	Reference	Jrnl	Trans Description	Debit Amt	Credit Amt	Balance
12000-00	3/1/07			Beginning Balance			26,036.83
Inventory	3/1/07	VCM30009	PJ	Stanley Shipping E		71.70	
	3/1/07	VCM30009	PJ	Stanley Shipping E		31.90	
	3/1/07	ADJ301	INAJ	BGS Landscaping	11.95		
	3/1/07	1621A	COG	Aldred Builders, In		15.95	
	3/1/07		COG	Golden Gardens - I		15.90	
	3/2/07	B1021	PJ	Clooney Chemical	23.85		
	3/2/07	10211	COG	Holland Properties		300.00	
	3/2/07	10211	COG	Holland Properties		437.50	
	3/2/07	10211	COG	Holland Properties		120.00	
	3/2/07	10211	COG	Holland Properties		300.00	
	3/2/07	10211	COG	Holland Properties		100.00	
	3/2/07	10211	COG	Holland Properties		200.00	
	3/2/07	10337	COG	Freemond Country		300.00	
	3/2/07	10337	COG	Freemond Country		100.00	
	3/2/07	10337	COG	Freemond Country		200.00	
	3/2/07	10337	COG	Freemond Country		15.90	
	3/2/07	10337	COG	Freemond Country		120.00	
	3/2/07	10337	COG	Freemond Country		437.50	
	3/2/07	10337	COG	Freemond Country		300.00	
	3/3/07	B1003	PJ	DPH Web Design -	25.50		
	3/3/07	B1003	PJ	DPH Web Design -	25.50		
	3/3/07	B1003	PJ	DPH Web Design -	25.50		
	3/3/07	101	ASB	Garden Hoe Kit		31.20	
	3/3/07	101	ASB	Garden Hoe Kit		21.30	

Figure 15-1: See all transactions affecting your accounts in the General Ledger report.

Table 15-1 General Ledger Source Codes

Jrnl Code	*Stands For*	*Source*
SJ	Sales journal	Sales/Invoicing
CRJ	Cash receipts journal	Receipts
PJ	Purchase journal	Purchases/Receive Inventory
CDJ	Cash disbursements journal	Payments and Write Checks
PRJ	Payroll journal	Payroll entry
INAJ	Inventory adjustment journal	Inventory Adjustments
COG	Cost of goods sold journal	Sales/Invoicing
ASB	Assemblies adjustment journal	Assemblies
GEN	General journal	General Journal entry

Purchase orders, quotes, and sales orders do not affect general ledger accounts.

When printing or previewing the General Ledger report for multiple months, you may find the option Hide Period Totals on Multi-Period Report useful. You can select this check box on the Filter tab when you set up the report's options.

Like most Peachtree reports, you can double-click on a line to open the window in which Peachtree created the original transaction.

Peachtree provides two trial balance reports. The first report, called General Ledger Trial Balance, shows each account and its balance as of the last day of the current period. The report displays the account ID and description as well as the debit or credit balance.

The other trial balance report is Working Trial Balance. This report provides a worksheet where you can list adjusting entries. Each account includes the current balance and a series of lines where you can write down any necessary adjusting amount. Referring to your handwritten trial balance entries speeds up data entry when you need to make adjusting entries.

Using Segments and Masking

In Chapter 3, we show you how to set up your chart of accounts to better track departments or locations. In that chapter, you see how important the numbering sequence is when setting up the chart of accounts, especially if you want to report on your different company areas, or segments.

In Peachtree Premium edition, you can formally divide your accounts into segments. In other Peachtree editions, you set up your accounts in a pattern where you could utilize report masking. *Masking* is the ability to limit information in certain reports to a single division, department, location, or type code.

You can use masking and segmenting in financial statements and in most general ledger reports.

For a review of designing your chart of accounts for masking or segmenting, see Chapter 3.

Report masks use a wildcard character, the asterisk (*), to represent all the other digits of the account number *except* the digits you want on the report. For example, Bellwether Garden Supply references two departments as Aviary and Landscape Services; these departments are represented as AV and LS in the chart of accounts. 40000-AV is the account number for the

Aviary sales account, and 40000-LS is the account number for the Landscape Services sales account. So a mask for the Aviary department look like *****-AV and a mask for the Landscape Services appears as *****-LS. On many standard general ledger reports, you can use the mask when you set the report options.

If you're using Peachtree Premium edition, you can take advantage of the segments feature. Using segments over masking means you don't have to remember the wildcard character or the number of digits. You need to remember only what you called the segments, such as *department* or *location*.

From the Select a Report window, select the general ledger or financial statement report you want to view. Click the Preview button to display the Options dialog box.

If you're using Peachtree Premium and have segments activated, you'll see an options box such as the one in Figure 15-2. You first select the segment type you want to review. Then, in the From and To boxes, select the segments you want.

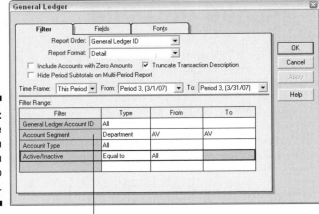

Figure 15-2:
Select the segment on which you want to report.

Account Segment type

If you're not using Peachtree Premium, or if you do not have segments activated, you'll see an options box for masking. You can create a mask such as the one you see in Figure 15-3, which uses the asterisk wildcard.

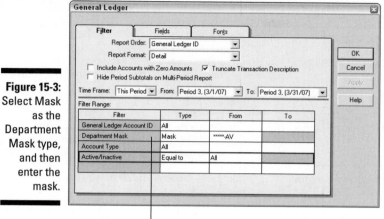

Figure 15-3:
Select Mask
as the
Department
Mask type,
and then
enter the
mask.

Department Mask type

Producing Financial Statements

You display or print financial statements through the Select a Report window in the same manner as reports. Peachtree provides a number of predefined financial statements, including a balance sheet and an income statement. Similar to other reports, you can preview them, print them to a printer or a PDF file, e-mail them, or send them to Excel.

Table 15-2 provides a list of all the Peachtree provided predefined standard financial statements. If any of these statements don't fit your needs, look in the next section to find out how to customize them.

Table 15-2	Furnished Financial Statements
Report Name	*What It Does*
<Standard> Balance Sheet	Lists your company assets, liabilities, and capital.
<Standard> Cash Flow	Shows the cash receipts, cash payments, and change in cash in a business.
<Standard> GL Account Summary	Shows the account number and description, beginning balance, activity, and ending balance for each account.

(continued)

Table 15-2 *(continued)*

Report Name	What It Does
<Standard> Income 2 yrs	Compares revenue and expenses for the current month totals to the same month last year, and the current year's totals to last year's totals.
<Standard> Income Stmnt	Sometimes referred to as a P&L (profit and loss) statement. Shows income and expenses and the difference between them.
<Standard> Income/Budgets	Compares income and expenses balances to the budgeted amounts.
<Standard> Income/Earnings	Shows income and expense activity as well as retained earnings information.
<Standard> Retained Earnings	Shows beginning and ending retained earnings amounts, adjustments to retained earnings in the period, and the detail for all Equity-gets closed accounts.
<Standard> Stmnt Changes	Describes changes in a company's overall financial position.
<Standard> Budget vs History	Shows budget amounts, current actual amounts, and last year's actual amounts. This report comes standard only in the Premium edition.
<Standard> Monthly Variance	Compares income and expenses to the amounts budgeted for a given time period. Displays the variance as an amount and a percentage. This report comes standard only in the Premium edition.
<Standard> Balance Sheet/Budg.	Lists actual and budget amounts for all assets, liabilities, and capital accounts as of a specific date. This report comes standard only in the Premium edition.

As we mention earlier in this chapter, the two most frequently used financial statements are the Balance Sheet and the Income Statement. Here are a few suggestions to assist you when working with your financial statements:

✔ All statements and reports appear for the current period unless you select a different date range in the Options dialog box.

✔ Open any financial statement by double-clicking the desired report, change the date range or other options, including segments, and then click OK.

✔ Double-clicking an account displays the underlying details for the selected account through the General Ledger report.

✔ If you're using Peachtree Premium, you can access the monthly variance statement also through the Maintain⇨Budgets window.

✔ The option to select a segment does not appear if you do not have segments setup in General Ledger defaults.

Modifying Financial Statements

In this section, we take a look at Peachtree's third designer — the Financial Statement designer.

You can create customized financial reports using the Financial Statement Wizard or by the conventional method of customizing a statement yourself in the Financial Statement Design window. The Financial Statement Design window gives you more individual control over each aspect of the financial design process, but the Financial Statement Wizard provides a grasp of the basic elements of a statement and how to put them together effectively.

Using the Financial Statement Wizard

The Financial Statement Wizard can assist you with great detail in creating a financial statement. At every point in the process, the wizard makes your choices clear so you know what effect each choice has on the finished statement. The following steps show you how to use Peachtree's Financial Statement Wizard:

1. **In the Select a Report window, choose Financial Statements.**

2. **Click the Financial Statement Wizard button.**

   The Financial Statement Wizard button is the big gray square (yep, that's a button!) in the lower-right corner. An introduction screen appears, showing you the processes you can specify by using the wizard.

3. Click Next to see the Financial Statement Name screen.

Similar to customized forms and reports, customized financial statements must have their own name. Additionally, you start customization by basing your report on one that already exists, as shown in Figure 15-4. This saves you *tons* of time!

Figure 15-4:
The
Financial
Statement
Name
screen.

4. In the drop-down list, choose an existing financial statement design to use as the model for your new statement, and type a unique name for the new statement.

Optionally, type a report description.

5. Click Next.

Each screen of the Financial Statement Wizard defines a specific area of your financial statement:

- **Headers and Footers:** Enter the text of each header and footer you want to include.

- **Dates and General Ledger Account Masking:** Choose the range of dates you want the statement to cover. If you've set up your general ledger accounts for department masking, you can enter an account mask that limits reporting to just one of your departments. In the next section, we show you how to create a departmental income statement using the Financial Statement Design window.

- **Column Properties:** Select the type and properties of data that appears in up to 30 columns.

- **Column Options:** For each type of column you set up in your statement, you can determine secondary titles, the width, and the alignment for the column.

- **Fonts:** You can choose the fonts that Peachtree uses to display or print each of the sections of your statement.

- **Formatting and Default Printer:** You can tell Peachtree which printer you want to use, whether you want to print page numbers, show zero dollar amounts, center the report on the page, and so forth.

- **Congratulations:** Decide whether you want to display the newly created statement, modify the new statement in the designer window, or create another financial statement using the Financial Statement Wizard.

6. **Click Finish.**

   The designed financial statement appears for your review on your screen.

Creating customized financial statements

Earlier in this chapter, you can see that Peachtree Premium edition users who also use account segments can enter the segment in the dialog box that appears when they select a financial statement. But what about those of you who aren't using segments? Can you create a departmental financial statement? Well, yes. In fact, you could use the Financial Statement Wizard to create departmentalized statements. But you can also create your own quickly and easily by using the standard statements provided with Peachtree.

Suppose that you want to compare the current period with the year-to-date information for only one department. The standard income statement compares current period information to year-to-date information for your entire company. The upcoming steps outline how to create a departmental version of the standard income statement, using the department mask.

Creating a new financial statement by using an existing financial statement as a model is always easiest. To avoid accidentally damaging the model, make a copy by saving it under a new name in the Design window. Then, modify the properties of the column heading to include a department mask.

For a review on designing your chart of accounts for masking, see Chapter 3. The following steps show you how to create a customized financial statement:

1. **Choose Reports⇨Financial Statements.**

   Peachtree displays the available financial statement report formats in the Select a Report window.

2. **Select the financial statement you want to modify and then click the Design button.**

   In the example, we're using the <Standard> Income Statement. Peachtree's Financial Statement Designer window for the Income Statement appears (see Figure 15-5).

3. **Click the button marked Column Desc and then click the Property button.**

   The Column Description dialog box appears, as shown in Figure 15-6.

Column Description

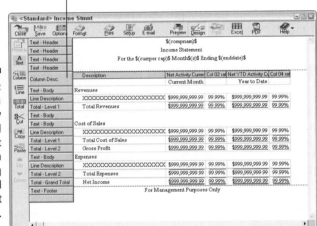

Figure 15-5:
Create a new financial statement by using an existing financial statement as a model.

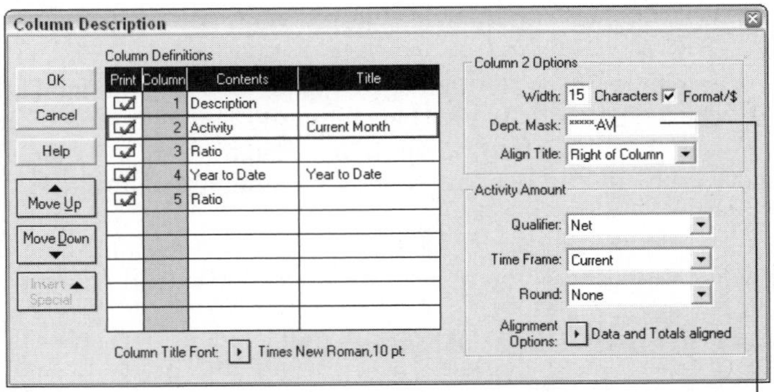

Figure 15-6:
Add a department mask to print this report for only one department.

Department Mask

4. **Click the row for Column 2 Activity to select it, and display the Dept. Mask field.**

   Just like in the earlier section, "Using Segments and Masking in Reports," you create the mask by using the asterisk (*) wildcard character to represent all the other digits of the account number *except* the digits you want displayed.

5. **Add an appropriate mask.**

   To mask for just the Aviary department, for example, enter *****-AV.

6. **Repeat the mask for other activity columns, such as Column 4 Y-T-D Activity.**

7. **Click OK to redisplay the report design.**

8. **Click the Save button to display the Save As dialog box.**

   Peachtree will not allow you to overwrite a <Standard> financial statement. You must supply a different name.

9. **In the Name box, type a new name for the report.**

   For example, you might type Income Statement — Aviary.

10. **Optionally, enter a Description.**

11. **Click OK.**

    Peachtree changes the report title in the title bar.

Now when you print or preview the report, it includes information only for the department you specified.

Delete any customized financial statement by highlighting the financial statement name and clicking the Delete button.

Copying Reports and Financial Statements

You'll find customized reports (in any report area) and financial statements available only in the company you created them in. However, you can copy reports and financial reports you create in one company to another company. This feature comes in particularly handy if you create a second company and would like to use a customized report or financial statement that you created in the first company.

Peachtree makes customized forms (invoices, checks, purchase orders, and so on) available in *all* companies, regardless of which company you used to create them.

To copy reports or financial statements between companies, begin by opening the company that does *not* have the necessary report. In the Select a Report window, click the Copy button on the toolbar. In the Select a Company to Copy from list box, select the company containing the report you want to copy. Enter a name for the report and then click the Copy button. See Figure 15-7.

Figure 15-7:
Use this box
to copy
custom
reports and
financial
statements
from one
company to
another.

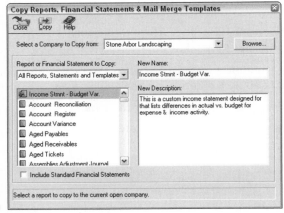

Visit this book's Web site for more information on Peachtree.

Chapter 16

When the Bank Statement Arrives

*E*ach month, the mailman delivers with an envelope full of checks. Don't get too excited; unfortunately, they aren't checks written to you. They're checks or copies of checks you've written to others.

So why is the bank sending you this information? Well, the bank is obligated to tell you each month how much money you have in your account. "Uh . . . okay, so what?" you ask.

Well, if you're smart, you'll want to make sure that the bank thinks you have the same amount of money *you* think you have. After all, banks make mistakes, and you wouldn't want to "give your money away" to the bank just because you didn't take the time to check their accounting and find their error. The process of comparing the bank's balance to yours is called *reconciling*.

Face it; accounting is not exactly a barrel of laughs. And reconciling your bank statement probably wins the award for the least fun thing you can do when working with your company's books. However, reconciling is an important function because it's the only way to confirm that you and the bank agree on the amount of money you have in your account.

Anyone who has ever tried to reconcile a bank account knows that the process can be at best tedious, and at worst, a nightmare when you just can't make the bank's numbers match yours. When you reconcile your bank statement using paper and pencil, you add "time-consuming" to the list of negative adjectives.

So, let Peachtree help you. At least when you reconcile your bank statement electronically, you finish more quickly. This chapter shows you how to use Peachtree's Account Reconciliation feature — and how to track down problems when things don't balance on the first try.

Understanding the Concept of Balancing

Along with the checks in that envelope, you'll find a statement that summarizes the transactions the bank has processed for you during the month. These transactions include checks you've written, deposits you've made, and actions the bank has taken, such as charging your account for checks you ordered or adding interest to your account.

You need to use the statement to compare the balance that the bank says you have with the balance you think you have. In the best of all worlds, they should match. If they don't match, you need to figure out *why* they don't match and then take some action (which we talk about later in this chapter) to make them match — that's the part that most people think isn't fun.

After you record the transactions the bank has entered (check order charges, service charges, and the interest), the difference between your account balance and the bank statement's balance should be the total of the uncleared transactions. *Uncleared transactions* are any checks you've written or deposits you've made since the cutoff date on the bank statement. You can think of uncleared transactions as transactions about which the bank doesn't know, according to the information on the statement. To reconcile your account, you add to the bank statement balance any deposits you've made since the bank prepared the statement. Similarly, you subtract from the bank statement balance any checks you've written since the bank prepared the bank statement.

Typically, the bank's cutoff date for a business checking account is the last day of the month; this date coincides with the end of an accounting period for most businesses. So, when you reconcile your bank statement, you effectively determine your actual cash balance as of the last day of the accounting period. Your accountant needs to know your cash balance on the last day of the accounting period to prepare accurate financial statements, so reconciling your bank statement helps your accountant prepare financial statements.

When you reconcile using paper and pencil, you list and total all checks you've written that don't appear on the bank statement and all deposits you've made that don't appear on the bank statement so that you can subtract and add them to the bank's ending balance to determine whether you and the bank agree on your account balance. Initially, the listing and totaling is the most time-consuming part of the process (if your account doesn't balance, finding the error can become the most time-consuming part of the process). Peachtree shortens the listing and totaling part of the process by doing the math for you.

Before You Start Reconciling

Before you start reconciling, you need to address two issues. First, when you receive your statement from the bank, make sure you're working in the accounting period covered by the bank statement. Check the Peachtree Toolbar (see Figure 16-1), which typically appears at the bottom of your screen, to determine the current accounting period.

Figure 16-1:
Look at the toolbar to determine in which period you're working.

The period in which you are working appears here.

If you need to change the accounting period, follow these steps:

1. **Click the box in the toolbar that displays the current period.**

   If you prefer, you can choose Tasks➪System➪Change Accounting Period. The Change Accounting Period dialog box appears.

2. **Click the period you want to reconcile.**

3. **Click OK.**

   Click No if you see a prompt asking if you want to print invoices or reports.

For details on changing the accounting period, see Chapter 17.

Second, for deposits, some bank statements list individual items rather than the deposit ticket total. Most banks, however, list deposit ticket totals rather than individual items. If your bank lists individual items and you group receipts using the deposit ticket ID field available in the Receipts, Receive Payments, and Select for Deposit windows, you can print the Bank Deposit report, shown in Figure 16-2, to match individual items to deposit ticket totals.

Figure 16-2:
This report lists the individual items that were included on each bank deposit ticket.

Bank Deposit Report

Close | Save | Options | Hide | Print | Setup | E-mail | Preview | Design | Find | Excel | PDF | Hel

Bellwether Garden Supply
Bank Deposit Report
For the Period From Mar 1, 2007 to Mar 31, 2007
10200 - Regular Checking Account

Filter Criteria includes: Report order is by Deposit Ticket ID. Report is printed in Detail Format.

Deposit Ticket ID	Date	Reference	Description	Amount
030207	3/2/07	CH31703	Kenton Golf and Tennis Center	160.50
	3/2/07	CC0003	Everly Property Management	149.97
	3/5/07	CH5000	Holland Properties, Inc.	26.50
	3/7/07	CC0001	Chapple Law Offices	40.25
	3/7/07	CC0002	Cannon Heathcare Center	158.74
	3/13/07	CC0006	Snyder Securities	99.98
			Total Deposit	635.94
030307	3/3/07	4452	Williams Industries	220.31
			Total Deposit	220.31
030407	3/4/07	31114	Snowden Interior Design	97.57
			Total Deposit	97.57
030507	3/5/07	2231	Everly Property Management	186.88
	3/5/07	CASH030503	Retail (Cash) Sales	528.56
			Total Deposit	715.44
031207	3/12/07	CASH031203	Retail (Cash) Sales	763.82
			Total Deposit	763.82

In the Account Reconciliation window, Peachtree lists individual items if you don't fill in the deposit ticket ID field or if you have items you have not yet selected for deposit. If you fill in the deposit ticket ID field, Peachtree lists the deposit ticket total rather than each individual item. The Bank Deposit Report helps you tie back the individual items to a particular deposit so that you can properly identify deposits that clear the bank. To print the report, follow these steps:

1. **Choose Reports⇨Account Reconciliation.**

   The Select a Report window appears, showing the available account reconciliation reports.

2. **On the right side of the window, select Bank Deposit Report.**

3. **Click the Print button.**

4. **In the Cash Account ID field, select the correct cash account.**

5. **Click OK.**

The Bank Deposit Report doesn't display deposits made through journal entries.

Starting Account Reconciliation

In the previous section, which we strongly suggest that you read, we discuss two housekeeping tasks you should complete to prepare for reconciliation. With those two housekeeping tasks out of the way, you're ready to reconcile. It won't be painful. Honest. Or at least it won't be as painful as it used to be. To start the reconciliation process, follow these steps:

1. **Choose Tasks⇨Account Reconciliation.**

   Peachtree displays the Account Reconciliation window.

2. **Click the list box selector next to the Account to Reconcile box to display the list of your accounts.**

3. **Select the account you want to reconcile.**

4. **Click OK.**

In Peachtree, you can balance _any_ account, not just a checking account. For example, you can balance savings accounts, petty cash accounts, and credit card accounts.

After you select an account, Peachtree shows you all the transactions available for reconciliation for the period (see Figure 16-3). Any checks you voided already have check marks in the Clear column. In the Checks and Bank Debits section at the top of the window, checks you've written appear. In the Deposits and Bank Credits section at the bottom of the window, the deposits you've made appear.

Service charges box

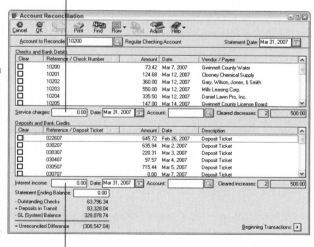

Figure 16-3:
After you select an account, Peachtree shows you the transactions you can clear.

Interest income box

#2 PEACHTREE

Reconciling for the first time

If you're reconciling for the first time in Peachtree, you may find checks and deposits on your bank statement that you haven't entered in Peachtree because the transactions occurred *before* you started using Peachtree. Your very first action after opening the Accounts Reconciliation window should be to enter these outstanding transactions. In the Account Reconciliation window, click the Beginning Transactions button in the lower-right corner of the window. Peachtree displays the Beginning Transactions dialog box shown in the figure.

Enter unreconciled transactions that appear on your bank statement but occurred before you started using Peachtree. In the top portion of the window, enter unreconciled checks that were written before you started using Peachtree. Remember that "unreconciled checks" includes checks remaining unreconciled from prior bank statements *as well as* checks that appear on the bank statement you're about to reconcile. In the lower portion of the window, enter unreconciled deposits that were made before you started using Peachtree. Like unreconciled checks, "unreconciled deposits" includes deposits remaining unreconciled from prior bank statements *as well as* deposits that appear on the bank statement that you're about to reconcile.

For checks, assign the check number as the Reference number. For deposits, the Reference number doesn't really matter; just make sure that you enter the deposit amount as it appears on your bank statement. Click OK when you finish. The transactions you entered will appear in the Account Reconciliation window so that you can mark them as cleared and reconcile your bank statement.

Beginning Transactions

| ⊗ Cancel | ✓ OK | ▦ Row ▾ | 🖨 Help ▾ | | | |

| Account to Reconcile: | 10200 | | Statement Date: | Mar 31, 2007 | |

Beginning Withdrawals

Amount	Description	Reference	Date
25.43	Office supplies	1243	Feb 18, 2007

Beginning Deposits

Amount	Description	Reference	Date
4,650.00	Various customers	022807	Feb 28, 2007

The Account Reconciliation window also shows journal entries that affect the account you are reconciling. So, in the strictest sense, you see more than checks and deposits in this window. In the top of the window, you see transactions that credited (oops, there's that C word) the account, and in the bottom of the window, you see transactions that debited (you knew that was coming) the account.

You can maximize this window to see more information, and you can sort the information in the window by any column in the window — just click the column heading. And, if you're looking for a particular transaction, you can click the Find button on the Account Reconciliation window's toolbar to search for it.

Marking Checks and Deposits

Okay, back to the bank statement. Stop looking at the Account Reconciliation window for a minute and look at your bank statement. That's it — that piece of paper you got from the bank. Not the computer screen. (It's so easy to get glassy-eyed whiling reconciling a bank statement . . . we got glassy-eyed while writing this chapter.) The bank statement shows checks and deposits that have cleared the bank, along with those other miscellaneous transactions that the bank may have recorded (service charges, interest, and so on). When you compare it to the Account Reconciliation window (that's right, you can look back at the computer screen now), you'll see some transactions in Peachtree that don't appear on the bank statement, and you may also see some transactions on the bank statement that don't appear in Peachtree.

You need to mark the cleared transactions that appear on the bank statement as cleared in Peachtree's Account Reconciliation window. Follow these steps to continue the reconciliation process:

1. **In the Statement Ending Balance box (at the bottom of the window), enter the ending balance that appears on the bank statement.**

2. **In the Service charges box (below the Checks and Bank Debits portion of the window), enter any bank service charges.**

   Assign the date of the bank statement to the service charges and select the appropriate expense account for the service charges.

3. **In the Interest Income box (below the Deposits and Bank Credits portion of the window), enter any interest you earned.**

   Assign the date of the bank statement to the interest and select the appropriate income account for the interest income.

4. **Click in the Clear box at the left edge of a Checks and Bank Debits entry if the entry appears on the bank statement.**

   Peachtree places a check mark in the box, indicating that the bank has processed the item. You can match cleared checks on the bank statement to checks in Peachtree using the number assigned to each transaction. In the Account Reconciliation window, you'll find the number for checks in the Reference/Check Number column in the top half of the window. Remember, you can sort the information in the window by any column heading by clicking the column heading.

   Instead of clicking one transaction at a time, you can mark groups of transactions. If a consecutive range of checks — either by check number or check date — cleared, you can click the Range button and enter the range of numbers or transaction dates for Peachtree to mark. Or, as a shortcut, if most of the transactions in either portion of the window cleared the bank, click in that portion of the window, click the Row button, and then click the All button. Peachtree marks all transactions cleared. You can then remove check marks by clicking the Clear box next to the transactions that did not clear the bank.

5. **Click in the Clear box at the left edge of a Deposits and Bank Credits entry if the entry appears on the bank statement.**

Most people use amounts to match deposits on the bank statement to deposits in Peachtree. If you're having trouble matching deposits on your bank statement to deposits in the Account Reconciliation window, Peachtree probably grouped a deposit differently than the deposit you presented at the bank. You can drill down on a deposit in the Account Reconciliation window to open it in the Select for Deposit, Receipts, or Receive Payment window (wherever it was created). Then if necessary, change the deposit ticket ID number so that all items you deposited in the bank on the same deposit ticket have the same deposit ticket ID number in Peachtree. Also, use the bank deposit report we showed you earlier in Figure 16-1 to help identify the receipts included in each deposit in Peachtree.

You can use the same shortcut methods just described in the previous tip to mark deposits cleared.

6. **Repeat Steps 4 and 5 until you have accounted for each transaction that appears on the bank statement.**

7. **Check the Unreconciled Difference value — your goal is to make that value equal to 0.**

8. **If the Unreconciled Difference value equals 0, you've reconciled and you're finished (pat yourself on the back); just click OK to save your work.**

9. **If the Unreconciled Difference value doesn't equal 0, read on (sorry).**

When the Account Doesn't Balance

What do you do when you've marked everything but the Unreconciled Difference does not equal 0? Well, you do a little detective work. Go dig your detective hat and magnifying glass out of the closet so you can prepare to snoop around. We'll wait. . . .

Items to review

The Unreconciled Difference may not equal 0 for several reasons:

✓ **The bank may have recorded a transaction that you haven't recorded in Peachtree.** Look for bank charges such as check reorder charges, other service charges, or interest payments if your account is interest-bearing.

✔ **The bank may have recorded a transaction *for a different amount than you recorded in Peachtree.*** Compare the amounts of checks you've recorded in Peachtree to the amount the bank cleared for the check. Similarly, compare deposit amounts you recorded in Peachtree to deposit amounts on the bank statement.

Add the digits of the unreconciled difference and see whether they equal 9 or a multiple of 9. If so, the odds are good that you have transposed the digits on one or more checks or deposits. We don't know why this works, but it does.

✔ **You may have cleared a transaction that didn't clear the bank.** Review the transactions you have cleared. If you used the Range button, double-check the check numbers in the range both in Peachtree and on the bank statement. Occasionally, you'll write a check and forget to post it in Peachtree, and the check will clear the bank. When you mark a range, finding that transaction can be difficult.

✔ **You may have recorded the Statement Ending Balance incorrectly.** Make sure you typed the amount correctly.

You can sort the information in the Account Reconciliation window by any column in the window — just click the column heading. And, if you're looking for a particular transaction, you can click the Find button on the Account Reconciliation window's toolbar to search for it.

If you determine that you need to correct an existing transaction or enter a check or receipt, you can leave the Account Reconciliation window open while you edit or add the transaction in the appropriate window. Repeat: *There is no need to close the Account Reconciliation window.* To edit a check or deposit, double-click it in the Account Reconciliation window, and Peachtree opens it in the window where you created it. To enter a check or deposit, just ignore the Account Reconciliation window for a minute and choose Tasks ➪ Payments to open the Payments window, or choose Tasks ➪ Receipts to open the Receipts window. If you determine that you need to record either a bank service charge or an interest payment, you can make an adjustment — read on.

Making adjustments

You make adjustments when you can't find the problem and you decide to write it off as a lost cause.

Accountants do not frown on adjusting to reconcile the account when the difference is small (less than $5). You need to weigh the trade-offs: Is it worth spending hours to find a nickel? We have to believe that your time is worth more if you're doing something other than looking for a dime or a quarter. On the other hand, don't write off large unreconciled differences and don't make a practice of writing off unreconciled differences; eventually, they will come back to haunt you.

To record an adjustment, follow these steps:

1. **Click the Adjust button to open the General Journal Entry window.**

   Yep, that's right, adjustments are journal entries. Don't panic.

2. **Record a journal entry.**

   On one line of the entry, select the cash account you're reconciling for the GL account. On the other line of the entry, select an income or expense account for the GL Account. Record additional withdrawals for check reorder charges as credits to the cash account and additional deposits like interest earned as debits to the cash account.

   Record the same amount on the other line that contains the income or expense account. For additional withdrawals, select an expense account like Bank Charges. For additional deposits, select an income account like Interest Income. If you aren't sure what account to select, ask your accountant.

   What about when you're "off" by a small amount that you want to write off? Remember this rule: If the Unreconciled Difference is negative, you need to record a journal entry that credits the cash account for the Unreconciled Difference amount. If the Unreconciled Difference is positive, you need to record a journal entry that debits the cash account for the Unreconciled Difference amount.

3. **When you finish, click Save and then click Close to redisplay the Account Reconciliation window.**

4. **Place a check mark in the box next to each adjusting entry to mark them as cleared and to balance your account.**

   Each debit or credit on the journal entry that affects the cash account appears as a separate entry in the Account Reconciliation window.

5. **When the Unreconciled Difference equals 0, you can consider the account reconciled. Click OK to close the Account Reconciliation window.**

If you later find the source of the problem that caused you to make the adjustment and you want to delete or change the adjustment, open the General Journal Entry window and click the Open button. Double-click the adjustment transaction to display it; then edit it or click the Delete button.

Printing the Reconciliation Summary

After all your hard work, you'll want to print a record of the balanced reconciliation. Follow these steps:

1. **Choose Reports⇨Account Reconciliation.**

   The Select a Report window appears, showing the available Account Reconciliation reports.

2. **From the list on the right, select Account Reconciliation.**

3. **Click the Print button to produce a paper copy of the report.**

   Peachtree prints a report similar to the one you see in Figure 16-4, showing that the Unreconciled Difference is 0.

You may have noticed other available reports when you printed the Account Reconciliation report. You don't really need the Deposits in Transit, Outstanding Checks, or Outstanding Other Items reports, because all of that information appears on the Account Reconciliation report. We've already discussed the Bank Deposit Report; the Account Register report lists individual deposits and withdrawals in the selected account.

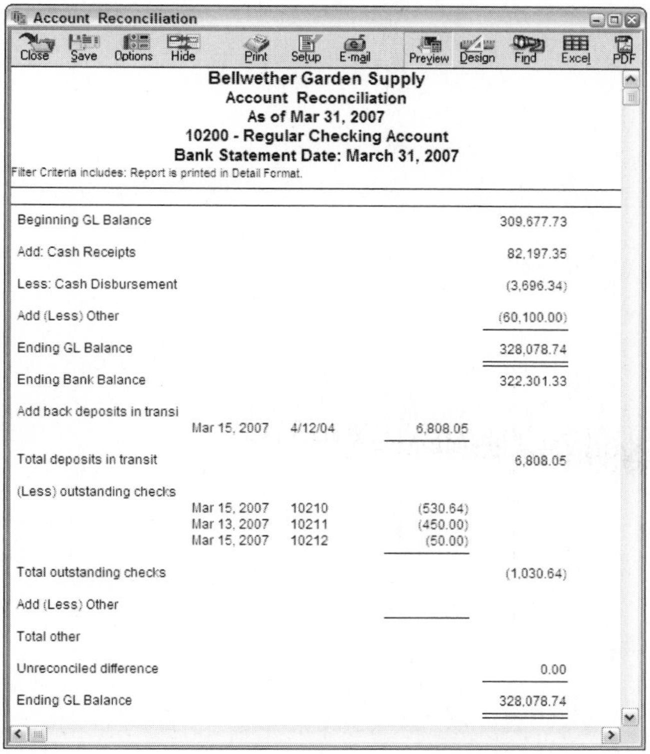

Bellwether Garden Supply
Account Reconciliation
As of Mar 31, 2007
10200 - Regular Checking Account
Bank Statement Date: March 31, 2007
Filter Criteria includes: Report is printed in Detail Format.

Beginning GL Balance				309,677.73
Add: Cash Receipts				82,197.35
Less: Cash Disbursement				(3,696.34)
Add (Less) Other				(60,100.00)
Ending GL Balance				328,078.74
Ending Bank Balance				322,301.33
Add back deposits in transi				
	Mar 15, 2007	4/12/04	6,808.05	
Total deposits in transit				6,808.05
(Less) outstanding checks				
	Mar 15, 2007	10210	(530.64)	
	Mar 13, 2007	10211	(450.00)	
	Mar 15, 2007	10212	(50.00)	
Total outstanding checks				(1,030.64)
Add (Less) Other				
Total other				
Unreconciled difference				0.00
Ending GL Balance				328,078.74

Figure 16-4: This report shows the matching ending balances as well as deposits and checks that have not yet cleared the bank.

In transit refers to checks you've written or deposits you've made that have not yet cleared the bank.

By the way, you can see the same information that appears on the Account Register report in the Account Register window. Choose Tasks➪Account Register to display the window. (The window reminds us of the register you use with a personal checking account to record deposits and withdrawals.) For the current period, it lists only transactions that affect the cash account. You can switch to a different cash account, and you can change the time-frame displayed in the window. To see the details of any transaction, double-click to drill down on it; Peachtree displays it in the window where you created it.

Visit this book's Web site for more information on Peachtree.

Chapter 17

When Accounting Cycles End . . . and Other Miscellaneous Stuff

. . . .

In This Chapter

▶ Changing accounting periods

▶ Making general journal entries

▶ Preparing the payroll quarterly report

▶ Completing year-end tasks

. . . .

A lot of stuff happens at the end of an accounting period — whether that period is a month, a quarter, or a year. Most of it deals with finishing the transactions that belong in the period that's ending. But you need to start working in a new period before you finish working in the old period. Why? Because you won't have all the necessary information to finish working in a period on the last day of the period. For example, you won't be able to reconcile your bank statement on the last day of the period because the bank hasn't mailed it to you yet.

In this chapter, we talk about the things you do at the end of each period — and some other topics that just don't fit well in any other chapter, such as (and here come those words!) making journal entries.

Changing Accounting Periods

When you open Peachtree, note the date that appears on the left side of the toolbar, next to the current accounting period. The date matches the system date on your computer, and Peachtree uses that date as the default date for every transaction you enter.

This is true, except when the accounting period changes. Look at an easy example: You use standard months in the calendar year for accounting periods, and your fiscal year matches the calendar year.

Fiscal year refers to the year your business uses. The fiscal year can be the same as the calendar year — and run from January 1 to December 31. Or the fiscal year might run from April 1 to March 31 or from July 1 to June 30. You and your accountant establish your fiscal year with the IRS.

Your current accounting period is January. All through the month, Peachtree will default transaction dates to the current day of the month in January. On February 1, Peachtree will correctly report the date in the lower-left corner of the screen, but the default date for transactions will not be February 1 — because you haven't changed the accounting period. The default date on transactions will be January 1 — and will remain January 1 for all subsequent days — until you change the accounting period.

So, what's the big deal? Well, you may be sitting around posting February transactions in the accounting period that runs from January 1 through January 31. That, of course, will misstate the financial condition of your business for both January and February. You need to change the accounting period on the first day of each new period.

"Is this a difficult thing?" you ask. Nope. "Don't you need to wait to change the accounting period until you've posted everything in the current period?" Nope. You can switch back to any open period at any time. "You mean that changing the accounting period doesn't close it?" Yes, that's what we mean. In fact, in Peachtree, you can't close a single accounting period; you can close only a fiscal year, a subject we talk about later in this chapter.

Although you can change to a prior accounting period, we don't recommend that you make changes to transactions in a prior period after giving your data to your accountant. Such actions tend to strain relationships.

If you enable security in Peachtree Complete or Peachtree Premium, a padlock symbol appears in the Change Accounting Periods dialog box next to prior periods. You can allow users to view prior period transactions but prevent them from editing those transactions using Peachtree's security settings. In the Maintain Users window, click the System tab. Then double-click the Tasks program area and set the Transactions in Prior Periods option to Read. For more information on Peachtree and security, see Chapter 18.

When you move forward to a new accounting period and operate on an accrual basis, Peachtree asks you whether you want to print invoices, checks, and reports before changing the period. (If you operate on a cash basis and have printed all checks and invoices, Peachtree asks only about reports.) If you haven't finished entering transactions for the period, you don't need to print anything. But we suggest that you simply answer no to these questions, even if you've entered all transactions. Then when you've finished entering everything for a period, use the Reports menu to print all the reports for the period — the journals discussed at the end of the chapters in Part II and the financial reports discussed in Chapter 15.

To make the report-printing process easier, create a report group that contains all the reports you want to print at the end of a period. Then you won't need to select and set up each report. To find out how to make a report group, see Chapter 14.

So, why do we suggest that you print reports using the Reports menu *before* you change the accounting period? Well, the window you see when you're selecting reports to print while changing the accounting period doesn't include a few reports that you might find useful, such as the Balance Sheet, Income Statement, Trial Balance reports. And although you can print these reports at any time for any period, printing them for an accounting period while you're working in that accounting period is easiest.

Second, for reasons we don't understand, when you print reports while changing the period, Peachtree displays reports from prior periods as well as reports from the current period. You may think the reports appear because you've changed a transaction in a prior period, but we can't prove that. We've found that printing reports using a report group is faster and easier.

Follow these steps to change the accounting period if you operate on an accrual basis:

1. **Click the Period button on the toolbar (the button that displays the current period) or choose Tasks⇨System⇨Change Accounting Period.**

   The Change Accounting Period dialog box appears, as shown in Figure 17-1.

2. **Click the new period you want to use, and then click OK.**

   Peachtree may display a dialog box asking whether you want to print checks or invoices.

3. **If the dialog box appears, select Yes if you won't be returning to this period; choose No if you'll be returning to this period to enter additional transactions.**

   If you select Yes, Peachtree simply redisplays the Change Accounting Period dialog box with the original period selected. You'll need to click Cancel and print invoices or checks. If you select No, Peachtree displays a dialog box asking whether you want to print reports.

   Peachtree changes the accounting period; you'll see the new period reflected in the lower-right corner of the screen.

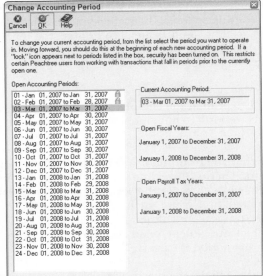

Figure 17-1:
Use this
dialog box
to switch to
a different
period.

If you operate on a cash basis and have no unprinted invoices or checks, Peachtree doesn't ask whether you want to print invoices and checks, but it does ask whether you want to print reports. Again, we advise that you *not* print reports at this time. Instead, create a report group to print the necessary end-of-period reports.

Making General Journal Entries

Okay, don't be freaked by the title of this section. Journal entries are nothing more than another type of transaction to enter in Peachtree — you just won't use journal entries as often as you do other types of transactions. In fact, here's a good rule to follow:

> *Don't* enter journal entries unless your accountant tells you to make the entry and you *really* know what you're doing.

You see, the truth is, you can usually find another way to enter the information. For example, when you pay your telephone bill of $37.50, you spend money from your Cash account and identify what you spent the money on by making an entry in your Telephone account. You don't need to use the General Journal Entry window; instead, you write a check from the Payments window or the Select for Payment window.

By the way, the example also demonstrates what accounting types mean when they talk about *double-entry bookkeeping*. The term simply means that each transaction conducted by your business causes you — and your accounting software — to make at least two entries. And here come those dreaded words: One entry is a *debit* and one entry is a *credit*. The most important thing to know about debits and credits is that they must equal each other. Do you *need* to know this? No. Peachtree will do most of it for you. Can it *hurt* you to know this? No. Who knows . . . knowing may even help you.

So, when *would* you use the General Journal Entry window? Well, you'd use it to record the depreciation of assets. Most businesses let their accountants figure the amount of the depreciation — and then the accountant gives you the journal entry information so you can enter the transaction. Or, if you use job costing (see Chapter 12), you can add overhead to a job using a journal entry.

If you're interested in the "how and why" of debits and credits, read the sidebar titled "The accounting equation — and how it works."

Okay, now that we've told you *not* to make journal entries unless you really need to make them, we'll show you how to make them:

1. **Choose Tasks➪General Journal Entry to display the General Journal Entry window (see Figure 17-2).**

2. **If necessary, change the date.**

3. **Enter a reference number to identify the transaction.**

   We used JE (for Journal Entry) and then the month and date (refer to Figure 17-2).

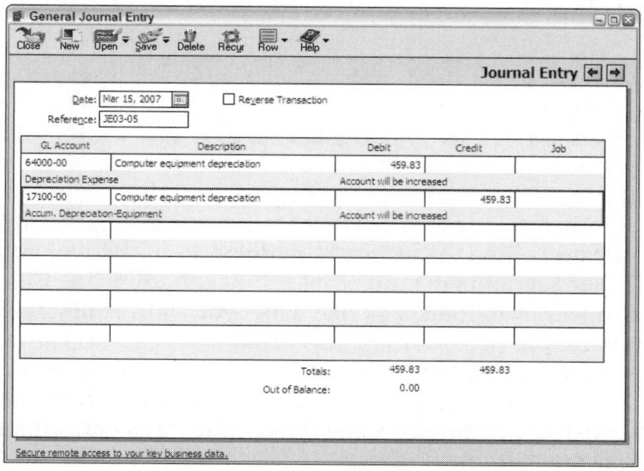

Figure 17-2:
To be able to record a journal entry, it must be in balance.

GL Account	Description	Debit	Credit	Job
64000-00	Computer equipment depreciation	459.83		
Depreciation Expense		Account will be increased		
17100-00	Computer equipment depreciation		459.83	
Accum. Depreciation-Equipment		Account will be increased		
	Totals:	459.83	459.83	
	Out of Balance:	0.00		

Date: Mar 15, 2007 ☐ Reverse Transaction
Reference: JE03-05

General Journal Entry
Journal Entry ← →

Secure remote access to your key business data.

4. **In the Account No. column, select the first account you want to change.**

Accountants like you to list debits first and then credits. Doing so is not a rule, but it will make you look more professional. We're going to assume that you want to look professional, so enter the debit first and then the credit.

5. **In the Description column, enter the reason for the transaction.**

Peachtree copies these words to the next line for you, saving you the typing. You can change them on the next line if you want.

6. **In the Debit column, enter the amount.**

7. **If necessary, assign a job to the entry.**

8. **Repeat Steps 4–7, but in Step 6, enter the amount in the Credit column.**

When you finish, debits should equal credits. If they don't, the amount you're out of balance appears at the bottom of the window.

9. **Click Save to save the journal entry.**

Peachtree won't let you save the entry if it's out of balance.

For some journal entries, you may need to enter multiple debits to offset one credit or multiple credits to offset one debit. That's fine. A journal entry consists of a set of debits and credits that equal each other. Also, your accountant may send you a list of entries to make before you close the fiscal year. You can make all the entries in one General Journal Entry transaction — maybe even with a description such as A "Adjustment per CPA." That is, you can keep entering lines in the General Journal Entry window using only one transaction number.

Accounting Behind the Scenes

If you chose the Hide General Ledger Accounts option for your company in the Maintain Global Options dialog box, then your transaction windows don't look like the ones we show throughout this book. In particular, you don't see any general ledger accounts in your transaction windows. See Chapter 13 for a comparison of what windows look like when you hide or display general ledger accounts.

In Chapter 5, we promised to tell you about a neat way to identify the accounts Peachtree updates as you enter transactions even if you don't display the general ledger accounts in your transaction window. Click the Journal button in the window, and Peachtree displays the Accounting Behind the Screens dialog box you see in Figure 17-3.

And yes, you *can* make changes in this dialog box to modify one or more of the accounts Peachtree updates for this transaction, but we don't recommend it. Notice that you can't change a debit to a credit or vice versa; if you change the accounts and you don't know what you're doing, you'll really mess up your company's books.

Figure 17-3:
The accounting Peachtree is doing "behind the screens" when you hide general ledger accounts.

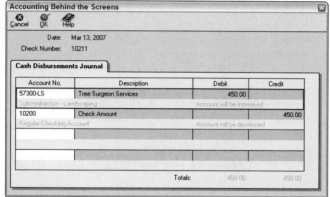

Batch Posting

People who like batch posting typically work in a multi-user environment and want to review transactions before updating the general ledger. When you use batch posting in Peachtree, you save transactions as you enter them, but they don't update your accounts — or appear on reports — until you post. You choose batch or real-time posting in the Maintain Company window. See Chapter 2 for more information.

Okay, so you know you need to post to update your accounts. You also need to make sure you post all journals before you try to change the accounting period. If you use batch posting, follow these steps to post:

1. **Choose Tasks⇨System⇨Post to display the Post dialog box you see in Figure 17-4.**

2. **Select the journal you want to post, or leave the check mark in All Journals to post everything.**

3. **Click the OK button.**

   Peachtree displays a bar across the screen as it posts and then redisplays the main Peachtree window when posting finishes.

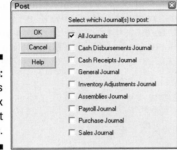

Figure 17-4:
Use this
dialog box
to post
journals.

Before producing many reports, Peachtree asks batch posting users if they want to post before viewing the report.

Preparing the Payroll Quarterly Report (941)

This one's easy. You're gonna love it. To prepare the payroll quarterly report (941), you just print a form. Actually, you need to print the form onto the IRS form you receive in the mail. (See Chapter 14 for information on aligning information on forms.) If you're afraid you're going to mess up the IRS form, print Peachtree's version to paper and transfer the numbers (be sure to put everything in the right box).

We recommend that you print the 941 Worksheet (or the 941B Worksheet if appropriate) before you print the Federal Form 941. The worksheet will show you the amount you were supposed to deposit during the quarter — and we assume that you make your payroll tax deposits in a timely fashion, as required by law. You'll need the amount you deposited to print an accurate Federal Form 941. You can take advantage of the Print Preview feature and display the 941 Worksheet on-screen to see get the amount you should have deposited.

To print the appropriate forms, follow these steps.

1. **Choose Reports⇨Payroll to display a list of payroll reports.**

2. **From the Report List on the right, click the Federal Form 941 folder to display the available versions of the 941 and 941B report.**

3. **Highlight the version you want to print, and then click the Print button.**

   Peachtree displays a dialog box showing the options for the form.

4. **Supply the total tax liability amount you paid for the current payroll quarter.**

5. **Make sure that you're printing the form for the correct quarter.**

6. **Click OK.**

7. **When Peachtree prompts you to select a printer, do so and then click OK again.**

Peachtree prints the form.

If you need to complete form 941B — the second page of the payroll tax liability form — repeat these steps, choosing the correct form in Step 3.

If you don't want to mess with form alignment and you don't want to write in the numbers, get fill-in forms from the IRS Web site. You can type your 941 information while displaying the fill-in form in Adobe Acrobat Reader 3.0 or later, and then print the completed form. You can't save the forms using Acrobat Reader; if you want to save the forms, you must purchase Adobe Acrobat Approval, available at the Adobe Web site (www.adobe.com) for a nominal fee.

Printing W-2s

Printing W-2's is similar to printing the 941 quarterly report. W-2s are forms that you print, and you'll need to purchase W-2 forms and load them into your printer.

You can purchase your forms from your local office supply store or printer (the people who print forms, not the machines), or you can use the offers you receive in your Peachtree software box. Chapter 21 lists Web contact information on a few sources for forms. (If you contact Deluxe Forms at 800-328-0304 and reference this book and discount code R03578, you'll receive 20 percent off your first order.)

By default, Peachtree automatically includes all employees that you've paid during the current year when you print W-2s, even if you've marked an employee as inactive.

You mark an employee inactive in the Maintain Employees/Sales Reps window when the employee no longer works for you. But if the employee worked for you during any part of a calendar year, you must provide the employee with a W-2. Also, by marking the employee inactive, you make the employee a candidate for purging, which we talk about later in this chapter.

You must print W-2s before you close the Payroll Tax year. If the federal government has changed the W-2 form, you'll need to modify it (see Chapter 14). Or you can subscribe to Peachtree's Payroll Tax Table Service; toward the end of December, the service will provide you with the latest update, including any form modifications. (You find out more about updating payroll tax tables later in this chapter.)

To print W-2s, follow these steps:

1. **Choose Reports⇨Payroll to display a list of payroll reports.**

2. **From the Report List on the right, click the Federal Form W-2 folder.**

   Peachtree displays available versions of the W-2 — 4 per page and Standard. The form you select should match the form you purchased.

3. **Highlight the form you want to print, and then click the Print button.**

   Peachtree displays the options dialog box for the form.

4. **If necessary, make changes in the options dialog box.**

   You can (but shouldn't need to) change the form to print, select employees by ID, or change the year for which you want to print W-2s (you can select any open year).

5. **Click OK.**

6. **When Peachtree prompts you to select a printer, do so and then click OK.**

   Peachtree prints the W-2s.

If you're printing W-2s on laser forms, you need to print the forms several times, one for each copy of the W-2 that should be produced.

Printing 1099s

I know it's beginning to sound like a mantra, but 1099s are forms that you print. You'll need to purchase 1099 forms and load them into your printer.

You can purchase your forms from your local office supply store or printer (the people, not the machines), or you can use the offers you receive in your Peachtree software box. Chapter 21 lists Web contact information on a few sources for forms. (If you contact Deluxe Forms at 800-328-0304 and reference this book and discount code R03578, you'll receive 20 percent off your first order.)

By default, Peachtree automatically includes all vendors who meet both of the following criteria:

✔ You've selected Independent Contractor or Interest in the 1099 Type field of the Maintain Vendors window

✔ You've paid more than $600.00 or more than $10.00 in interest during the calendar year

Refer to Chapter 5 for information on setting up vendors and the 1099 Type field.

You must print 1099s before you close the payroll year. If the federal government has changed the 1099 form, you'll need to modify it (see Chapter 14). Or you can subscribe to Peachtree's payroll tax table service; toward the end of December, the service will provide you with the latest update, including any form modifications. (You find out more about updating payroll tax tables later in this chapter.)

You use the same steps to print 1099s that you use to print W-2s, except that the forms appear in the 1099 Forms folder under Accounts Payable in the Report list.

Peachtree supports producing 1099s for only two types of vendors: Interest (1099-INT) and Independent Contractors (1099-MISC). If you need to produce 1099s for more than two types of 1099 vendors, workarounds exist, but they are beyond the scope of this book. So, once again, if you *like* this book, contact Wiley and tell them that you want them to hire us to write a Peachtree Bible.

Updating Payroll Tax Tables

To calculate payroll accurately, Peachtree uses tax tables. Each tax table is associated with the current year. The name of the table ends with the last two digits of the current year, which means that as you begin a new calendar year, you must have new tax tables with names that include the last two digits of the new year. In addition, the calculations in the tax table may have changed, and you need to make sure that the tax tables will calculate correctly. So, how do you do this? We suggest that you subscribe to the Peachtree Payroll Tax Table Update service. Whenever the government makes changes to payroll tax tables or payroll forms, the service sends you a disk that you load to update your tax tables. For more information on the service and subscribing, call 800-336-1420 or visit `www.peachtree.com/html/tax_pca.cfm` to order tax tables online.

Peachtree doesn't come with global tax tables when you purchase the product. Global tax tables include the tables that calculate federal income tax, Social Security, and Medicare. To use payroll, you *must* have these tables. So, either set them up yourself or pop for the Payroll Tax Table Update service.

You will need to manually update the User-Maintained tax tables. Since most tax tables you see in the User-Maintained Payroll Tax Tables window don't change drastically from year to year, you can use last year's tax table as a model to create this year's table. For details on creating a user-maintained tax table, see "Union Dues" in Chapter 19.

Understanding Closing

Closing the Payroll Tax Year and the Fiscal Year are not difficult or time-consuming. The activities you should complete *before* closing, however, can be time-consuming. Before we jump into describing those activities, you should understand what happens when you close in Peachtree.

Closing in Peachtree automatically does the equivalent of manually preparing and posting closing entries to the general ledger. In addition, Peachtree resets all your vendors', customers', and employees' year-to-date totals to zero. That way, you can begin monitoring the new year's purchases with each vendor, sales with each customer, and wages, benefits, deductions, and taxes with each employee.

Why does Peachtree enable you to close the payroll tax year separately from the fiscal year? The payroll tax year is based on a calendar year. When you close the payroll tax year, Peachtree zeros out year-to-date wage and tax information for employees and year-to-date purchasing information for vendors — the information that appears on W-2s and 1099s. The fiscal year may or may not be a calendar year. When you close the fiscal year, Peachtree zeros out other information (such as year-to-date customer information) and closes everything, including the general ledger. If your fiscal year is the same as your calendar year, you still need to let Peachtree close both years to close everything.

Even if you don't use payroll, you need to close the payroll year to zero-out year-to-date vendor purchase information.

When you close, Peachtree automatically closes the first 12 periods, which make up the oldest open year.

Timing is everything when you talk about closing. Typically, no one is ready to close a year on December 31. But because Peachtree allows you to have two years — 24 periods — open simultaneously, you should have no trouble moving forward to the new year while leaving the prior year open. Therefore, closing should not become a pressing issue unless you find that you're working in Period 24 and need to move to a new open period. If you find yourself in this situation, you need to close both the Payroll Tax Year and the Fiscal Year — and Peachtree will close Periods 1 through 12 and then renumber so that the periods that used to be 13–24 become 1–12.

To identify the years you have open, click the Change Accounting Period button on the toolbar. The open Fiscal and Payroll Tax Years appear on the right-side of the box (see Figure 17-5).

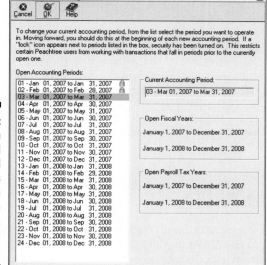

Figure 17-5:
The open Fiscal and Payroll Tax Years appear in the Change Accounting Period dialog box.

Payroll

Before you close the payroll year in Peachtree, you must finish payroll processing for the year you intend to close. You should check employee background information, wage information, and tax information. Printing W-2s should be the last task you perform for the year you intend to close so that you can be sure that the information on the forms will be accurate.

If you have adjustments or fringe benefits that should be reflected on W-2s, you can include them in the last payroll of the year, or you can run a separate payroll. We recommend that you try to include them in the last payroll of the year. See Chapter 9 for information on setting up and paying bonuses.

Accounts payable

In addition to printing 1099s before closing the payroll year, the end of the year is a good time to consider identifying any vendors with whom you no longer do business and marking them inactive in the Maintain Vendors window. You also should review open purchase orders and close any that you know you won't fill, making them candidates for purging along with inactive vendors.

Inventory

There are no special year-end procedures for inventory in Peachtree. However, many businesses perform a physical inventory count at this time of year. Peachtree's Physical Inventory List report contains space for you to enter actual counts, which makes taking physical inventory easier.

Be sure to print an Inventory Valuation Report after you adjust your quantities to the physical count. See Chapter 11 for details on inventory and Chapter 14 for details on printing reports.

Accounts receivable

In accounts receivable, you simply need to clean up your files. You should review customers and, in the Maintain Customers/Prospects window, mark inactive those with whom you no longer do business. Review open quotes and sales orders and close any that you know you won't fill, making them candidates for purging. You should also review your Aged Receivables report for possible bad debts and write off any amounts that you know you won't collect.

Job cost

Job cost helps you track costs and revenues over the life of a project. By its very nature, job costing doesn't run on a calendar or fiscal year basis and has no end-of-year procedures. But while you're housekeeping, you might want to review existing jobs and mark appropriate ones as inactive using the Maintain Jobs window.

Account reconciliation

We recommend reconciling your December bank statements before you close the fiscal year to make reconciled checks and deposits candidates for purging. Unreconciled transactions remain in the system.

General ledger

You'll probably want to wait to close the fiscal year until you've had time to make year-end adjustments — and you get those from your accountant after he or she has prepared the income tax return for the business. You also should review your chart of accounts for accounts you're no longer using and mark those accounts inactive.

Even though Peachtree purges inactive transactions, the program retains enough information to produce comparative financial statements.

Archiving your data

If you're using Peachtree Premium, you can archive your company data at any time, but the end of the year is a good time to create an archive copy of your company data. When you archive data, Peachtree creates a read-only copy of your company that you can use to print reports and review transactions. From your accountant's perspective, the good news is that you can't add, change, or delete anything in an archived company. Accountants really *don't* like it when you make changes to a closed period (it kind of makes them nuts) and, if you create an archive copy of your data to use for prior year research right before you close, you will make your accountant *very* happy.

Choose File⇨Archive Company. In the Archive Company window, supply a name for the company. Peachtree suggests the name Archive-XXXXXX, where the Xs represent today's date in six digit format. If you're following our advice, you'll name your archive company file using the numeric form of the year that you are archiving. Then, click Archive, and Peachtree creates the archive company.

You many want to change the period to the last month (typically December) of the year you are archiving before you create the archive file. If you change periods as we suggest, Peachtree displays that month when you open the archive file.

To use an archived company, choose File⇨Open Archived Company. Peachtree displays the Open Archived Company dialog box, which lists all archived companies you've created. Select the one you want to open and click OK. Your company name along with the archive date appear in the title bar of the window.

After you review reports or transactions, choose File⇨Open Previous Company to view a list of companies you can open. Select your company from the list. Note that archive companies do not appear in this list.

Peachtree stores archived companies in a folder called Archives, which appears inside your company folder after you create your first archive company. Should you happen to be housecleaning and get the urge, you can delete old archives from the Archives folder.

Using the Year-End Wizard

We suggest that you print any year-end reports you want before you start the Year-End Wizard. When you close the payroll tax year, Peachtree doesn't prompt you to print any reports, and when you close the fiscal year, Peachtree selects the reports for you that you can print. To retain some choice in this matter, print all your reports before you start the Year-End Wizard.

It's also important to understand that you can't cancel the year-end closing process once you click the Begin Close button in the Year-End Wizard. Restoring from a backup becomes the only way you can "undo."

In addition to the backup that Peachtree will force you to make before closing, we suggest that you use the archiving feature available in Peachtree Premium and described in the "Archiving your data" section so that you'll have access to reporting and transaction details in closed years. If you're using a version of Peachtree other than Peachtree Premium, we suggest that you create a prior year company as described in Chapter 19 so that you can print reports and view transaction details in closed years.

Don't forget that the closing process closes the first 12 periods. By the time you close these periods, you won't be working in them anymore; instead, you'll be working in Period 13 or later. It's safe to close the first 12 periods if you've finished all the work for those periods.

Closing the payroll year

Peachtree asks you to back up during the closing process, so make sure you have disks available if you back up to floppy disks.

Even if your company's fiscal year doesn't match the calendar year, payroll always operates on a calendar year basis. Therefore, sometime in January, after you've created your last payroll for the preceding year, confirmed that your payroll data is complete, and printed your W-2s, you're ready to close your payroll information for last year.

You won't be able to cancel this process after the first screen.

Follow these steps to close the payroll year:

1. **Choose Tasks➪System➪Year-End Wizard.**

   Peachtree displays the current open years; fiscal years appear on the left side of the window and payroll tax years appear on the right.

2. **Click Next to display the Close Options dialog box shown in Figure 17-6.**

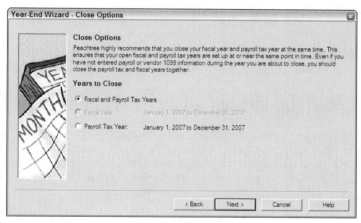

Figure 17-6:
This is where you identify what you want to close.

3. **Select Payroll Tax Year and click Next.**

   Payroll Tax Year is not an option if the oldest open year is the current year.

   If you have any unprinted payroll checks or if you have not yet printed W-2s or 1099s, Peachtree prompts you to print them before you continue. Click Cancel, print the appropriate forms, and restart the closing process. Once you close, you won't be able to print them.

   Peachtree displays the Back Up Company Data window.

4. **Click the Back Up button.**

   Peachtree displays the Back Up Company window, where you can choose to include your company name in the backup file name. For details on creating the backup, see Chapter 18.

When Peachtree finishes the backup, you see the Back Up Company Data window again.

5. **Click Next.**

   If you use Peachtree Premium, the Archive Company window appears, where you can archive your data before you close. See "Archiving your data," earlier in this chapter, for details on archiving.

   Peachtree displays a window where you can confirm that you are closing the payroll tax year for last year.

6. **Click Next.**

   The Begin Close-Year Process window appears. This is your final chance to cancel before closing.

7. **Click Begin Close.**

   Peachtree closes the oldest open payroll tax year and displays a window where you see the new open years, both fiscal and payroll.

8. **Click Finish.**

   You can now continue to enter payroll information into the next year.

Closing the fiscal year

If you've finished processing and made all adjustments to a fiscal year, you need to close that fiscal year in Peachtree. You'll probably postpone closing a fiscal year until well after you start a new one. For example, if your fiscal year matches the calendar year, you probably won't close last year any earlier than March of the current year.

Before Peachtree will let you close a fiscal year, you must not have any purchases that are "Waiting on a Bill" from the vendor in the year that you want to close. Typically, you will have received all bills by the time you want to close the fiscal year, but if you haven't, you should change these transactions. Choose Tasks⇨Purchases/Receive Inventory. Then click the Open button. For any purchase that contains a Y in the Waiting? column, remove the check mark and post the transaction.

Depending on the amount of data in your company, closing can take awhile. You can't interrupt the process.

Before you start the Year-End Wizard, make sure you print any year-end reports you want.

To close the fiscal year, follow these steps:

1. **Choose Tasks⇨System⇨Year-End Wizard.**

   Peachtree displays the current open years; fiscal years appear on the left side of the window and payroll tax years appear on the right.

2. **Click Next to display the Close Options window.**

3. **Select Fiscal Year and click Next.**

   If you did not previously close the payroll tax year, select Fiscal and Payroll Tax Years.

   Peachtree displays the Fiscal Year-End Reports window.

   If you have any unprinted checks, Peachtree prompts you to print them before you continue. Click Cancel to print them and then restart the closing process. You won't be able to print them after you close.

4. **If you followed our advice and printed all your reports before you started, uncheck all the reports listed in the box and click Next.**

   Peachtree displays the Back Up Company Data window.

5. **Click the Back Up button.**

   Peachtree displays the Back Up Company window, where you can choose to include your company name in the backup file name.

   When Peachtree finishes the backup, you see the Back Up Company Data window again.

6. **Click Next.**

   If you use Peachtree Premium, the Archive Company window appears, where you can archive your data before you close. See the "Archiving your data" section earlier in this chapter for details on archiving. After you make choices in this window, click Next.

   Peachtree displays a window where you can view and change the new open fiscal years. Usually, it is *not* necessary to change any of these dates, since Peachtree adjusts them for you.

7. **Click Next.**

   Peachtree displays a window where you can confirm that you are closing the year(s) you are closing.

8. **Click Next to display the Begin Close-Year Process window.**

   This window represents your final chance to cancel before closing.

9. **Click Begin Close.**

   Peachtree closes the oldest open year(s) and displays a window where you see the new open years, both fiscal and payroll.

10. **Click Finish.**

Purging

You can purge information from your company data files at any time, but most people like to tie purging with other year-end activities. Peachtree lets you purge transactions in closed years of your company, and you can purge payroll and 1099 transactions only when you've closed both the fiscal and payroll tax years during which you entered those transactions.

Purging can take quite a long time, depending on the size of your data, the speed of your computer, and the age of the transactions you choose to include in the purge. Peachtree's purge process doesn't have a limit to the number of passes it makes, or the time it takes to go through the journal file. We strongly recommend that you start this process before leaving for the night or weekend.

If your Peachtree journal file is large, you may want to purge every month. To determine the size of your journal file, choose Help⇔Customer Support and Service⇔File Statistics and look at the Size in Kbytes column for the Jrnl Rows file. If this file is larger than 50 MB, you'll probably want to purge in small increments.

Peachtree purges two types of data:

- **Transactions:** Quotes, invoices, sales orders, receipts, purchases, purchase orders, payments, paychecks, and general journal entries from previous years that are no longer needed. If you use Peachtree Premium or Peachtree Complete, Peachtree also purges time and expense tickets.

- **Inactives:** Customers, vendors, employees, inventory items, jobs (and phases and cost codes if you use Peachtree Premium or Peachtree Complete), and general ledger accounts that you've marked as Inactive in the Maintain windows.

If you plan to purge inactives, you should also purge transactions because Peachtree won't purge inactives if any transactions apply to them.

Follow these steps to purge information:

1. **Choose Tasks⇔System⇔Purge Wizard.**

   Peachtree displays a screen that tells you the earliest date you can use to purge data.

2. **Click Next.**

   Peachtree displays the Back Up Company Data window.

3. **Click the Back Up button.**

   Peachtree displays the Back Up Company window, where you can choose to include your company name in the backup file name, For detailed instructions on creating a backup, see Chapter 18.

   When Peachtree finishes the backup, you see the Back Up Company Data window again.

4. **Click Next.**

   Peachtree displays the Old Transactions window shown in Figure 17-7.

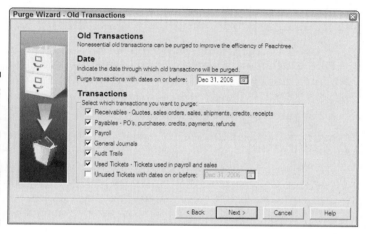

5. **Select the date Peachtree uses to identify transactions to purge as well as the types of transactions to purge, and click Next.**

   The choices concerning Audit Trails and Tickets appear only if you're using Peachtree Premium or Peachtree Complete.

6. **In the Account Reconciliation window, indicate whether you use the Account Reconciliation feature. If you do, select the accounts you reconcile.**

   Double-click the arrow in the Use column for any account type — most people reconcile cash accounts at a minimum — to display the account numbers. Then add a check mark next to each account you reconcile. Peachtree purges all unreconciled transactions dated earlier than the purge date you established in Step 5.

7. **Click Next.**

   The Inactive Maintenance Records window appears.

8. **Check the box next to each type of inactive maintenance record you want to purge.**

   Maintenance records are the ones you create for customers, vendors, employees, general ledger accounts, inventory items, and jobs in the windows that open when you select a command on the Maintain menu.

9. **Click Next.**

   The Summary of Options window appears, and you see a list of the choices you made in the wizard.

10. **Click Begin Purge.**

    You can stop a purge as long as the Stop button is available in the Purge Is in Progress window. When that button appears dimmed, you can't safely interrupt the purge. Yes, that means turning off your computer at this point is *not* recommended.

11. **When the purge finishes, click Close.**

    You can click the Log button to see a file in the Windows Notepad listing your selection criteria and information about what did and did not purge (see Figure 17-8).

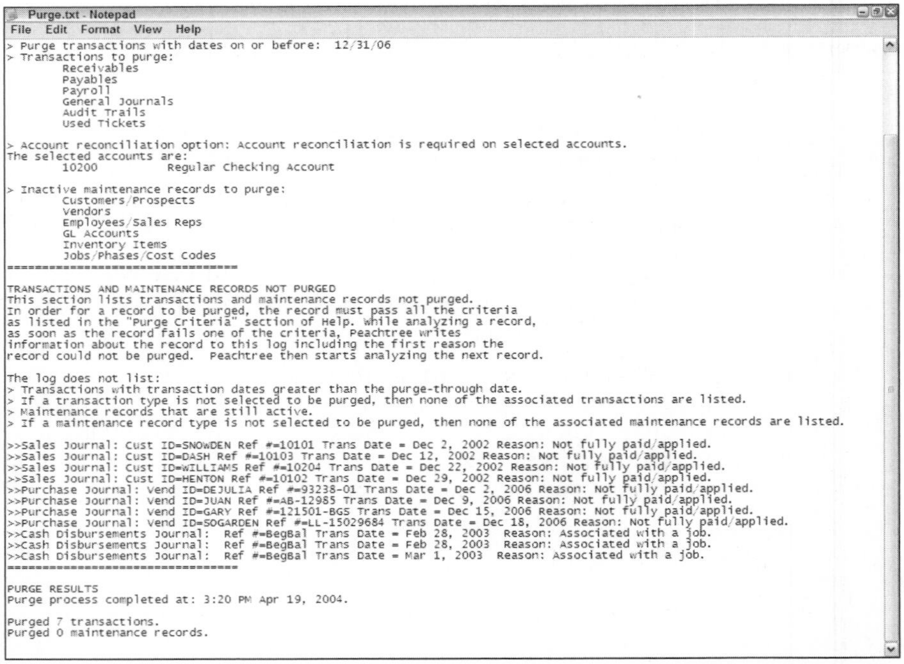


```
> Purge transactions with dates on or before:  12/31/06
> Transactions to purge:
        Receivables
        Payables
        Payroll
        General Journals
        Audit Trails
        Used Tickets

> Account reconciliation option: Account reconciliation is required on selected accounts.
The selected accounts are:
        10200           Regular Checking Account

> Inactive maintenance records to purge:
        Customers/Prospects
        Vendors
        Employees/Sales Reps
        GL Accounts
        Inventory Items
        Jobs/Phases/Cost Codes
=================================

TRANSACTIONS AND MAINTENANCE RECORDS NOT PURGED
This section lists transactions and maintenance records not purged.
In order for a record to be purged, the record must pass all the criteria
as listed in the "Purge Criteria" section of Help. While analyzing a record,
as soon as the record fails one of the criteria, Peachtree writes
information about the record to this log including the first reason the
record could not be purged.  Peachtree then starts analyzing the next record.

The log does not list:
> Transactions with transaction dates greater than the purge-through date.
> If a transaction type is not selected to be purged, then none of the associated transactions are listed.
> Maintenance records that are still active.
> If a maintenance record type is not selected to be purged, then none of the associated maintenance records are listed.

>>Sales Journal: Cust ID=SNOWDEN Ref #=10101 Trans Date = Dec 2, 2002 Reason: Not fully paid/applied.
>>Sales Journal: Cust ID=DASH Ref #=10103 Trans Date = Dec 12, 2002 Reason: Not fully paid/applied.
>>Sales Journal: Cust ID=WILLIAMS Ref #=10204 Trans Date = Dec 22, 2002 Reason: Not fully paid/applied.
>>Sales Journal: Cust ID=HENTON Ref #=10102 Trans Date = Dec 29, 2002 Reason: Not fully paid/applied.
>>Purchase Journal: Vend ID=DEJULIA Ref #=93238-01 Trans Date = Dec 2, 2006 Reason: Not fully paid/applied.
>>Purchase Journal: Vend ID=JUAN Ref #=AB-12985 Trans Date = Dec 9, 2006 Reason: Not fully paid/applied.
>>Purchase Journal: Vend ID=GARY Ref #=121501-BGS Trans Date = Dec 15, 2006 Reason: Not fully paid/applied.
>>Purchase Journal: Vend ID=SOGARDEN Ref #=LL-15029684 Trans Date = Dec 18, 2006 Reason: Not fully paid/applied.
>>Cash Disbursements Journal:  Ref #=BegBal Trans Date = Feb 28, 2003  Reason: Associated with a job.
>>Cash Disbursements Journal:  Ref #=BegBal Trans Date = Feb 28, 2003  Reason: Associated with a job.
>>Cash Disbursements Journal:  Ref #=BegBal Trans Date = Mar 1, 2003  Reason: Associated with a job.
=================================

PURGE RESULTS
Purge process completed at: 3:20 PM Apr 19, 2004.

Purged 7 transactions.
Purged 0 maintenance records.
```

Figure 17-8: The purge log shows you what information was and wasn't purged.

When Stuff Doesn't Purge

Sometimes, after purging, you'll find information still in the system that you think should have been purged. Peachtree follows some extensive rules when selecting information to purge.

We don't have room to list all the rules Peachtree follows, but we do list the ones that we believe affect the majority of transactions that don't purge. Anything Peachtree leaves in your database we call a *saved* transaction, and we refer to the date you specify while setting up a purge (the one that identifies the latest transaction date Peachtree will purge) as *the purge through date*. Peachtree saves the following:

- All transactions dated later than the purge through date.
- All transactions in any open year.
- Purchases and invoices that are not completely paid as of the purge through date.
- All cash disbursements or receipts applied to a saved purchase or invoice.
- All purchases and invoices that are related to saved cash disbursements or cash receipts.
- Purchases or invoices related to unpurged jobs.
- Open sales orders and purchase orders.
- All quotes with a transaction date or good-through date later than the purge through date.
- Unreconciled transactions (as of the purge through date) associated with an account you designate as one you reconcile.
- For Peachtree Premium and Peachtree Complete, time or expense tickets dated later than the purge through date or available as reimbursable expense tickets. If you have not chosen to purge unused time tickets, Peachtree also saves unused tickets for employees paid using time tickets and tickets tied to customers where the ticket status is HOLD.
- Inactive jobs (and phases and cost codes for users of Peachtree Premium and Peachtree Complete) with saved transactions that refer to the inactive job.

Use the purge log to review what Peachtree purged and what it didn't purge. The log will even tell you why an item wasn't purged. Peachtree stores the purge log (purge.txt) in your company data folder. You can open it at any time by locating it using Windows Explorer and double-clicking it.

Visit this book's Web site for more information on Peachtree.

Chapter 18

Keeping Your House Safe

*A*s with any financial software, a business has a lot at stake with Peachtree data. After all, it holds the financial picture of the business. In this chapter, we show you how to protect that data. You discover how to protect your data from computer failure as well as from unauthorized entry. We even show you how to play detective and snoop on what others are doing to your financial data. We don't provide the detective hat, overcoat, and spyglass. Those you need to provide for yourself.

Backing Up Your Data

You know the silly (but popular) little saying, "Stuff Happens." (That's not exactly how it goes, but you get the idea.) Well, it's true. Things happen. Now, we don't mean to sound pessimistic here, but computers do fail, data gets deleted or corrupted, and disasters like fire or theft can occur.

Well, you can always get another computer and reload Peachtree, but even for millions of dollars you can't buy all the work that you've put into Peachtree. That's why backing up your company data files on a regular basis is important. You can then restore your data if necessary.

By backing up company data within Peachtree Accounting, your company data files and customized forms are backed up by using the Peachtree format. You can save your Peachtree backup to a floppy disk, a hard drive, or other mediums, such as Flash or Zip drives, tapes, or recordable CDs.

If you choose to back up your company data to a tape device, you must exit Peachtree and use the tape backup to copy the company files. To make backups to those mediums, refer to the tape instruction manual. However, we really don't recommend this method.

Establish a regular policy for backing up your data. Backups are the only way to guarantee the safety of the accounting records that you create in Peachtree. Without backups, you run the risk of losing weeks, months, or even years of work. Do you really want to take that kind of risk?

The general rule is that if you used Peachtree that day, back it up that day. Backing up data doesn't take long, and in case of a catastrophe, you'll be glad you did. Disks are inexpensive, even Zip disks, especially when compared to the costs of reconstructing and reentering data.

In Table 18-1, we show you an ideal plan for backing up. That's the one that we really suggest that you use. However, we're also realistic. We show you an absolute minimum strategy for backing up in Table 18-2. If you don't follow Plan A (the ideal), at the very least, follow Plan B (the minimum). Believe us — you won't regret it. Backing up is the cheapest form of insurance that you can have.

When we refer to backup disks, they can be floppy disks, Zip disks, Flash drives, recordable CDs, or tapes.

Table 18-1	Plan A: An Ideal Backup Strategy
Number of Disks	*Backup Plan*
Ten sets of daily disks	Back up onto a set of different disk(s) each day (Monday through Friday) for two weeks, and then begin again with the same set of disks.
Twelve sets of monthly disks	At the end of each month, back up to one of these sets of disks. Keep the monthly disk sets off site.

Table 18-2	Plan B: The Minimum Backup Strategy
Number of Disks	*Backup Plan*
Five sets of daily disks	Use one set of disks for each day of the week and then start reusing them again the following Monday.
Two sets of monthly disks	At the end of each month, back up to one of these sets of disks. Again, alternate them. For example, use one disk in January, and then use the second disk in February. Reuse the January disk in March. Keep the monthly disk sets off site.

Label each disk with the day of the week. If a backup uses more than one disk, be sure to number the disks so that you know which disk is Disk 1 of the backup.

To back up your Peachtree data and customized forms, use the following procedure:

1. **Choose File⇨Back Up or press Ctrl+B to display the Back Up Company dialog box.**

   No other users can work in Peachtree during the backup process.

   Select the Reminder check box if you want Peachtree to prompt you to back up in a specified number of days. When the specified number of days has elapsed, Peachtree displays a reminder message as you close the company or exit the program.

   In a moment, Peachtree suggests a name for the backup file, but first, Peachtree wants to know whether it should include the company name as part of the backup filename. We recommend that you *do* include it, especially if you have multiple companies. That way, you won't confuse the backups of one company with another. If you do want to include the company name as part of the backup, select the Include company name in the backup file name check box.

   Peachtree can also backup your archived data if any is available. Find out more about archiving data in Chapter 17.

2. **Click the Back Up button to display the Save Backup As dialog box.**

3. **In the File Name text box, type a filename for the backup set or leave the one Peachtree suggests.**

   Peachtree backup files use the $*$.ptb (for *Peachtree backup* — clever, huh?) file extension. Peachtree automatically adds the current date to the backup file name. If you elected not to include the company name as part of the backup filename, Peachtree includes the letters BU as part of the filename. (In case you're wondering, BU stands for *backup* — also clever.)

4. **From the Save In list box, choose a location for the backup set.**

   We recommend backing up to a floppy disk (through the A: drive), a Flash drive or CD drive, a Zip disk, or a different computer.

   For data protection, don't back up the Peachtree data to the same hard drive where the current data resides. If the hard drive crashes, you'll have two sets of unrecoverable data, and that won't do you one bit of good.

5. **Click the Save button.**

   Peachtree displays the estimated size in megabytes (MB) of your backup, or if you're backing up to a floppy disk, Peachtree displays the estimated number of floppy disks needed for the backup.

6. **Click OK.**

   If you're backing up to floppy disks, Peachtree prompts you to insert the first and subsequent disks as needed.

7. **Click OK.**

   The system displays the backup progress.

Depending on the quantity of data, the speed of your computer, and the backup device that you use (floppy drives back up more slowly than any other kind of device), the backup process might take several minutes to complete. Don't interrupt the process. Interrupting the backup process could corrupt the data — and then you'd have a useless backup.

If you're backing up to floppy disks, you probably need to erase those disks before you use them again. Refer to your Windows documentation for procedures on erasing floppy disks.

If you're backing up to a Zip disk, rewriteable CD or a Flash drive, at some point the disk might become too full to hold another backup, so you'll want to erase the oldest backup file. Refer to your Windows documentation for directions on deleting files.

If you have a server making automated backups for you, be sure that you don't make incremental backups. You cannot backup individual files, because each file relates to another. You must backup the entire Peachtree company data. In fact, we suggest that you let the server back up everything and that you back up Peachtree independently by using the steps that we provide — it's safer, and we're into safety, especially when it's Peachtree data we're talking about.

Restoring Information

We sincerely hope that you never ever have to restore your data. If you do, it probably means that something really bad happened, and we just don't want those kinds of incidents to materialize.

But if something does happen . . . you'll be so glad that you read this chapter and found out how to back up and restore your data.

If you backed up company data by using an alternate utility (for example, a tape program), you must use that program to restore your company data.

No other users can use Peachtree during the restore process. Use the following steps to restore your data:

1. **Open the company that you want to restore.**

Any data that you entered after making the backup isn't part of the backup and so is lost.

2. **Choose File⇨Restore to launch the Restore Wizard.**

   Peachtree displays the Select Backup File window, as shown in Figure 18-1.

   If the file that you want to restore doesn't appear, click the Browse button and then locate and click the name of the backup file that you want to restore. Peachtree backup files use the `*.ptb` file extension.

   Many compression programs, such as WinZip, can open and extract PTB files.

3. **Click Next.**

   The Select Company screen appears. You can restore the backup file over the currently open company data, or you can restore it to a new separate company folder.

4. **Select the option that you want, and then click Next.**

   What data gets restored? Peachtree works differently from some of the accounting programs that you might have used. When you restore data, you're restoring *all* the information that was previously backed up; all the Receivable, Payroll, Payable, Inventory, and Job Cost information together. *Everything.* The process replaces all the current data files with those that have been previously backed up. You cannot restore individual files because each file relates to another. However, you can restore your customized forms, such as invoices or checks, separately from your data.

5. **Click the options that you want restored, and then click Next.**

   A confirmation screen appears.

6. **Click Finish.**

   Peachtree displays the progress of the restoring data files. If you restore data from floppy disks, Peachtree prompts you to insert any subsequent disks as needed.

Figure 18-1:
Peachtree automatic-
ally displays
the last file
that you
backed up.

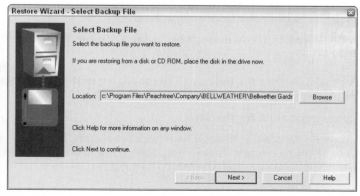

Depending on the quantity of data, the speed of your computer, and the backup device that you use, the restoration process could take several minutes to complete. Don't interrupt the process. Interrupting the restoration process could corrupt the data.

Securing Your Data from Prying Eyes

Because accounting data is highly sensitive and confidential, you might want to prevent unauthorized persons from accessing your data. Peachtree includes a security system that allows you to set accessibility parameters for each user that you identify. Peachtree security makes use of user IDs and passwords.

Setting up users

Peachtree can allow tailored access for different individuals. With the security feature activated, Peachtree requires each user to enter his or her ID and password before opening and working with company data. With the correct user ID and password, users can access the areas of the program to which they have rights.

If you choose to set up users, you must set up at least one user with access to the Maintain Users window. Typically, this user is considered a system administrator who has the access rights to all Peachtree features, including setting up and maintaining company users and their passwords.

While setting up users, no other users can be using Peachtree.

To set up users, follow these steps:

1. **Choose Maintain⇨Users.**

   With the first user ID created, Peachtree displays an information box.

2. **Click OK to close the information box.**

3. **In the Maintain Users dialog box, enter a unique ID for the first user.**

   Set up the system administrator first.

   Typically, you use the first name or initials, or in the case of the administrator, try something like *admin* for the user ID.

4. **Enter a password for the user.**

   This is the user's secret code to access Peachtree. The password can be up to 13 alphanumeric characters. Don't use a slash (/) as part of the password.

Passwords and user IDs are both case sensitive and must be unique: Joe, joe, and JOE are all different. Two users can't have the same password.

5. **Click Save.**

   With the first user ID created, a message box appears.

6. **Click OK to close the message box.**

Don't lose the password! If you do lose your user ID or password, and no one else can open the Peachtree company, you have no back-door way to access the passwords. You'll need to back up your data and send it into Peachtree Technical Support for them to locate the information. This process can take several weeks!

7. **To enter additional users, click the New button.**

8. **Enter the next user ID and its corresponding password.**

   From here, you can customize the rights for each user (see the following section) or click the Close button to close the Maintain User dialog box.

Customizing user rights

When setting up users, you can select an access level to each program area for an individual user. For example, if you have a clerk who mainly makes Accounts Receivable entries, you might want to restrict that clerk from accessing Accounts Payable, Payroll, or General Ledger information. Perhaps you have a person who receives inventory, but you want to restrict him or her from editing the information after it's entered or from printing Inventory Valuation reports.

By customizing the user rights, you give each user specific access. The rights vary depending on the feature. Through the Maintain Users window, you can choose from the following options when deciding how much access you want to allow a user:

✔ No Access at All to the Feature

✔ Only the Ability to View the Data

✔ To View and Add to the Data

✔ To View, Add to, or Edit the Data

✔ Full Rights, which allows the user to view, add, edit, or erase data.

The security that we describe here is for the Complete and Premium editions. If you're using Peachtree Accounting, your choices are limited to setting security selections for an entire module (Accounts Receivable, Accounts Payable, Payroll, and so on).

With the exclusion of the system administrator (the first user that you set up), by default, Peachtree provides each user full access to all areas of Peachtree except access to Maintain Users.

We recommend that you have only one administrative user with access to the Maintain Users window. This setup prevents multiple users from accessing other users' passwords, changing other users' records, or inadvertently erasing users.

To quickly restrict access to a primary program area, such as Payroll, select a control level in the Summary tab of the Maintain Users dialog box. For example, in Figure 18-2, we restrict all rights to Payroll by clicking the Summary tab and selecting No Access from the Control drop-down list.

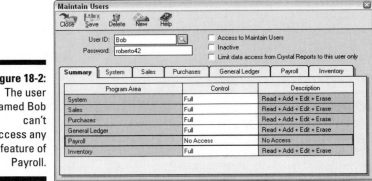

Figure 18-2:
The user named Bob can't access any feature of Payroll.

Follow these instructions to be more specific in user accessibility:

1. **Click the tab for which you want to set restrictions.**

   Peachtree displays a list of the program areas.

2. **To expand the list of program areas in the grid, double-click the triangle to the left of the program area and then click the Control area you want to modify.**

   The access choices vary depending on the feature. For example, if you click the Sales tab and open the Control drop-down list for Receipts, you find that you can select Full, No Access, Read, Add, or Edit. But if you open the Control drop-down list for Master Lists under the Reports program area, you can select only Full or No Access. In Figure 18-3, the user named Alex can enter or view Inventory transactions but cannot edit or erase them.

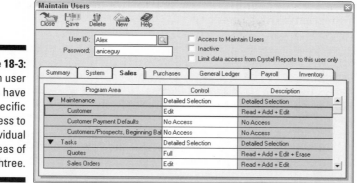

Figure 18-3:
Each user
can have
specific
access to
individual
areas of
Peachtree.

3. Click Save.

Any changes that you make take effect the next time you open the
company.

Removing users

When users leave or change positions, you can stop them from accessing
Peachtree data. You have the option of deleting users or making them inactive. When you make users inactive, their user ID profiles remain in Peachtree,
but you disable their access to the company. Deleting users erases their user
IDs and passwords.

To remove a user, choose Maintain⇨Users to display the Maintain Users
window. Enter or look up the user record that you want to remove, and then
select the Inactive check box or click OK to delete the user.

If multiple users still exist, and you attempt to delete the only administrative
user with access to Maintain Users, Peachtree displays an error message. You
cannot remove the administrator user until you have removed all other user
records.

Any changes that you make take effect the next time you open the company.

Logging on as a user

After user IDs exist, when you or anyone on your Peachtree network (if you're
on a network, that is) tries to open your Peachtree company files, Peachtree
prompts you for a user ID and password.

Enter your user ID in the User ID text box, and then enter your password in the Password text box. Press Enter.

User IDs and passwords are case sensitive.

The user ID system works like this: Say you give user Bob no access to Payroll, but user Alex does have Payroll access. No matter whose computer Bob uses — his own computer or Alex's computer — he doesn't have access to Payroll when he logs on as Bob.

To prevent unauthorized access to your data, exit the Peachtree program when you leave your computer unattended.

Using the Audit Trail Report to Track Actions

Peachtree includes an audit trail security feature that tracks when a person enters new data, maintains (edits) existing data, and removes data. The audit trail provides accountability of users, discourages users against fraudulent activity or mistakes, and tracks transaction history. The Audit Trail report traces all activity and adjustments; from this report, you might find that transactions were completed without your knowledge.

Only the Peachtree Complete or Premium editions contain the audit trail feature.

Turning on the audit trail

Before you can begin using the Audit Trail report, you need to tell Peachtree to begin tracing your steps:

Choose Maintain⇨Company Information to open the Maintain Company Information dialog box. Then select the Use Audit Trail check box and click OK.

If you haven't set up users with password protection, a message appears, suggesting that you do so to personalize audit trail activity. We recommend that you set up users as we describe earlier in this chapter in the aptly named section, "Setting up users." Peachtree can associate the user currently working in the Peachtree company with the data being entered or maintained, consequently providing a more comprehensive audit trail.

If you activated the audit trail feature and implemented password security, limit access to the Maintain Company Information window to one or two users. This action can prevent other users from inadvertently removing audit trail functionality to enter or maintain company data in a fraudulent manner.

Viewing the Audit Trail report

The Audit Trail report displays the date and time a Peachtree action took place as well as who did it and what he or she did.

To view the Audit Trail report, choose Reports⇨Company to display the Select a Report dialog box, and then double-click the Audit Trail report to display the report on-screen.

Like other Peachtree reports, you can customize the Audit Trail report. See Chapter 14 for instructions on customizing reports.

By default, this report displays only the transactions that took place on the current date, but you can click the Options button to select a different time frame. You can even specify the user ID that you want to review.

Visit this book's Web site for more information on Peachtree.

Chapter 19

Real-Life Ways to Use Peachtree

- -

In This Chapter

▶ Dealing with customer prepayments

▶ Making a prior year company

▶ Moving to a new computer

▶ Handling retainage

▶ Organizing employee loans, garnishments, and other odds and ends

- -

This book wouldn't be complete if we didn't provide you with solutions for some common situations. Given the limited space we have in the book to present Peachtree to you, we worked really hard to make room for these "real-life situations."

Handling Customer Prepayments

Under certain conditions, your customers may pay you before you actually deliver the goods or services you promise. For example, in the building business, customers often provide down payments that builders use to purchase construction materials. Some service providers, such as lawyers and CPAs, request retainers before performing work. If your customers pay you in advance, you're accepting money that is a liability to your business, and you must account for it as a liability until you deliver the promised goods or services.

Deposits and *prepayments* — interchangeable terms — are, by definition, payments received before you deliver goods or services. Your method of accounting — cash or accrual basis — has no bearing on how you handle these prepayments. Prepayments from customers are actually your liabilities.

Because you receive the money before you supply the goods or services, you now have an obligation (a liability) to the customer to complete the transaction. Deposits are unearned revenue.

First, you need a G/L account in which to record customer prepayments when you receive them. To handle customer deposits, from the Maintain Chart of Accounts window, set up Customer Deposits as an Other Current Liability type account. (See Chapter 3 to review adding accounts.)

Second, set up a nonstock inventory item for deposits. Use the Customer Deposits G/L account you created for all three G/L accounts (Sales, Salary/ Wages, and Cost of Sales), and be sure to select an exempt Item Tax Type. See Chapter 11 to review setting up inventory items. When you receive a prepayment from your customer, create a receipt to track the deposit by following these steps:

1. **Choose Tasks⇨Receipts to display the Receipts window.**

2. **Enter the deposit ticket ID, customer ID, reference number, date, payment method, and cash account as you normally enter receipts.**

   Refer to Chapter 8 for details on entering receipts.

3. **On the Apply to Revenues tab, enter a quantity of 1.**

4. **In the Item drop-down list, select Deposits.**

5. **Enter the amount of the deposit.**

6. **Click Post to save the transaction.**

This transaction debits Cash and credits Customer Deposits. The balance sheet shows the Customer Deposits account and the Cash account increased by the amount of the prepayment.

After you perform the work, you want to send your customer an invoice. Add a final line item on the invoice showing a quantity of –1 using the Deposits item for the amount of the prepayment (see Figure 19-1). If the amount of the invoice you create equals the amount of the prepayment, the customer owes you nothing. If the invoice amount exceeds the prepayment amount, the customer owes you the difference between the invoice amount and the prepayment amount.

On the line showing the deposit, be sure to enter a negative number (–1) for the quantity but use a positive number for the unit price amount. Peachtree automatically converts the total amount to a negative number. When you receive the balance due from the customer, create another receipt. The amount that appears in the Receipts window is the remainder of the invoice amount.

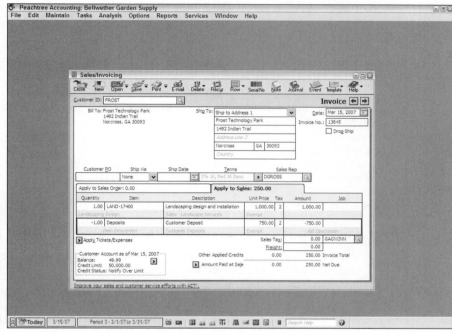

Figure 19-1:
The deposit reduces the amount owed against the invoice.

Creating a Prior Year Company

When you close and purge a fiscal year, the transactions and reports are no longer accessible. Before you close your year, you should archive your company data if you're using Peachtree Premium. If you're using any other edition of Peachtree, you should create a prior year company so that you can print reports, look for transactions, and so on. The big picture? You create a backup of your existing company, create a new, empty company, and then restore the backup into the new, empty company.

To find out how to close and purge a fiscal year, turn to Chapter 17.

Follow these steps *before* you close the fiscal year.

1. **Open your company in Peachtree.**

2. **Choose File➪Back Up and then click Back Up.**

3. **In the File Name text box, leave your company name but replace today's date with the last open fiscal year (so that you can easily identify the data in the backup).**

4. **Under Save In, select the folder on your C drive where you store your Peachtree company data.**

   If you work in a network, save the backup to the My Documents folder on your C drive.

5. **Click Save to back up.**

When the backup is complete, you need to restore it and simultaneously create a new company.

The following technique works with Peachtree 2004 or later. If you have an older version of Peachtree, you need to create a new, empty company before you restore, and then restore the backup into that company.

To restore the backup, follow these steps:

1. **Choose File⇨Restore to start the Restore Wizard.**

2. **On the Select Backup File screen, click Browse and navigate to the location where you stored the backup.**

3. **Select the backup file (its name ends with .ptb) and click Open.**

4. **Click Next to display the Select Company screen.**

5. **Click the A New Company option button and click Next.**

6. **On the Restore Options screen, check all appropriate boxes.**

   Peachtree automatically checks Company Data; if you have Customized Forms or Web Transactions, check those boxes as well.

7. **Click Next.**

8. **On the Confirmation screen that appears, click Finish.**

   Peachtree creates a new company for you and restores the backup into it.

9. **When Peachtree finishes the process, choose Maintain⇨Company Information and change the name of the new company.**

   Use an obvious name, such as FY*XXXX* Company Data, where *XXXX* is the last open fiscal year in the company. This step makes the second copy of your company appear as a separate name in the Open Company window.

You can now open your regular current company by choosing File⇨Open Company. When you need to refer to the prior-year company, you can find it in the Open dialog box.

Handling Retainage

Suppose that you receive partial payment at the beginning of a job and the balance when the job is completed. If you work this way, you have *retainage,* and you need to know how to correctly bill customers and track both billed and unbilled amounts owed to you.

You need only one extra account on your balance sheet — an Other Current Asset account called Retainage Receivable. See Chapter 3 to review adding accounts.

Suppose that the terms of your contract specify that you will earn $10,000 and get paid 90 percent at the beginning of the job, with 10 percent, or $1,000, held as retainage. You need to prepare an invoice for $9,000 and account for the $1,000 retained by the customer:

1. **Choose Tasks⇨Sales/Invoicing to display the Sales/Invoicing window and select the customer for whom you need to prepare the invoice.**

2. **In the line item section of the invoice, create two lines.**

3. **Fill in the total sale amount ($10,000 in our example) and post the line against an income account.**

4. **On the second line, post the retainage amount as a negative number to the Retainage Receivable account.**

   This transaction credits an income account for $10,000, recognizing the revenue you will generate from the contract. It also debits Accounts Receivable for $9,000, the amount the customer owes immediately, and Retainage Receivable for $1,000, the amount the customer will pay when the job is completed.

When the customer pays you for the original invoice — $9,000 in this example — record the receipt in the same way that you'd record any receipt in the Receipts window. When you finish the job, you need to bill the customer for the final amount — the retainage amount of $1,000 in this example. Record an invoice, posting the line item for the retainage amount as a positive number against the Retainage Receivable account. As a result of this invoice, Peachtree debits the Accounts Receivable account and credits the Retainage Receivable account, reducing the amount of retainage the customer owes but increasing the customer's regular Accounts Receivable balance.

To use the following method to track retainage balances, we suggest that you use an invoice number for the retainage bill that is the same as the original invoice number, followed by an *R*.

When the customer pays this bill, record the receipt the same way you would record any receipt in the Receipts window.

To help you identify clients who have unbilled retainage amounts, we suggest that you take advantage of Peachtree's Account Reconciliation feature, which allows you to reconcile *any* account, not just bank accounts. Follow these steps to reconcile an account:

1. **Choose Tasks⇨Account Reconciliation to display the Account Reconciliation window.**

2. **Select the Retainage Receivable account.**

   Note that some amounts appear in both the top and the bottom portions of the window. For example, the Vendor/Payee at the top and the Description at the bottom are the same. The entry at the bottom of the window occurred when you prepared the original invoice that held back the retainage amount. The entry in the top portion of the window occurred when you billed the retainage.

3. **When you see a pair of like entries in the top and bottom portions of the window, check them off as we've done in Figure 19-2, because they represent billed retainage amounts.**

   You don't need to enter the Statement Ending Balance, because you don't have a statement; the Unreconciled Difference should always be zero, because you're checking off matching entries in both the top and bottom of the window.

4. **When you finish marking off matched pairs, click OK.**

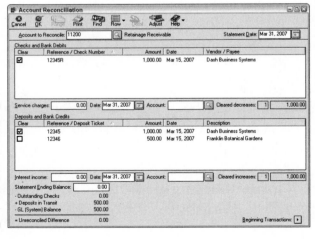

Figure 19-2: Match retainage amounts to help identify billed retainage.

Use the Account Reconciliation Other Outstanding Items report to identify the clients and retainage amounts you didn't mark off in Account Reconciliation. These are the amounts that you have not yet billed. Choose Reports⇨Account Reconciliation and highlight the Other Outstanding Items report. On the Filter tab, choose the Retainage Receivable account. When you print the report, you'll see only retainage amounts that you haven't yet billed.

Paying for Purchase Orders by Credit Card

Here's the situation: You ordered goods using a purchase order and, at the time that you placed the order, you hadn't made a decision about how you wanted to pay for the goods. The goods arrive, and you now decide that you want to pay for them using a credit card. You need to make sure that you account for everything properly in Peachtree.

We assume that you have a Credit Card Payable account — an Other Current Liability account — on your chart of accounts so that you can record credit card purchases in Peachtree. If you don't have a Credit Card Payable account — yours might be called Visa Payable or American Express Payable — set one up using the Maintain Chart of Accounts window.

The process starts when you decide to buy a product and you issue a purchase order. You create the purchase order the same way that you create any purchase order. Some time passes, and the goods you ordered arrive. You need to receive the goods into inventory and establish that you owe the vendor money. Enter a purchase against the purchase order in the same way that you enter a purchase against any purchase order.

So far, you haven't done anything unusual. But when you pay for the goods using a credit card, you need to make some changes from your usual procedures. Follow these steps:

1. **Choose Tasks⇨Payments to display the Payments window.**

2. **Select the vendor.**

3. **Find the appropriate purchase to pay and click in the Pay column.**

4. **Change the Cash Account from your checking account to the Credit Card Payable account (see Figure 19-3).**

5. **Enter a dummy check number and click Save to save the transaction.**

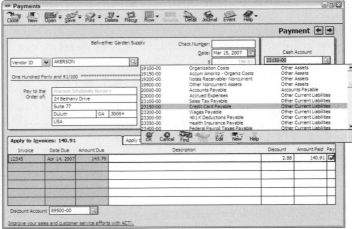

Figure 19-3:
Apply the
payment to
the pur-
chase and
select your
Credit Card
Payable
account.

When the credit card bill arrives, you need to make sure that you post the items on it correctly in the Purchases/Receive Inventory window. Typically, you post each line item to its appropriate expense account. But for goods you ordered on a purchase order and paid for using a credit card, you need to assign the purchase order charge on the credit card bill to the Credit Card Payable account (see Figure 19-4).

When you're ready to pay the credit card bill, use the Payments window or the Select for Payment window. Make sure that you use your regular cash account when you print the check to pay this bill.

For those of you who care, we'll explain the debits and credits posted to the general ledger with these transactions. If you don't care, you can quit reading here.

Entering the purchase order had no effect on the general ledger; no purchase order affects the general ledger. When we entered the purchase to receive the goods into inventory and post a payable for the vendor, we debited expense (or inventory) accounts and credited Accounts Payable.

When we paid the vendor's bill, we debited Accounts Payable (reducing our debt to the vendor and washing out the Accounts Payable account) and credited the Credit Card Payable account (increasing the credit card liability).

When we recorded the line on the bill from the credit card company for the goods purchased using the purchase order, we debited the Credit Card Payable account (washing out the Credit Card Payable account) and credited Accounts Payable (increasing our debt to the credit card vendor).

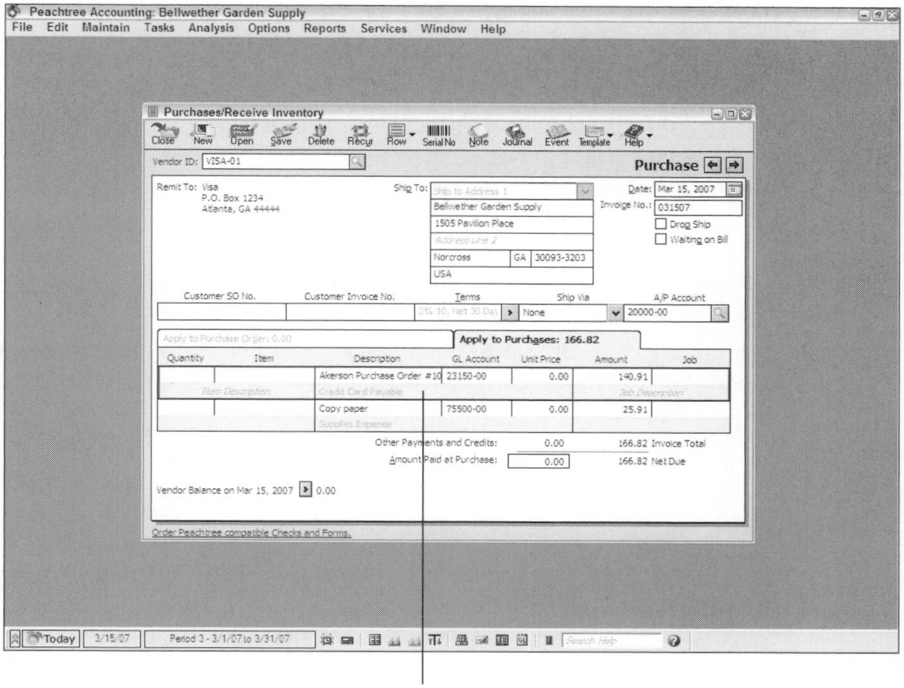

Figure 19-4:
Assign card transactions for purchase order goods to the Credit Card Payable account.

Credit Card Payable

Last, when we paid the credit card bill, we debited Accounts Payable (reducing Accounts Payable and washing out the balance owed to the credit card vendor for the credit card bill), and we credited Cash (reducing the balance in our checking account).

For you visual people, Table 19-1 summarizes the debits and credits.

Table 19-1 — Debits and Credits for Paying Purchase Orders by Credit Card

Action	*Debit*	*Credit*
Recording the purchase for goods on the purchase order	Expense	A/P
Paying the vendor's bill by credit card	A/P	Credit Card Payable
Recording the credit card bill for the goods purchased on the purchase order	Credit Card Payable	A/P
Paying the credit card bill	A/P	Cash

Real-Life Payroll Situations

There are dozens of real-life payroll situations, so we picked the ones we figure occur most frequently and therefore would be of the most use to you. In the pages that follow, we show you how to set up some common payroll deductions and taxes.

Payroll deductions, in general

For all payroll deductions, you need at least two elements: the payroll field for the deduction and a general ledger account that you tie to the field. Because you assign a general ledger account to a payroll deduction, we usually suggest that you first set up the general ledger account and then set up the deduction.

In many cases, you also need a third element: a payroll tax table to calculate the amount of the deduction. And you assign a payroll tax table to a deduction. So, when a deduction requires a payroll tax table, we suggest that you first set up the general ledger account, then set up the payroll tax table, and finally set up the deduction.

"But what does a payroll tax table have to do with a deduction?" you ask. Well, Peachtree uses payroll tax tables to calculate more than just federal, state, or local taxes due. The name "payroll tax table" is somewhat of a misnomer, because these tax tables store calculations that you need for payroll — even if the calculation is not for a tax. You can set up payroll tax tables to calculate 401(k) deductions, health insurance deductions, union dues deductions — you can see where we're going with this concept.

Remember one important fact when you create a payroll tax table for your own use: Create the tax table in the User-Maintained Payroll Tax Tables window. Why? To protect your payroll setup. You see, when you subscribe to Peachtree's payroll tax table update service, Peachtree will *replace* the tax tables you see in the Peachtree-Maintained Payroll Tax Tables window. But it won't touch the tax tables you see in the User-Maintained Payroll Tax Tables window. If you store your calculations in the Peachtree-Maintained Payroll Tax Tables window, your calculations will be wiped out when you update payroll tax tables at the end of the calendar year.

Finally, you also need to define the elements of Adjusted Gross Income so that Peachtree can calculate payroll deductions or additions. You find out how to define the elements of Adjusted Gross Income later in this chapter in Health Insurance and Union Dues.

Employee loans

Suppose that you loan money to an employee. You can set up a payroll deduction so that the employee can repay the loan from his or her paycheck. And, depending on the repayment amounts, you can either manually enter the repayment amount on each paycheck or Peachtree can automatically deduct a fixed amount from each paycheck until the loan is repaid.

The general ledger

You need at least two elements for a payroll deduction: the general ledger account and the deduction. For the employee loan, you don't need the third element — the payroll tax table.

To track a loan, set up another current asset account on your Chart of Accounts, and call the account, say Employee Loans or Employee Advances.

If you intend to loan money to more than one employee, we suggest that you use Peachtree's masking feature (if you're using Peachtree Premium, use the segmenting feature) and set up individual accounts for each loan that would roll up into the Employee Advances account. For example, if you created 14100 for your Employee Advances account, the account number for a loan to Dorothy Beckstrom might be 14100-01, and the account number for a loan to Elliot Adams might be 14100-02. See Chapters 3 and 15 for information on masking.

Writing a loan check

When you write the check for the employee's loan, use the Payments window. You don't need to set up the employee as a vendor; simply type the employee's name in the Pay to The Order Of box. On the Apply to Expenses tab of the Payments window, fill in the employee's loan account as the G/L account.

The payroll field

You need to use the manual repayment method if the repayment amounts differ from paycheck to paycheck.

Set up a payroll deduction for the loan by following these steps:

1. **Choose Maintain⇨Default Information⇨Employees.**

2. **Scroll to the bottom of the EmployEE Fields tab.**

3. **In the Field Name column, add a field called Loan (see Figure 19-5).**

    The name must not contain spaces. The name you use will appear on the paycheck stub.

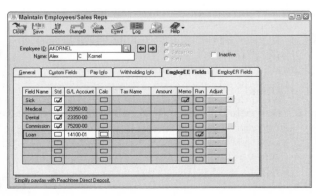

Figure 19-5:
Setting up a payroll field.

4. **In the G/L Account list, select the main account you set up for employee loans.**

   In our example, we selected 14100.

5. **Place a check mark in the Run column.**

   Peachtree will now maintain a running total for the deduction even when you close the payroll year.

6. **Click OK.**

Next, use these steps to assign the loan payroll field to the employee to whom you are making the loan:

1. **Choose Maintain➪Employees/Sales Reps.**

2. **Select the employee to whom you are making the loan.**

3. **On the EmployEE Fields tab, remove the check mark from the STD column (see Figure 19-6).**

Figure 19-6:
Make changes for employees who don't use the standard defaults.

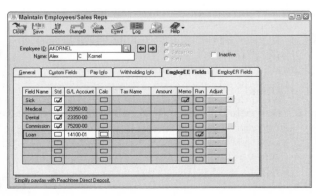

4. **Change the G/L account to the account for the employee.**

5. **Click Save.**

Repaying the loan

When you create a paycheck for the employee, fill in the repayment amount on the paycheck as a negative number. To track the amount the employee has repaid, customize the Yearly Earnings report; using the Fields tab, show only the payroll field for the loan and the Amount field. On the Filter tab, check the Show Totals Only check box.

If you can divide the loan amount into equal installment payments, then you can let Peachtree automatically record the loan payment on the employee's paycheck. Set up the general ledger account and the deduction as we describe. However, when you edit the employee's record in the Maintain Employees/Sales Reps window, also fill in the loan repayment amount as a negative number in the Amount column on the EmployEE Fields tab.

Garnishments

Occasionally, you need to hold back money from an employee's check as a legal garnishment. *Garnishments* are another form of payroll deduction similar to employee advances; however, garnishments typically use all three elements of the payroll deduction. For the general ledger account, use an other current liability account in the case of a garnishment instead of the other current asset account you set up for an employee loan. You also need to set up the payroll deduction, and you'll probably use a payroll tax table to calculate the garnishment amount. Later in this chapter, in Health Insurance and Union Dues, you see some examples of setting up payroll tax tables.

Different states have different requirements for garnishments; the garnishment might be a percentage of adjusted gross pay or a percentage of net pay. Check with your accountant to determine the correct way to calculate the garnishment.

Health insurance

For health insurance deductions, you need two elements: the general ledger account and the payroll deduction. But health insurance deductions come in two basic types: after-tax deductions (non-qualified plans) and before-tax deductions (qualified plans such as cafeteria plans). And for cafeteria plans, you need to take an extra step and include the field when Peachtree calculates the adjusted gross amount it uses for taxes.

As the employer, you must pay the amount you deduct for health insurance to the insurance company that supplies the plan. Therefore, the amount is a liability to you, and you need to set up an other current liability account in your Chart of Accounts.

You set up the health insurance deduction in the same way that you set up the deduction for an employee loan. On the EmployEE Fields tab of the Employee Defaults dialog box, type a name (no spaces allowed) for the health insurance deduction. Remember that the name you type will appear on the paycheck stub. Supply the liability account for health insurance.

You handle this next part in the same way you handle employee loans, as we describe in the preceding section. If you deduct the same amount for most employees, enter the amount in the Amount column on the EmployEE Fields tab of the Employee Defaults dialog box as a negative number. To supply amounts for employees who don't pay the standard amount or who don't pay anything, open the Maintain Employees/Sales Reps window and select the employee. Click the EmployEE Fields tab and remove the check mark from the STD column for the health insurance deduction. Then supply the appropriate amount as a negative number in the Amount column (refer to Figure 19-6).

A new payroll field can affect the calculation of existing payroll fields. Whenever you add a tax-sheltered deduction or an addition that is taxable, you need to click the Adjust button for *other payroll fields* that are affected by the new field. For example, suppose that an addition field — perhaps an automobile benefit — is subject to Social Security and Medicare. You need to click the Adjust buttons for Social Security and Medicare and select the Use box for the new addition field (the automobile benefit in our example) to make sure that Peachtree includes the addition field when calculating adjusted gross wages for Social Security and Medicare.

Tax-sheltered deductions — such as a health insurance deduction for a cafeteria plan — are typically deducted from Gross Pay before calculating taxes. So you need to click the Adjust button next to Federal Income Tax, Social Security, Medicare, and any state and local taxes. In the Calculate Adjusted Gross dialog box, shown in Figure 19-7, you select the Use box next to the health insurance deduction. Then Peachtree will subtract the health insurance deduction from gross pay before calculating taxes. If you're not sure whether a deduction is taxable, check with the plan administrator.

You'll find ADJUSTED_GROSS in the formulas of many payroll tax tables. When you use one of these payroll tax tables, you need to identify the fields that Peachtree should include when calculating ADJUSTED_GROSS to make Peachtree actually calculate something. You identify these fields by clicking the Adjust button next to the new field you're adding and then selecting the Use box next to the fields that Peachtree should add or subtract when calculating ADJUSTED_GROSS. As a rule, whenever you create a payroll field for which you don't supply an amount in the Amount column, you should always click the Adjust button for the new field and select the Use box for the Gross field. The Gross field is the first field in the left column — you can't see it in Figure 19-7. A formula that includes ADJUSTED_GROSS in its calculation makes Peachtree calculate something; if the formula doesn't include ADJUSTED_GROSS, you won't hurt anything.

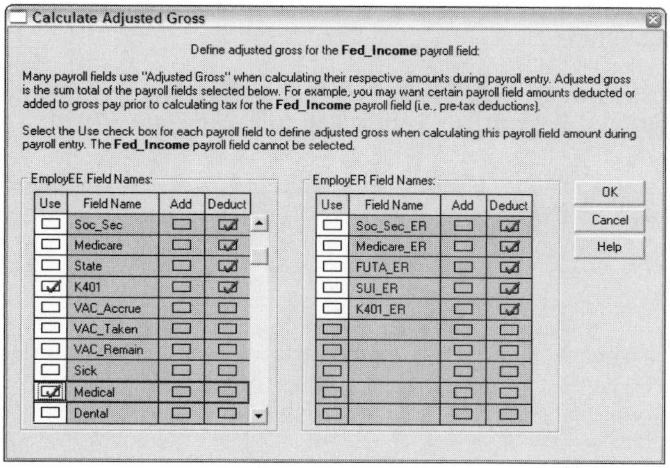

Figure 19-7:
Selecting the payroll elements Peachtree should include when calculating adjusted gross income.

Union dues

Deducting union dues from an employee's paycheck can be tricky simply because so many different ways exist to calculate union dues. In this section, we examine how to set up payroll to calculate and deduct union dues, and examine four different ways of calculating the amount:

- Deducting a flat amount per month
- Deducting a number of hours of pay per month
- Using an hourly rate based on hours worked
- Using a percentage of gross pay

To calculate union dues, you need all three elements of the payroll deduction: the general ledger account, the payroll field, and the payroll tax table to calculate the union dues amount.

As an employer, you handle union dues deductions in the same way you handle federal income tax deductions — you collect the money due from the employee and turn it over to the proper authority. So, to track the union dues collected that must be paid to the union, you need an other current liability account on your Chart of Accounts. See Chapter 3 for help creating the account.

Setting up a payroll tax table

For most union dues calculations, we think you'll find it easiest to use payroll tax tables to calculate the amount to deduct from an employee's paycheck. Follow these steps:

1. **Choose File⇨Payroll Tax Tables⇨User-Maintained to display the User-Maintained Payroll Tax Tables window (see Figure 19-8).**

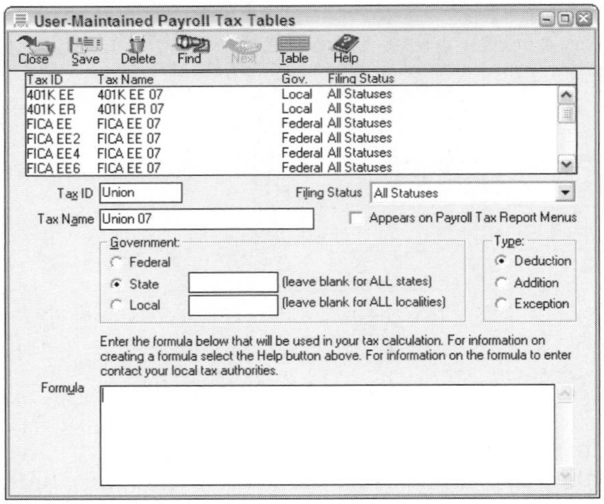

Figure 19-8: The User-Maintained Payroll Tax Tables window, where you store calculations you use in payroll that are specific to your company.

2. **Type an ID for the tax table.**

   Use a name such as Union *XX,* where *XX* represents the last two digits of the current year.

3. **Type a name, adding to the end of the name a space and the last two digits of the year for which the tax table will be applicable.**

4. **Even though the Government box has nothing to do with union dues (no jokes please), select State or Local in the Government box.**

5. **Enter the appropriate formula for the calculation you want Peachtree to make (see the next section).**

6. **Click the Save button to save the tax table.**

Figuring out what goes in the Formula box

The information in the Formula box will change, depending on how you need to calculate union dues. And many of the formulas we show you use EMP_SPECIAL1_NUMBER or EMP_SPECIAL2_NUMBER. These two fields represent variables that you set for individual employees. To set the values for these variables, open the Maintain Employees/Sales Reps window, select the employee, and click the Withholding Info tab. As needed, supply values in the rows for Special 1 and Special 2.

If you're supplying a percentage, make sure you type the percentage as a percentage. For example, if the percentage is 2.65%, type 2.65; don't type .0265, which is the rate, not the percentage.

If the formula you use requires different rates for each employee, the formula will reference EMP_SPECIAL1_NUMBER or EMP_SPECIAL2_NUMBER, and you'll need to enter each employee's rate in the employee's record. However, if the formula calls for the same rate for each employee, you should substitute that rate in the formula as a value instead of using EMP_SPECIAL1_NUMBER or EMP_SPECIAL2_NUMBER.

To calculate union dues as a percentage of adjusted gross pay, use the following formula for both salaried and hourly employees:

```
ANSWER = -ADJUSTED_GROSS*EMP_SPECIAL1_NUMBER/100
```

If you need to calculate union dues based on a number of hours worked, use the following formula for hourly employees, where REGULAR, OVERTIME, and SPECIAL are the pay levels you set up in your company:

```
ANSWER = -(REGULAR+OVERTIME+SPECIAL)*EMP_SPECIAL1_NUMBER
```

If you pay your employees a salary instead of an hourly wage and need to calculate union dues based on a number of hours worked, use the following formula, where pay periods are biweekly and consist of 80 hours. If you pay some employees weekly, some biweekly, and some semimonthly, you'll need separate tax tables, one for each pay frequency. In the weekly tax table, change 80 to 40; in the semimonthly table, change 80 to 88.

```
ANSWER = -80*EMP_SPECIAL1_NUMBER/100
```

If all employees pay the same percentage, you can substitute that percentage for EMP_SPECIAL1_NUMBER/100 in the formula.

Suppose that you must deduct an amount equal to two hours of pay per month for an hourly employee. In the following formula, you enter the annualized amount you need to deduct in the Special 1 field on the Withholding Info tab in the Maintain Employees/Sales Reps window. Peachtree then prorates the annualized amount so that the correct amount is deducted from an employee's paycheck based on the frequency you pay. For example, if an employee earns $10 per hour, union dues would be $20 for the month or $240 for the year — and that's the number you enter in the Special 1 field. If you pay your employees weekly, you'd want to deduct $4.62 per paycheck. Using the PRORATE function tells Peachtree to divide the annualized amount ($240 in our example) by the number of pay periods in the year (52 in our example) to determine the amount to deduct per pay period.

```
ANSWER = -PRORATE(EMP_SPECIAL1_NUMBER)
```

If you must deduct a flat amount — say 5 cents per hour — based on the number of hours worked, use the following formula:

```
ANSWER = -(REGULAR+OVERTIME+SPECIAL) * .05
```

REGULAR, OVERTIME, and SPECIAL are the pay levels you set up in your company.

If you must deduct a flat amount per month, regardless of the number of hours the employee works, you don't need to set up a payroll tax table. Instead, calculate the total amount due for the year and divide that number by the number of pay periods in the year. When you set up the deduction for each employee, supply that number.

Creating the payroll deduction for union dues

You create the payroll deduction for union dues on the EmployEE Fields tab of the Employee Defaults dialog box, using the same steps that you used to create the deduction for health insurance. Remember that the name you type appears on paycheck stubs and cannot contain spaces. Supply the liability account for union dues and, if you created a payroll tax table to calculate union dues, place a check mark in the Calc column. The Tax Name column will then become available, and you can select the payroll tax table that you created. Last, be sure to click the Adjust button and select the elements of pay that Peachtree should include in ADJUSTED_GROSS when calculating union dues. At a minimum, select the Use box next to Gross.

If you didn't create a payroll tax table to calculate the union dues deduction, supply the liability account for union dues when you create the field, but don't place a check mark in the Calc column. If most employees pay the same amount for union dues, type that amount as a negative number in the Amount column, remembering to supply the amount *per pay period*. Peachtree will assign the amount you type in the Maintain Employee Defaults dialog box to *all* employees. For an employee who don't pay the standard amount, select the employee in the Maintain Employees/Sales Rep window and click the EmployEE Fields tab. Then remove the check mark from the STD column, and type the amount per pay period that you want to deduct as a negative number in the Amount column.

Showing employer contributions on paycheck stubs

Suppose that you want to display the employer's contribution on the employee's paycheck stub. No problem. In fact, although we use union dues as the example, you can display *any* employer contribution to *any* program on the employee's paycheck stub.

By default, the paycheck stub shows only the information that appears on the EmployEE tab of the Employee Defaults dialog box. But employer's contributions appear on the EmployER tab of the Employee Defaults dialog box. To make an employer contribution appear on the paycheck stub, you create a field on the EmployEE tab. To avoid affecting the employee's paycheck, make the field a memo field.

Remember that you use the memo field *in addition to* (not instead of) the EmployER field.

Employer contributions to benefit plans are handled as liabilities on the balance sheet. As such, to calculate correctly, the formula you use usually generates a negative number. If you don't mind showing the contribution as a negative value on the employee's paycheck stub, you can use the same formula for the memo field as you use for the employer's contribution. However, you may prefer to show the contribution as a positive number on the check stub — so that employees doesn't mistakenly think you deducted the money from their paychecks. In this case, create another formula that looks just like the employer contribution formula. However, make sure that you

 ✔ Remove the negative sign from the portion of the formula that calculates the deduction

 ✔ Set up the formula type as an Exception rather than a Deduction

Don't forget to click the Adjust button for the new memo field. Also, make sure that you include the same fields when calculating the memo field that you included when calculating the actual employer contribution.

Adding a 401(k) plan to an existing company

Suppose that you've been using payroll for a while and your company decides to implement a 401(k) plan. We're not going to walk you through setting up a 401(k) plan; you have the Payroll Wizard to help you do that.

The Payroll Wizard assumes that you want to assign contribution percentages individually to each employee in the Maintain Employees/Sales Reps window. If your employees' contribution rates vary greatly, you don't have much choice. Choose Maintain➪Employees/Sales Reps and select an employee who participates in the plan. On the Withholding tab, supply the employee's contribution percentage in the 401k% field.

However, if most of your employees contribute the same percentage, you can save yourself some work (and time). Simply change the 401K EE tax table that Peachtree creates to calculate the 401(k) contribution using the percentage that most employees contribute. That way, you need to set up specific percentages only for those employees who contribute the different rate — let Peachtree use a default rate that matches the rate contributed by most employees. Follow these steps to modify the 401k EE tax table:

1. **Choose File➪Payroll Tax Tables➪User-Maintained.**

2. **Highlight the 401K EE tax table to see its formula (see Figure 19-9).**

3. **Add the following three lines, placing them at the top of the tax table or immediately below the first line of the tax table that specifies the limit (the line begins** LIMIT=**):**

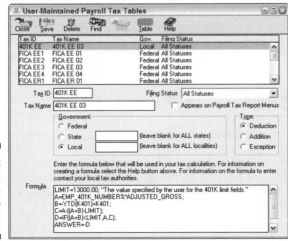

Figure 19-9:
The formula Peachtree creates for a 401K field.

Be sure you *don't* type anything while the formula is highlighted.

To add lines below the first line, place the insertion point at the end of the first line and press Ctrl+J to start a new blank line. Make sure you include a semicolon at the end of each line you add.

```
E=2%;
F=EMP_401K_NUMBER%;
G=If (F=(0),E,F);
```

In the first line, type the fixed percentage used by most employees — in our example, we made the percentage 2%.

4. **Edit the line that contains the information for the A variable and replace** EMP_401K_NUMBER% **with** G. **After you edit the line, it should look like this:**

```
A=G*ADJUSTED_GROSS;
```

5. **Click Save.**

Next, edit *only* the records of employees who don't use the standard rate (2% in our example) and employees who don't participate in the 401(k) plan. For the employees who *don't* use the standard rate, choose Maintain⇨Employees/Sales Reps. On the Withholding tab, supply the correct rate in the 401k% field. For the employees who don't participate in the 401(k) plan, open the same window and click the EmployEE Fields tab. Then remove the check mark from the STD column and the Calc column next to the K401 payroll field.

The modifications to the 401K EE payroll tax table that we suggest change the way Peachtree calculates the 401(k) contribution. Using our modifications, Peachtree first checks the rate in the 401k% field on the Withholding Info tab of the Maintain Employees/Sales Reps window. If an employee's rate is 0, Peachtree uses the default rate specified in the formula stored in the 401K EE payroll tax table (in our example, 2%) to calculate the employee's 401(k) contribution. On the other hand, if Peachtree finds a percentage in the 401k% field in the Maintain Employees/Sales Reps window, Peachtree uses that percentage to calculate the 401(k) contribution.

Multiple state withholdings

If your business is located on the border of a state, you might employ people who live in both the state in which your company is located and in the neighboring state. In this case, your payroll is affected at two levels:

✔ Typically, you need to pay state unemployment insurance (SUI) for only the state in which your business is located.

✔ You must deduct correct state income taxes for employees based on where *they* reside, not where your business is located.

Look first at SUI. When you set up Payroll, Peachtree automatically creates a payroll field for state unemployment insurance for the state in which your business is located. Peachtree makes the calculation for each state based on the employee's state of residence. So, you need to edit your payroll setup to tell Peachtree to include all employees, regardless of their residence, when calculating state unemployment for your company's state. Follow these steps:

1. **Choose File➪Payroll Tax Tables➪User-Maintained to display the User-Maintained Payroll Tax Tables window.**

2. **Highlight the state unemployment tax table.**

   Typically, the table's name is comprised of your two-letter state abbreviation and the characters *SUI*. The state unemployment insurance tax table for Florida, for example, is FLSUI.

3. **In the State box, delete the characters that represent the two-letter abbreviation for your state.**

4. **Click the Save button to save the tax table.**

Next, you need to make sure that Peachtree uses the correct state unemployment insurance tax table. Follow these steps:

1. **Choose Maintain➪Default Information➪Employees.**

2. **Click the EmployER Fields tab.**

3. **Highlight your state unemployment insurance tax table.**

4. **In the Tax Name box, select your state's payroll tax table.**

   In our example, we'd select FLSUI instead of **SUI ER.

5. **Click OK.**

Last, you need to make sure that all employees' records use the correct state.

1. **Choose Maintain➪Employees/Sales Reps to display the Maintain Employees/Sales Reps window.**

2. **Select an employee.**

3. **On the Withholding Info tab, make sure that the state code matches the state in which the employee resides.**

Local taxes

During the initial payroll setup, you have the opportunity to set up local taxes as well as state taxes. But suppose your employees live in a variety of localities instead of just the locality in which your business is located. You need to set up additional tax tables for those other localities and assign them to the appropriate employees.

The process is similar to setting up payroll for multiple state withholdings. First, make sure you have another current liability account for local taxes set up in your Chart of Accounts. Then confirm that you have a Local tax payroll field set up, and assign it, if necessary, to the correct box on the W-2.

1. **Choose Maintain➪Default Information➪Employees to display the Employee Defaults dialog box.**

2. **Click the EmployEE Fields tab.**

3. **If you don't find a "Local" field, type** Local **on a blank line and assign the Local field to the appropriate Other Current Liability account.**

4. **Click OK to save the field.**

5. **Reopen the Employee Defaults dialog box by repeating Step 1.**

6. **On the General tab, click the W-2s button to display the Assign Payroll Fields for W-2s dialog box.**

7. **Select the Local payroll field you created from the Local Inc Tax list box (the last box in the dialog box).**

8. **Click OK twice to close both dialog boxes.**

Next, set up additional local tax tables by following these steps:

1. **Choose File➪Payroll Tax Tables➪User-Maintained.**

   Peachtree displays the User-Maintained Payroll Tax Tables window.

2. **Enter a tax ID.**

   For Marion county, for example, you might use something like Marion*XX*, where *XX* represents the last two digits of the current year.

3. **In the Tax Name box, enter the tax ID and follow it with the last two digits of the current year.**

   In our example, we'd type MarionXX XX; where the first set of X's is part of the Tax ID you created in Step 2, and the second set of X's again represents the last two digits of the current year.

4. **Set the Government type to Local. In the Local box, type a name for the locality.**

   The name can be up to 15 characters long.

5. **In the State box (above the Local box), type the two-letter abbreviation for the state.**

6. **In the Formula box, type the formula for the locality.**

Remember to place a semicolon (;) at the end of every line except the last line and press Ctrl+J to start a new line. The last line should begin with ANSWER = . A local tax formula might look something like this:

```
PERCENT = .7;
ANSWER = - PRORATE ((ANNUAL (ADJUSTED_GROSS)) * PERCENT%)
```

You'd change the percentage amount in the first line to match the percentage for your local tax.

7. **Click the Save button to save the tax table.**

8. **Repeat Steps 2–7 for each local tax you need to create and then click Close.**

Last, make sure that you assign each employee to the correct local tax. Follow these steps:

1. **Choose Maintain⇨Employees/Sales Reps.**

2. **Select an employee.**

3. **On the Withholding Info tab, check the following:**

   • The State/Locality box for the State field contains the two-letter abbreviation for the state in which the employee resides

   • The State/Locality box for the Local field contains the name of one of the localities you created in the preceding steps

4. **Click the EmployEE Fields tab.**

5. **Find the Local payroll field, remove the check mark from the STD column and place a check mark in the Calc column.**

6. **Based on the employee's locality, select the appropriate payroll tax table you created in the preceding set of steps.**

7. **Click the Adjust button for the Local field and place check marks in the Use boxes for all fields that you want Peachtree to include when calculating Adjusted Gross Income.**

   At a minimum, place a check mark in the Use box next to Gross. Ask your accountant about the others if you're unsure.

8. **Click Save.**

Visit this book's Web site for more information on Peachtree.

Part IV
The Part of Tens

The 5th Wave   By Rich Tennant

"Oh yeah, he's got a lot of money. When he tries to check his balance online, he gets a computer message saying there's 'Insufficient Memory' to complete the task."

In this part . . .

Move over David Letterman. Your competition is here. *Not!* Our top ten lists aren't as funny as his, but they clearly serve a practical purpose.

This part provides remedies to common Peachtree error messages and offers locations of helpful Web stuff. Ain't that special?

Chapter 20

Ten Common Error Messages (And What You Can Do about Them)

In This Chapter

▶ Surviving and mastering common errors

Sometimes computer programs just don't act the way that you want them to. At any moment in time, error messages might pop up, throwing most people into a state of near panic.

This might sound a little strange, but frequently you can fix a problem if you simply exit Peachtree and restart your computer. Always try shutting down your computer before any other step. If the problem remains after restarting your computer, and you're on a network, try restarting your server. If the problem still remains after that, look at this chapter or contact technical support for a resolution.

Although most error messages are easy to fix, if an error occurs because of data problems, you might need to run a program called Data Verification. Contact Peachtree or your Peachtree consultant *before* you attempt to run Data Verification or its more powerful counterpart, Integrity Check. You might notice that we don't even include the instructions for running Data Verification or Integrity Check anywhere in this book. We leave it out on purpose!

Here's a valuable piece of advice: Don't run Data Verification or Integrity Check unless you *really* know what you're doing and *always* make a backup before you run the program. We don't mean to scare you, but trust us on this one . . . we found that out the hard way.

Period Changed to ## Due to Unposted Entries There

Our clients call us about this error message more than any other. This error usually occurs when you're using the real-time posting method and when you're trying to change your accounting period. It means that Peachtree improperly posted one or more transactions. Usually, but not always, the error occurs if you interrupt Peachtree's posting process. You can usually repair the problem by changing to a batch posting method, posting all journals and changing back to a real-time posting method.

To correct the error, follow these steps:

1. **Choose Maintain⇨Company Information to display the Maintain Company Information dialog box.**

2. **Click the arrow next to Posting Method to display the Posting Method dialog box.**

3. **Change the Posting Method to Batch posting and then click OK twice.**

4. **Choose Tasks⇨System⇨Post to display the Post dialog box.**

5. **Click OK.**

   Peachtree now posts any unposted entries.

6. **Repeat Steps 1 through 3, selecting Real-time posting in Step 3 instead of Batch posting.**

   Now you're able to change your accounting period.

Not a Valid Date in This Period

This error occurs when you attempt to enter a transaction with a date in a prior period. Peachtree allows you to date a transaction in the current period or in a future period but gives you this error message if you attempt to create and post a transaction to an earlier period. You have three choices at this point:

- ✔ Change the accounting period to the period in which you need the transaction posted.

- ✔ Go ahead and post the transaction with a date in the current month, and then edit the transaction in question and put a prior period date on it. Peachtree gives you a warning message that you're modifying a transaction that's not in the current period. Click Yes, and Peachtree posts the transaction in the previous period. This method is our personal favorite, although Peachtree doesn't allow this method in Payroll Entry.

✔ Leave the transaction dated in the current period (not recommended if you really want the transaction dated in a prior period).

The Record You Are Trying to Access Is Currently in Use

This error, which also includes the message "Please try again when it is available," occurs when you attempt to select, use, or modify a customer, vendor, item, employee, job, and so on when you or another user on your network has the respective Maintain window open. To access the record in question, the user who has the maintenance window open needs to close it.

No Forms to Print

Peachtree displays this message in a couple of different situations:

✔ **If you try to print forms, such as invoices or checks, and Peachtree determines no transactions meet the requirements you specified.** For example, you tell Peachtree to print invoices, but no invoices exist without an invoice number. (Remember that Peachtree chooses invoices or checks that need to be printed if they don't have a reference number.) Sometimes Peachtree displays the No forms to print message if when you created these transactions, you dated them for a future date, such as tomorrow. Unless you change the Last Date for which the invoices will print in the options dialog box, Peachtree assumes that you want to print only the forms dated today or earlier.

✔ **If you try to reprint a customer statement after updating the customer file.**

This Program Has Performed an Illegal Operation

First of all, you haven't done anything illegal. Rest assured that you don't have to live in fear that the software police are going to knock at your door and haul you away to jail (or the hoosegow, as grandma called it).

Frequently, programs just decide that they won't play nice any more, so you see this error message. There are too many reasons to list that can cause a program to crash, but usually you can just restart the program. If that doesn't work, reboot your computer and then start the program. If *that* doesn't work, try reinstalling the program, and if that *still* doesn't work, you need to contact a consultant or Best Software, the company that manufactures Peachtree.

GL Does Not Foot

This message occasionally appears when you attempt to print a General Ledger report. To correct the error, you need to access and run Peachtree's Integrity Check and run the Data Synchronization Test for Chart of Accounts/Journal.

Don't run Integrity Check unless you *really* know what you're doing. We suggest that you contact Peachtree or your Peachtree consultant *before* you run Integrity Check, and *always* make a backup before proceeding.

Could Not Find the xxx Single (Or Married) Calculation

This message occurs when you're trying to generate a paycheck and the payroll tax tables haven't been updated. We cover updating the tax tables in Chapter 17.

File System Error 11 or 35

This message usually appears if you're on a network and the network has lost connection to the Peachtree data file location or lost mapping to a network drive. It can also occur if you move your Peachtree data files to a different drive or folder. If it occurs because of a network issue, contact your network administrator.

If you've recently moved the Peachtree data files, you need to modify Peachtree's INI file (pronounced *inny*). You need to know the location of the Peachtree data files before you can modify the INI file.

1. **Open the Windows Explorer program, locate the Windows folder, and locate the following file:**

   - Peachtree First Accounting R2004 — PFA110.INI
   - Peachtree First Accounting R2005 — PFA120.INI
   - Peachtree Accounting R2004 — PAW110.INI
   - Peachtree Accounting R2005 — PAW120.INI
   - Peachtree Complete Accounting R2004 — PCW110.INI
   - Peachtree Complete Accounting R2005 — PCW120.INI
   - Peachtree Premium Accounting R2004 — PPA110.INI
   - Peachtree Premium Accounting R2005 — PPA120.INI

2. **After you locate the correct INI file, double-click the filename to open it in the Windows Notepad program.**

3. **Look for the line that reads** `DATAPATH=`.

4. **Change this line to the correct Peachtree data directory.**

   For example, suppose that you originally stored the Peachtree data files on your local hard drive and you moved them to the network drive `F:` into the ACCTG folder.

   The datapath line in the INI file originally reads something like this: `DATAPATH=C:\PEACHW\`.

   After you modify the line to the preceding scenario, it reads `DATAPATH=F:\ACCTG\`.

   Don't include your company folder in the data path. Doing so overwrites tax files and confuses Peachtree as to which files are program files and which files are your company data files.

5. **Choose File⇨Save.**

6. **Choose File⇨Exit.**

7. **Restart Peachtree.**

There Was No Room to Store Those Printer Setup Parameters in the Form File

This message almost always appears when using a customized form and certain printers. Switch to a generic version of the printer driver. Also make sure that you're using a newer version of Peachtree. The older versions *really* don't play well with newer printers.

I/O Errors

I/O errors are Input/Output errors and mean that Peachtree might be having a problem reading or writing data to your computer's hard disk. Frequently, this means that there's a problem with your disk drive or transmission across your network. Contact your hardware specialist to check your system. I/O errors can cause irreparable data corruption. If your data becomes corrupted, you must restore a backup, restart your Peachtree company from scratch, or send your data out for repair. See Chapter 21 for information on data repair resources.

Chapter 21

Ten Things You Can Get from the Web

In This Chapter

▶ Getting support

▶ Communicating with companies and other users

▶ Surfing and finding helpful, interesting, and fun Web sites

*T*hrough the outstanding power of the Internet, you can find an entire world of information only a few mouse clicks away. We found numerous Web sites that are beneficial to Peachtree users. What are you waiting for? Ready . . . Set . . . Get clicking. . . .

Please keep in mind that this was a tough chapter to write. So many wonderful Web sites exist, but we have room enough to list only a few.

Peachtree Software

www.peachtree.com

Well, of course we suggest this Web site. Lots of information is accessible from the Peachtree Web site. From this site, you can access support options such as searching through the Peachtree Knowledge Center for answers to many frequently asked questions. You can click Contact Us and send suggestions and enhancements for the future versions of Peachtree. (They really do listen to what the users want!)

You can also find detailed information on the many Web-based services that you can purchase from Peachtree. For example, you can find information on Peachtree's direct deposit service that enables you to offer your employees the benefit of paychecks directly deposited into their bank accounts.

Peachtree For Dummies, 2nd Edition, Extra Information

`www.dummies.com/go/peachtreefd`

We have so much information to share with you about Peachtree, but there just isn't enough space in the book to put it all. The kind folks at Wiley have posted a companion Web site for some of this additional information. We think that you'll find it very useful.

Just in case you didn't see the commercial announcements that we make in this book, we're giving you one more. Visit Wiley's Web site to purchase additional copies of this book and check out all the other great *For Dummies* books available (`www.dummies.com`).

The (Infernal) Internal Revenue Service

`www.irs.gov`

Visit the IRS Web site for all the forms and publications that you might need, such as the Circular E, Schedule C, or Form 1040. You can also find taxpayer help and information on electronic services, such as e-filing.

Just for fun, check out the Tax Stats section, which consists of data compiled from all kinds of returns and sorted in a variety of ways. The IRS groups statistics together by various topics and downloads them in a Lotus 1-2-3 or Microsoft Excel format. And if you're actually turning to tax statistics for Internet fun, may we recommend `www.bored.com`.

Peachtree Extra

`www.peachtreeextra.com`

Okay, we admit it. We're a little biased about this one because Elaine is the editor and writes most of the articles for Peachtree Extra, a monthly newsletter that's designed to help you use Peachtree more efficiently. (Diane has written several articles for them, too!) The publication tries to address the ways that people can use Peachtree to handle real business situations. The subscription price is money well spent.

PeachtreeUsers Forum

www.peachtreeusers.com

This site is an online community of Peachtree users and experts providing support in the Peachtree discussion forums (message boards). You can share tips, questions, answers, and comments about Peachtree accounting software.

Small Business Administration

www.sba.gov

America's 23 million small businesses employ more than 50 percent of the private workforce, generate more than half of the nation's gross domestic product, and provide the principal source of new jobs in the U.S. economy.

The U.S. Small Business Administration (SBA) provides financial, technical, and management assistance to help Americans start, run, and grow their businesses. With a portfolio of business loans, loan guarantees, and disaster loans, the SBA is the nation's largest single financial backer of small businesses. Last year, the SBA offered management and technical assistance to more than one million small business owners and played a major role in the government's disaster relief efforts by making low-interest recovery loans to both homeowners and businesses.

Checks and Forms

www.deluxeforms.com

For more than 80 years, Deluxe Forms has supplied businesses with business checks and forms that work seamlessly with Peachtree software. When ordering, reference this book and discount code R03578 to receive an additional 20 percent off your first order.

Stamps.com

`www.stamps.com`

Stamps.com is a fee-based service that you can use to print postage from your computer. It interfaces directly with Peachtree (the software that you need to use Stamps.com comes on the Peachtree CD), enabling you to print stamped envelopes for customers and vendors directly from various task windows.

Just for the Fun of It

`www.funnymail.com`

Has the computer got you down? Are you feeling major stress and need a break? Check out this site for jokes, puzzles, cartoons, games, sounds, and just plain fun. Each joke is rated on a scale similar to the movie ratings. Lighten up a little!

Our Own Web Sites

Diane's Web site provides links to contact her for Peachtree support, including data repair:

`www.thepeachtreelady.com`

Elaine's Web site, while currently under construction, offers information about Elaine and some of her projects. (Elaine isn't terribly imaginative, which her Web address indicates, but she does have a sense of humor.) You can find her site here:

`www.marmelenterprises.com`

You've already seen how shameless we are when it comes to promoting what we want. What better way to promote both of our services than through our own Web sites? Can't get enough of us? Please drop by for a visit!

Index

• *N* •

• *O* •

FOR DUMMIES®

The easy way to get more done and have more fun

PERSONAL FINANCE & BUSINESS

0-7645-2431-3

0-7645-5331-3

0-7645-5307-0

Also available:

Accounting For Dummies
(0-7645-5314-3)

Business Plans Kit For Dummies
(0-7645-5365-8)

Managing For Dummies
(1-5688-4858-7)

Mutual Funds For Dummies
(0-7645-5329-1)

QuickBooks All-in-One Desk Reference For Dummies
(0-7645-1963-8)

Resumes For Dummies
(0-7645-5471-9)

Small Business Kit For Dummies
(0-7645-5093-4)

Starting an eBay Business For Dummies
(0-7645-1547-0)

Taxes For Dummies 2003
(0-7645-5475-1)

HOME, GARDEN, FOOD & WINE

0-7645-5295-3

0-7645-5130-2

0-7645-5250-3

Also available:

Bartending For Dummies
(0-7645-5051-9)

Christmas Cooking For Dummies
(0-7645-5407-7)

Cookies For Dummies
(0-7645-5390-9)

Diabetes Cookbook For Dummies
(0-7645-5230-9)

Grilling For Dummies
(0-7645-5076-4)

Home Maintenance For Dummies
(0-7645-5215-5)

Slow Cookers For Dummies
(0-7645-5240-6)

Wine For Dummies
(0-7645-5114-0)

FITNESS, SPORTS, HOBBIES & PETS

0-7645-5167-1

0-7645-5146-9

0-7645-5106-X

Also available:

Cats For Dummies
(0-7645-5275-9)

Chess For Dummies
(0-7645-5003-9)

Dog Training For Dummies
(0-7645-5286-4)

Labrador Retrievers For Dummies
(0-7645-5281-3)

Martial Arts For Dummies
(0-7645-5358-5)

Piano For Dummies
(0-7645-5105-1)

Pilates For Dummies
(0-7645-5397-6)

Power Yoga For Dummies
(0-7645-5342-9)

Puppies For Dummies
(0-7645-5255-4)

Quilting For Dummies
(0-7645-5118-3)

Rock Guitar For Dummies
(0-7645-5356-9)

Weight Training For Dummies
(0-7645-5168-X)

Available wherever books are sold.
Go to www.dummies.com or call 1-877-762-2974 to order direct

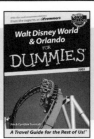

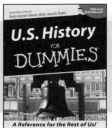

FOR DUMMIES®

Plain-English solutions for everyday challenges

HOME & BUSINESS COMPUTER BASICS

0-7645-0838-5

0-7645-1663-9

0-7645-1548-9

Also available:

Excel 2002 All-in-One Desk Reference For Dummies
(0-7645-1794-5)

Office XP 9-in-1 Desk Reference For Dummies
(0-7645-0819-9)

PCs All-in-One Desk Reference For Dummies
(0-7645-0791-5)

Troubleshooting Your PC For Dummies
(0-7645-1669-8)

Upgrading & Fixing PCs For Dummies
(0-7645-1665-5)

Windows XP For Dummies
(0-7645-0893-8)

Windows XP For Dummies Quick Reference
(0-7645-0897-0)

Word 2002 For Dummies
(0-7645-0839-3)

INTERNET & DIGITAL MEDIA

0-7645-0894-6

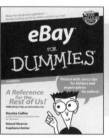
0-7645-1642-6

0-7645-1664-7

Also available:

CD and DVD Recording For Dummies
(0-7645-1627-2)

Digital Photography All-in-One Desk Reference For Dummies
(0-7645-1800-3)

eBay For Dummies
(0-7645-1642-6)

Genealogy Online For Dummies
(0-7645-0807-5)

Internet All-in-One Desk Reference For Dummies
(0-7645-1659-0)

Internet For Dummies Quick Reference
(0-7645-1645-0)

Internet Privacy For Dummies
(0-7645-0846-6)

Paint Shop Pro For Dummies
(0-7645-2440-2)

Photo Retouching & Restoration For Dummies
(0-7645-1662-0)

Photoshop Elements For Dummies
(0-7645-1675-2)

Scanners For Dummies
(0-7645-0783-4)

Get smart! Visit www.dummies.com

- **Find listings of even more Dummies titles**
- **Browse online articles, excerpts, and how-to's**
- **Sign up for daily or weekly e-mail tips**
- **Check out Dummies fitness videos and other products**
- **Order from our online bookstore**